Writing: The Bridge Between Us
A Step-by-Step Guide to Writing Well

Marcy McDonald

Popular
Weasel
Press.

Writing: The Bridge Between Us
A Step-by-Step Guide to Writing Well

Unattributed quotations are by Marcy McDonald or by students.

Printed in the United States of America

Book Cover Design: Greta Matus Design
Book Design and Typesetting: McDonald Communications

ISBN: 0-9715781-0-9

Contents

PART I: PROCESS

Section 1   What Is a Bridge?

Section 2   How To Build a Bridge

Section 3   Why Build a Bridge?

Section 4   Cleaning up the Construction Site

PART II: APPLICATION

Section 5   Bridge-Building in Action

Acknowledgements

This book would not have existed if I hadn't been given the opportunity to work with two county school systems in Virginia; I'm grateful for their faith in me as a writer and the chance to review several thousand essays.

Thank you to Greta Matus, for her incredible design work and unfailing sense of humor. I'm grateful to Ted Cheney for invaluable editing advice. Without Robin Allen of Dogwood Graphics and Linda Roggli of Exclusive Writes, I would never have managed the graphic elements; thank you both for rescuing me a million times.

I can't ever sufficiently thank my parents, Forrest and Ellen McDonald, for their help in developing the content of this book. They taught me how to organize, write, and revise when I was in high school, and they're still teaching me. The hourglass principle described herein comes from my father; I have used it countless times, including to plan this book. Thanks, Dad. And thank you, Ellen, for being my chief editor and cheerleader throughout the many drafts of this book and the many years it took to finish it.

Lastly, I thank my husband, John Funai, for his generous support of my writing and his patience with me, his eccentric wife.

Dedication

This book is dedicated to the determined parents out there who are giving their children an exceptional education, including my sister Kathy. And to great teachers everywhere, particularly my own best: Joan Tomaszewski (Latin), Alma Fleming (Literature), Kris Vervaeke (Writing), Miss Putnam (Biology), and above all, Forrest and Ellen McDonald, who homeschooled in their own way (Writing, History, and Life).

About the Author

Marcy McDonald, a summa cum laude graduate of Virginia Commonwealth University, has been a freelance writer and editor for more than twenty years. Her clients include schools, investors, bankers, lawyers, and doctors; she has also written for newspapers and magazines. She has published more than 100 articles, and as a weekly columnist she wrote on such diverse topics as art, gardening, and medicine.

During the eighties she worked as a consultant for a county-wide school system, assessing the effectiveness of its high school writing program. After reading and correcting thousands of essays, as well as reviewing a host of textbooks, she decided to write this book in her spare time. Spare time being rare, the book has been years in the making. It wasn't until Ms. McDonald homeschooled her son that she truly found the book's primary audience.

The author has won awards for her essays, poetry, and commercial work. She has also served as a writer-in-residence, working with talented and gifted students from grade school to high school. She taught them creative writing; they taught her a fresh approach to language. At the end of the session she edited and published a compendium of student works.

She lives with her family on a 117-acre farm in Virginia, which she is trying (in her spare time) to convert to native grasses and wildflowers. Her husband John is a cardiologist and, given the rural setting, is sometimes paid with whatever his patients can offer—chickens, peanuts, and once a handcrafted (and beautiful) belt buckle. Their children are Kiele, attending Goucher College in Maryland, Anjin (in high school), and Ian (in middle school). They live with their dog, a Great Pyrenees named Cody, and their cat Nekko, who thinks he is a dog too.

Homeschooling was a fruitful experiment, but Ian would rather see girls at lunch each day than his mom, and she doesn't blame him. Although he is back in school, she continues to teach him Latin, history, science, and writing at home. The author hopes other homeschoolers fare better and heartily endorses the movement.

Ms. McDonald has an additional book for homeschoolers due out in 2002, *The Kids' Work-Out Book*—an exercise program for adolescents.

Anjin and Ian at 16 and 12

Kiele and Anjin at 18 and 15

"In writing, as in so many pursuits, it is not the most gifted but the most determined who succeed."

Ralph Keyes

Preface: Letter to Parents and Other Teachers

Writing is one of the hardest subjects to teach, whether you have a class of one or twenty. It can be especially daunting for the homeschooler, who may not have much more confidence than the student about writing skills. Take courage: You are not alone. Others feel the same way, and others have mastered both their fears and the subject matter.

I urge you to do as many exercises as possible with your student(s), for tackling this tough subject together will improve not only their writing but yours. The better you understand it, the better you can teach it. Doing the exercises will also provide you with ample opportunities to get closer to your children (or other students) through deep discussion and revealing prose.

The course can be taught in a semester if you skip some of the exercises, and those teaching in a traditional setting (either high school or college) may want or need to do so. Otherwise, I encourage you to take as much time as possible. I mean for the student to do every exercise for maximum exposure to and practice of the elements of writing. If you can't, or if you have already covered some aspects thoroughly and don't need to repeat the experience, then by all means select the examples your students will most profit from or skim sections you've covered well previously. After all, flexibility is one of the best perks of homeschooling.

Regardless of how many exercises you assign, it is critical that your student(s) respond to *all* the questions in the SUM UP and REACT sections, in *all* the chapters, even if you do some of them verbally to save time. These questions lay the groundwork for developing the reading, analytical, and discussion skills that are essential for strong writing. If you must eliminate exercises, do so from the ACT section. (But again, try not to omit any.)

Besides the regular course work, daily reading should be mandatory. Good writers read, read, read. When I was homeschooling, the only homework I assigned was an hour of reading daily, plus upkeep on a reading log. The latter is something I suggest for all teachers. Have the student write the name of the book, the author, date read, and a one-sentence summary of the book (fiction and non-fiction). Doing so will sharpen the student's ability to write succinctly and clearly without absorbing much time. Actual book reports are covered in the text.

(By the way, I still require my two younger kids to read daily. Since we don't watch TV, we have plenty of time for this even with their regular homework.)

For vocabulary extension, use a dictionary rather than a thesaurus unless the text calls for it. Students can't choose the most precise wording if they have only a limited understanding of a word, which is all a thesaurus offers.

Whether in high school or college, students will reap great returns from discussing the textbook questions with other students. They will also glean considerable insights from exchanging their writing with at least one other person for peer review. Try to get together with other students at least once a week. If you are teaching in an isolated setting, you may have to act as the "peer." Be open to any writing criticism you receive, as editing someone else's work gives the student terrific practice. This work will be much harder if you're defensive, just as your job is harder if the student is defensive.

Nurture your student, but maintain high expectations. Notice first what is powerful, striking, or clear before you point out what is weak, insipid, or muddled. Keep suggestions concrete, relevant, and open-ended. Help the students find their own solutions. Particularly in the early chapters, understanding the concepts is as important as writing well. Remember, your student is just learning to write—as, perhaps, are you.

Writing is the best way to get to know what and how you think. Anyone blessed with a decent brain can become an organized and effective writer—even your students, even you. Writing is not a secret handed to a precious few. Like most other things, good writing is the result of hard and persistent work: Edison's 10% inspiration and 90% perspiration (his definition of genius). I didn't start out writing well, and neither will your students. But just as I did, so will they improve.

This is a demanding, rigorous course. At times you may feel that the challenge is too great. Take a break then, and do some playful writing exercises, go for a walk, or read aloud to one another. Come back to it when you and the student are more relaxed, and then plunge in with faith and enthusiasm. I guarantee that the work will pay off.

Good luck with the class, and try to have fun. If you have any questions or comments, feel free to write or e-mail me via the publisher.

For those desiring further teaching suggestions, a separate teacher's manual is available.

PART I: PROCESS

SECTION 1: WHAT IS A BRIDGE?

CHAPTER 1, WRITING: THE BRIDGE BETWEEN US

CHAPTER 2, SYNTAX: BUILDING BLOCKS

CHAPTER 3, CONTENT: THE BRIDGE ITSELF

"When an interviewer asked Anne Sexton what a writing class could offer students, Sexton replied, 'Courage, of course. That's the most important ingredient.'"

Ralph Keyes

one

Writing: The Bridge Between Us

You don't know me and I don't know you.

I don't know who you are, what you look like, or where you live.

Let's start with me.

I am sitting in an eight-foot by eight-foot room without air conditioning. It is 96 degrees. The fan is broken. My pencil's sticking to my fingers; my fingers are sticking to each other. Everything's sticking to something. The paper sticks to my elbow, the chair to my rear, my rear to my shorts. My legs stick to everything they touch, especially each other. My shirt is the smallest I could find, yet what there is of it is glued to my back. My hair is too short to stick to me, so it sticks in the air. It's too hot to breathe, never mind write. I'd rather be swimming. Instead, I'm trying to talk to you, although I don't know you and can't even picture you.

You, on the other hand, can suddenly picture me, something you couldn't do a mere fifty words ago.

I've just built a bridge.

Without ever seeing or speaking to you, I've taken words and created a bond between us.

You know what it's like to be hot. And you know what it's like to be trying to write when you'd rather be doing something else—anything. Those shared feelings connect us. We're sharing similar feelings, feelings that stretch across space and time, because I've built a bridge between this stifling office in Richmond, Virginia, and the place where you read my words, in this instant. I've built a bridge between me and you, between the writer and the reader. That's what writing is—bridge building.

Okay, you say. Fine. So you built a bridge, and now we're both hot and sweaty. Wouldn't it have been easier to phone?

If I had your number, if I knew you, and if we had time to talk, sure, I could have called. But in a single day I could never have reached as many people as I am reaching right now. (Besides, think of the bill. My parents don't pay it any more.)

Writing beats talking in a lot of ways besides no phone bill. I can work on my words until they say what I mean; I can't do that while I'm talking. What I blurt out vocally is what you hear, unrefined, undefined, and sometimes downright stupid. Spoken words come and go without revision. Written words can be erased. I find all kinds of possibilities in that, and choice. I like choice; we don't get enough of it in this world.

WHY WRITE?

You can express some things in writing that you cannot express as well in speech. When someone dies, you can't just say, "Sorry." Nor does a printed card alone explain your feelings. You might think that "Thanks" said over the phone does the same job in less time than a letter would, but sometimes a call is simply not enough. It's too casual and too easy a medium to carry the weight of some messages. You need words, your words, chosen and arranged according to your own style and history. For instance, when I was sixteen, trouble erupted in my family. Suddenly my mom was in the hospital, and I was the head of the household. A friend's mother helped me arrange temporary homes for my brothers and then took me in herself. She treated me with the same compassion that she treated her own children, even checking my homework and scrutinizing my dates. Her willingness to care helped keep me sane in the midst of chaos. Once I was home again, would a quick "Thanks, see you later" over the phone have been enough? No. I owed her a heartfelt letter, something that she could touch and cherish. I never sent her such a letter, and I regret it to this day.

At other times, words are the best presents to give; they can express love more deeply than any material object ever could. When I was first living on my own, I was only eighteen. I moved a thousand miles from home to prove my independence. I was independent, all right, but I was also broke. Come Mother's Day, all I could afford to send was a letter; the stamp took my last 13¢ (this was a while ago) until payday. My stepmother told me that the letter was the best gift she'd ever received.

Sentiment is best written, as are all the emotions. Through writing you can relive your joy and sort out your anger. You see on paper what it is that you are really thinking. In the case of anger, writing down your feelings will help you figure out what's bugging you. In the process you might let go of the anger. You might even realize that the issue is not so important after all, or that it *is* that important, and you need to take action. The action: An essay or letter written to persuade another that you are right, and why.

That "the pen is mightier than the sword" is no exageration. Its strength has been proven throughout history. Letters to editors, to city councils, to senators, kings, and presidents have changed lives and laws. The "Farmer's Letters" of John Dickinson, written in 1767 to the *Pennsylvania Chronicle*, were the most widely read publication by any American during the entire colonial period. These letters inspired the colonists to active resistance against the British government. Even if the fate of a country doesn't depend on it, you write for the same reasons Dickinson did—because you have something to say and because what you have to say is meaningful and important.

BUT I'M NOT A WRITER

At this point you may doubt that you have anything "meaningful" to say. You do. Writing is for anyone who wants an equal shake in life. Being treated fairly throughout your life can depend on your ability to write clearly and logically. Fighting for and winning a promotion you deserve, correcting unjust treatment, proving that you have dealt equitably with others—writing can serve you on the job and in life in many ways. For example, if you have a serious health problem, an accident, or something stolen, you will have to file an insurance claim. Winning that claim will be impossible if you can't relate in writing an exact sequence of events or a set of relevant circumstances. Getting stuck with junk merchandise—the tape recorder that won't rewind, the purse with a zipper that won't close, the bicycle with brakes that don't work—is a problem you can overcome when you can write a letter of complaint or file a petition with the Better Business Bureau or Small Claims Court.

The need to write cuts across all social and economic barriers. Indeed, the ability to write can remove barriers. Consider the changes wrought by the words of Charles Dickens against the harsh poverty of the working classes, or the words of William Lloyd Garrison against slavery, or of John Steinbeck in *The Grapes of Wrath*, speaking on the plight of migrants:

> There is a crime here that goes beyond denunciation.
> There is a sorrow here that weeping cannot symbolize.
> There is a failure here that topples all our success.

Words like these act on everyone's needs.

The effective writer has a natural advantage over others who cannot communicate well. If you can communicate clearly, you have power: power to get and hold a job, power to persuade others to your way of thinking, power to bring about change; power to build roads or to stop roads, to clean up rivers and air, to raise funds for research or to prevent research that you feel is immoral. If the content is lucid and well supported, the organization solid, the words rich and the style striking, what is written can live for centuries. Can you remember some of the words to Mark Antony's "Friends, Romans, countrymen" speech from Shakespeare's *Julius Caesar*; Martin Luther King's "I have a dream" speech; the Preamble to the Constitution: "We, the people of the United States..."; or the Gettysburg Address: "Fourscore and seven years ago..."? If you can recall a single line from any of these pieces, you prove how enduring writing can be.

The last quotation, from a speech by Abraham Lincoln, is a testament to the impact of writing. Lincoln was a man with a great mind but a terrible voice. He spoke in a high nasal twang, but he wrote eloquently and persuasively. Lincoln would have a hard time making it in politics today because of our emphasis on oral presentation and physical appearance. But what a politician speaks, even on television, is first written. In current times Lincoln would probably not be the man in front of the camera, but the man behind him: the speechwriter. As such he would still be the one whose words would be remembered. Ultimately, a person who controls language controls power.

Nonliterate individuals from the past are forgotten, yet we can reach back past Lincoln's time to the ancient Egyptians because of their written words. We can reach through twenty-three centuries to the great mind of Aristotle because of the written word. In language there is not only power, but immortality.

YOU CAN LEARN TO WRITE

The discipline of writing might not make you the next Aristotle or Willa Cather, but it will improve your capacity to speak, to think, and to manage your life as you go through the process of writing/responding/rewriting. By its very nature, to write clearly is to think clearly. It is a positive cycle. The more you write, the better you write; the more you improve your writing, the more thoroughly and critically you can read, respond, and rewrite. The better you can carry out each step of the process, the better you can carry out the overall process. Each step improves your concentration, your self-discipline, and your ability to think deeply.

Writing is a multi-level learning tool. From it and through it, you learn about yourself, you process what you have learned from others, and you apply what you learn to all your activities. Writing is essential as an act of communication, to yourself first and to others second. Because writing reaches into all aspects of your life, it is important enough to do well. What is more, anyone who can read and wield a pen or manage a typewriter or computer can learn to write—if willing to work at it. As Aristotle said, "For the things we have to learn before we can do them, we learn by doing them." The only way to learn how to write is to write. You start, of course, with words.

Words are like rocks. They litter the earth and hurt your toes until you pick them up and do something with them. Making a pile of rocks isn't enough; that's like handing someone the dictionary and saying, "Here, read this. There are some words in there that say what I mean." No, you must pick and choose your rocks with a single purpose in mind. *Pin your content down to one idea.* Assemble your rocks in a way that makes that idea clear. *Organize your content.* Pick out only those rocks which fit into your design. *Select words precisely and use them concisely.* Finally, you must know what to do first, how to begin. How do you build a bridge?

You must first learn what a bridge is and how it is put together, stone by stone and section by section. To build a bridge from one mind to another, you have to understand what English is and how it is put together, word by word and sentence by sentence. You may be terrified at this point, but you must meet yet one more requirement. You have to understand syntax, the pattern of sentence formation particular to English, because that pattern provides a model for all that you create.

In the next chapter, we'll start building. The first bridge is a sentence.

CREATING A JOURNAL

Trying to learn how to write without practice is like trying to learn how to tie your shoes without shoelaces. In this book you'll get your practice through exercises designed to improve all aspects of your writing and reading. The exercises are divided into three parts: SUM UP, REACT, and ACT.

Writers must be good readers. You must be able to discern the main ideas in what you have read (or experienced, for that matter), or you can't possibly write about them. The way to test your comprehension is simple: sum up what you have read, write it down, and then discuss it with others. The exercises in the SUM UP section test your understanding of the material in each chapter and your ability to express your thoughts about it.

Discussion is the next step for testing and enlarging comprehension of the material. Communicating your thoughts, feelings, and reactions to others and listening to their thoughts in return expands your own understanding. You have more to offer your reader—and yourself—when you develop and use discussion skills. The questions in REACT should help you to do so.

The exercises in ACT complete the process by providing ways to apply what you have learned. The place for the exercises will be a journal, while the forum for your discussions will be your classroom, whether that is a kitchen, den, or a room with thirty matching desks. The exercises will start out fairly simply and gain in complexity. They follow the pattern of the book's development and complexity and match your own developing skills.

NOTE: Some of you will be guided through this book by parents; others will have traditional teachers. For the sake of simplicity, I will refer to whoever is instructing as the "teacher." Likewise, regardless of group size, be it one or fifty, I will call you a "class."

Unless your teacher gives you specific instructions, you can pick for your journal any book style that you're comfortable with. You may use a lined or unlined "blank book" journal, a loose-leaf notebook, or a composition book. Whatever you choose should be thick and at least 5" x 7"; you'll be writing in it a great deal.

Follow these guidelines. First, because your ultimate goal in keeping the journal is to enlarge both your thinking and writing capabilities, write your entries in full sentences unless an exercise dictates otherwise. This is essential, so don't stint.

Second, date and identify all your entries (for example, January 4, 2004; Chapter 5; REACT; Question 2). Do this for all additions to your journal as well. An outside reader should be able to tell what you are working on, and you should be able to find particular entries when needed, for you will refer to earlier entries from time to time. Since you will sometimes add to your summary and response comments after class discussions, leave space after the entries.

Divide the journal into four sections, labeled according to exercise, and use these for your answers. (Call the fourth: Quotations.) Your teacher may want you to add two additional sections, one for vocabulary and one for outside reading. Right now it may seem unnecessary to split the exercises into sections, but in the long run it will be easier, as the exercises later in the book will dovetail into the earlier ones.

Use your journal as a bridge between yourself and your own mind. At the end of the course, it should be a record of your journey from a beginning writer to an accomplished one.

NOTE: Although the tone of this book is casual, that doesn't mean that I will avoid "big" words if they best say what I mean. If you don't understand the word, look it up. Yes, it's work. Yes, it's worth it.

SUM UP
1. State in one to five sentences the main points of the chapter.
2. Highlight or star the point you consider most important.
3. After class discussion, add any new points, and circle (or add, if you missed it) the point that the class agreed was most central to the chapter.

REACT
1. Do you agree with the author that "you can express some things in writing that you cannot express as well in speech"? Give the reasons for your response and at least two examples for each reason.
2. Give examples of occasions in history when the pen has been "mightier than the sword." State in a few sentences your thoughts about this statement.
3. Why is it necessary to be able to write clearly? Write a few sentences about a time when the ability or inability to write made a difference to someone you know. (If you can't think of an instance, make up an example of when it might make a difference.)
4. The central metaphor for the chapter and the book is that writing is a bridge between minds. What are some other metaphors for the process or aims of writing?
5. After class discussion, add any new points to your reactions.

ACT
1. Write a list of five or more words or phrases from the chapter or another source that "sound" good to you. Use each word or phrase in a vivid sentence of your own.
2. Record sentences from the chapter that describe something physical about the writer. Now write sentences that describe something physical about yourself. Do not merely state the color of your hair, eyes, or skin. Do not mention height in inches or weight in pounds; use non-numerical descriptions, and tell the kind of person you are.
3. Record one anecdote about the author's life. An anecdote is a true story, usually told to illustrate a point. Write one sentence stating the point of the anecdote. Next, write an anecdote (no shorter than three sentences and no

longer than ten) about yourself. In one sentence state the point of the anecdote.

4. Pick two writers, fiction or non-fiction, whom you admire. Write one sentence about each stating the author's name and why you respect that person. Then record one quotation (and the source) from each person that demonstrates your point.

"Let us define a plot. We have defined a story as a narrative of events arranged in their time-sequence. A plot is also a narrative of events, the emphasis falling on causality. 'The king died and then the queen died,' is a story. 'The king died, and then the queen died of grief,' is a plot."

E. M. Forster

two

Syntax: Building Blocks

All written thought relies on sentences. Without the idea of putting together nouns and verbs there could be no complete thought. All written thought she words complete thought. Whoops. What I just wrote is not a sentence; it is a gobbledygook of nouns, pronouns, and modifiers. Relies could wrote is. You see, all action and no nouns make no sense either. A sentence contains a subject and an action phrased in such a way that it expresses an idea clearly.

You should be able to boil down everything you write or read to one sentence, a sentence expressing the single basic idea of the composition. That sentence can be expanded into a larger body of thought, but it cannot be broken down any further. A car hauled to the dump can lose hubcaps, wheels, engine, windshield, seats, and dash, but when all is done, there will still be the chassis; it can be stripped no further. Likewise, a book, a screenplay, a movie, a letter, an essay, or a paragraph can be stripped down no further than to a sentence and have the idea remain clear.

Because the sentence is the foundation for all written language, because it is the first building block of the communication bridge, it is essential to understand its workings. Its components, its order, and its inherent logic—in other words, its syntax—are duplicated and magnified in every piece of writing.

ORDER UP A SENTENCE

Syntax is the arrangement of words in a sentence. A sentence is a group of words that expresses a complete thought. To express a complete thought, the succession of words must have a subject and a predicate. The subject is the person, place, object, idea, or abstraction that you are talking about.

Girl is a subject, but it is not a sentence, because we don't have any action. We can't answer the question, "What about the girl?"

Girl is the simple subject. You can describe the girl without relating her main thought or action: "The lonely girl sitting on the bleachers." Taken alone this phrase forms a fragment, not a sentence.

"The girl cried," is a sentence because it is a complete thought. There is a subject and an action (called the *predicate*, it is the verb *cried*). If you like, you can give the reader more details about both the subject and the predicate:

> The lonely girl sitting on the bleachers (Complete subject)
> cried while watching the runners. (Complete predicate)

Adding these details doesn't make the thought any more complete, however—just more complex.

On the other hand, you can also make a compound subject or compound predicate, which *will* change your basic idea. Two or more subjects joined by *and*, *or*, or *nor*, sharing the same verb, doing the same thing, and sharing the same situation or idea are called compound subjects.

> The girl and her lizard are dancing in the mall.
> [compound subject]   [complete predicate]

Two or more verbs sharing the same subject or compound subject and joined by *and*, *or*, or *nor* are known as compound verbs or compound predicates.

> The girl and her lizard are creeping and crawling through the mall's halls.
> [compound subject]   [compound predicate]

Forming a sentence is simple if you include both essential parts: the subject (the noun or pronoun and words describing it) and the predicate (the explanation of the action, condition, or effect of the subject). Together they form a complete thought. To work, however, they must not only form a complete thought, but form it in logical order. Try understanding this:

> Drives down the street the truck green.

If you were a Roman reading Latin, the above sentence would make sense. Or try this:

>The on the porch swing sitting girl was unhappy.

That word order would make sense in German, but it doesn't in English, any more than the Latin sentence did. For you, writing in English, the word order will typically put the subject first and the action second, even if secondary details are interspersed with the subject and predicate to create a mood or emphasize an idea.

Look at the slight shift in emphasis and content that rearranging syntax can create:

>He only batted for glory.
>Only he batted for glory.
>Glory, only he batted for.

While the placement of words within a sentence is somewhat flexible, the logic and order must always be accessible (available) to the reader and must reflect the essential logic and order of a sentence written in English: subject first, action second.

A SIDE ORDER OF LOGIC, PLEASE

English demands logic of thought as well as logic of order. What the words say when put together must form a complete thought that makes sense. Does the following?

>Birds type.

I can imagine this, but is it logical?

>Birds type scissors.

Since that has a subject, a verb, and a sort of object, it must be a complete thought. Or is it? Since it is illogical, it is a thought the reader can't understand. The sentence fails because there is no logic to the collection of words.

Granted, ideas can be distantly related and yet work together to create a lively image. Still, the interaction works only if the basic idea is recognizable by the reader.

> The bird pecks the tree for bugs.

This image is familiar to you, so it works. Both the order and the idea of the sentence are logical. Now that you are working with a reasonable idea, you can play with the language to enliven the image:

> The bird typed the tree, hunting and pecking for bugs like a one-fingered typist picking out the keys.

THESIS IS THE MAIN DISH

You can add to your thought in any number of ways to enrich it, explain it more fully, support it, or improve its style, as long as you keep at its base a single idea. In that base is the beginning of all writing, for if you can express a single clear idea in a single cohesive sentence, then you can write anything of any length simply by building on that sentence.

A sentence is a building block first because of its syntax and logic, which all communication uses. It is a building block second because it is a model of all story-telling. Within a complete sentence you find subject, action, and even plot. Try starting, for example, with the subject of a boy. Then tell a little about him: "The boy in the red and yellow sneakers," and add the action: "winked at the new girl while handing a love letter to his girlfriend"; then introduce the plot: "but when his girlfriend saw what he was doing, she threw the note back at him."

I have written a single sentence with a single idea. It is not only a story in itself, it has enough substance to be the basis of a larger story. That's because the sentence has at its core an idea. That idea can be stated more directly than in the story line above: "A boy expects that his words will speak louder than his actions, but they don't." My restatement is the essence of the idea, and it is from this essence that a writer would build a story.

This essence can be built up, but it cannot be pared down. All composition is founded on this principle, that everything is built upon and around one main idea. A clear statement of that idea is the basis of the introduction. The idea is then developed and supported to form the body. Finally it is summed up and restated in the conclusion. The essence is known as the thesis, the theme, the main idea, or the universal. Whatever you call it, a focused idea drives a composition.

Regardless of what form the writing takes, there must be a thesis. In a letter of application, the thesis is, "I am qualified for this job because I have the attitude, aptitude, and experience to fulfill the job's requirements better than anybody else." The writer fills in the specific details and builds on them throughout the letter, but every point is made to support the theme and prove it. The writing may be in the shape of a speech, as in Dr. Martin Luther King's "I Have a Dream" speech. King built image after image in that speech, but he based all of them on the one idea that freedom and equality will come with work, tolerance, and love. Similarly, short stories, essays, and books are built upon one principal thesis, even if they also discuss or develop a number of related or secondary ideas.

This doesn't mean that all themes are easy to figure out or that everyone always agrees on what the central theme is, especially in lengthy fiction. It means that regardless of the complexity of the piece, the rule holds. A single, central thesis must dominate, as the following examples demonstrate. In Herman Melville's *Moby Dick* the main idea is that a belief in love and human solidarity is stronger than the evils of greed and pride. Carson McCullers' *The Heart Is a Lonely Hunter* centers on the one idea that all individuals share the same need for love, compassion, and companionship, while the core of Toni Morrison's *Beloved* is that our past shapes us but does not have to hold us. In the non-fiction book, *Manage Your Time, Manage Your Work, Manage Yourself*, the theme is obvious. While these books vary widely in content, they nevertheless share one element: They are built on a single idea that could be expressed in a single sentence. (Of course, a single sentence is not a substitute for a book, any more than a single noodle is a substitute for a meal.)

You may disagree with my opinion about the themes of these books. Fine. Come up with your own single sentences stating the themes. The point is that you should be able to phrase the primary theme of any written work in one sentence. If you can't, chances are that you either need to reread the piece more carefully or the writer wasn't clear about the basic theme to begin with. The main implication for you as a writer (as distinct from a reader), is that you must be able to express your own theme in a single, relatively short sentence—either before writing or after writing.

Long or short, somber or witty, formal or chatty, all writing lays at its foundation a sentence that has logical syntax and content. Building on that sentence's single idea and following the development promised within it provides the structure for all written communication. If you can write a single sentence, you can write a thesis statement. If you can write a clear thesis statement, you can write sentences related to it. If you understand the basic order and logic of a sentence, you can give order and logic to all your sentences, both individually and as a whole. From one sentence you can build a stack of sentences, then paragraphs, chapters, sections, and whole books.

In short, a bridge can't become a bridge until you have in mind a single image of what that is—your own conveyance, of a particular shape and purpose. In writing, too, you begin with a singular shape and purpose. You start with one sentence that states the thesis in the most uncomplicated way possible. That sentence is the material from which your content will develop; it is the cement, sand, gravel, and water of your building blocks. From one block, you can build not only a bridge. You can build a world.

SUM UP
1. In three to five sentences write the main ideas in Chapter Two.
2. After class discussion, add to your understanding of these ideas by revising the sentences you wrote or writing additional ones.

REACT
1 Do you understand the idea that all writing is based upon a single sentence? Write a few sentences saying in your own words what this means. If you are confused about the idea, mention specific points from the chapter that are unclear.
2. What is meant by "logic of order"? Give two examples from the text that demonstrate this concept. In one or two sentences, say why logical order is important.
3. What is meant by "logic of thought"? What examples are given in the text that show illogical thought?
4. In a few sentences, explain what a thesis is.
5 After class discussion add to your responses.

ACT
1. Rewrite your summary of the chapter into a single thesis statement. Compare it to the previous summary.
2. Give an example of an illogical subject-and-verb combination. Write the subject and verb into an illogical sentence. Now rewrite the sentence, using the same subject and verb to create a logical idea.
3. Write at least three sentences that tell full (and different) stories; each should have a subject, action, and a plot. We'll cover plot more fully later, but for now you might view plot as something that complicates the action.
4. In the same section, write the thesis of three of your favorite novels in one sentence each; also, write the thesis of a favorite movie in one sentence.

5. Rewrite the following sentences so that they contain only one main idea that is clearly and logically expressed. (HINT: Sometimes you will be able to write two sentences with a different idea in each; with other sentences, you will have to drop some ideas altogether. Be sure to eliminate repetitive thoughts.)

1) Love cannot fill a vacuum of identity, and physical activity helps one face stress, because both things are important to mental and physical well being.

2) Knowledge that is applied is powerful, and although power is an elusive idea, it is attainable, but only if you use it well.

3) In order to be successful, a perfect situation, a great mind, and exceptional abilities are not necessary, but determination and confidence are, so long as you do not work so little that what you must do is overwhelming.

4) Setting limits gives people, from toddlers to law-abiding citizens to teenagers and even the elderly, something to define themselves against, measure up to, obey, and rules to abide by or rebel against.

5) Focusing attention on the speaker, when you want to listen effectively, you need to still your own inner dialogue, and observe the speaker's body language, too.

"You can write about *anything*, and if you write well enough, even the reader with no intrinsic interest in the subject will become involved."

Tracy Kidder

three

Content: The Bridge Itself

If writing is the act of building a bridge between minds, then content (the thoughts you are communicating) is the bridge itself. You can't write anything without content, just as you can't construct a bridge without building material. At the base of all content is a single idea—the rocks, the blocks, or the wood for the bridge.

Content is more than the subject; rocks are not a bridge. They must be selected and assembled with a purpose in mind. The rocks have the potential to become a tower, a wall, or a house, but your purpose is to create from them a bridge. Bear in mind that single purpose enables you to transform those rocks from a mere pile of rubble into a graceful arch that will connect two minds. Likewise, your content is the transformation of a subject as you give it focus and purpose, and as you direct that purpose toward a specific readership. Content is a subject with a direction and a focus, a bridge that leads to a particular place.

WITHOUT A DESIGN, THE WRITER WILL GO BONKERS

Say you really had to build a bridge. Assuming that you knew how to do so, and you had a pile of stones to work with, it would still be a daunting task until you had a clear design in mind (and preferably also on paper). Consider what would happen if you didn't have a vivid picture of what it should look like. Your design would change as you built it, your ideas converging and diverging willy nilly, and you would end up with—if it stood at all—a bridge that looked completely bonkers.

The same thing can happen with your writing. Without a specific idea of what you are to discuss, it is unlikely that you can write cohesively. The piece, like the bridge, wobbles. Your idea needs focus to guide your vision.

This focus, also called the "slant" or the "angle," asks, "What about the subject?" The question narrows the information involved to one idea. From a broad concept of "bridge," you design a specific bridge looking a certain way; from a broad idea of a topic you squeeze out a specific aspect of the topic, considering only certain related elements. Having a single idea makes it possible to figure out what material should be included, since everything must relate to that one idea. Include what's relevant. Exclude what isn't.

Let's get away from the bridge metaphor for a minute and consider how this principle might work in a writing assignment. Take, for example, an assignment to write about curfews. What about curfews? You could write a million things about them: how you hate them, how unfair they are, how only your little brother or sister or crazy neighbor should have them. You could write everything you know or could learn about curfews—hopping from curfews in England to American curfews in the 1800s to curfews in America today—but it would be a meaningless ramble covering so much information that you'd make no real point. You have to narrow the subject, picking one aspect to write about: how your parents' curfews have limited or did limit your social life; how curfews made you a more (or less) responsible person; how curfews in England during World War II helped save lives. First you've channeled the general idea of "curfews" to a more specific idea, "my curfews" or "curfews in England." That in turn allows you to refine it further, into a manageable, developable, single idea about some single aspect of curfews. This is your focus.

The writer in search of focus asks these questions:

"What is the one thing I want to get across?"
"What is the most important point?"
"What about this topic intrigues me enough to write about it?"
"What is significant to me?"
"How can I make the subject's significance clear to my readers?"

Focus is a narrowing-in process, some of which takes place before you write, some while you are writing. Imagine flying an airplane, with the whole world below. At first it seems as if you could land anywhere; then you realize that the choices are limited. You must choose one spot. You zoom in on the one small piece of land in the entire world for which you are aiming. You have narrowed your focus.

Or, imagine that you are a photographer taking pictures to sell colored contact lenses. The assignment could provide your big break into Madison Avenue, maybe even into international magazines, if you do it right. "Right" means that you don't pose your model on a hill a mile away and take pictures of the trees. You move up close, as close as you can get, and use a long lens to get even closer so that you can capture the significant detail: the big brown eyes that appear lavender. You have limited the subject matter, and by limiting it, given it meaning.

You can select for discussion a single, even tiny incident (event focus) or relate an account, step-by-step through time, of numerous events in order of occurrence (chronological focus). For event focus, you might describe a fumble in the fourth quarter of a football game that caused one team to lose. For chronological focus, you would recount all the major plays, perhaps mentioning the tension in the locker room the day of the game, or the history of the winning or losing team throughout the season. This method follows all the relevant steps, events, ideas, or information leading to one particular occurrence or idea. With either type of focus there must also be a thematic focus, for without a theme the information will not stick together to form a unit. Without a theme, all the facts in the world just add up to facts; the football game is just another game, no more and no less important than any other.

Your theme, also called the thesis, must be focused enough to keep you from rambling, yet broad enough to develop. It must have substance, reasons and reasoning. It needs general support for the assertion it makes. Is the theme so big that it contains more than can fit into a single essay? Is it so skimpy that you would struggle to write more than a few lines about it? (Many writers go ahead with insufficient material, only to repeat themselves for pages on end. This makes for deadly boring writing.)

Consider the following statements:

- Rain wets the earth.
- Everything around us operates according to basic principles of physics.
- Wrestling is a sport that requires discipline on and off the mat.
- Homeschooling is good.
- Performing in plays has given me confidence because I have faced and survived situations that used to terrify me.
- College entrance exams should be banned.
- It started when I was in the third grade. Nailbiting is a temporary solution to some other problem.
- For years I've kept a papier maché shoe that I made in kindergarten, for the shoe reminds me of a calmer, simpler time in life.
- The movie rating system is stupid.
- The more kinds of music the ear can appreciate, the more kinds of thoughts the mind can think, and the more kinds of emotion the soul can experience.

Which of these thoughts could be easily developed? Which ideas are fuzzy and which are focused? Some of them could be thesis statements because they are suitable for development, while others could not. Those that answer the questions, "Why?" and "What about the subject?" can be developed. The examination of an idea is an essential prewriting exercise, one that must settle yet another question: "How much can I say (of value) about this idea?"

Looking at the above ideas, ask whether you could write a paragraph about each one or whether some of the ideas fail to invite further thought. Which ones could be worked into many paragraphs? How many sub-ideas could you list for each one? These questions tell you whether your thesis has enough substance to develop and support beyond the statement you have already made. Ask yourself these questions whenever you're trying to find your focus and your theme, and you'll be one step closer to creating a bridge with solid footings.

LONDON BRIDGE IS FALLING DOWN

You can start with footings of concrete, but unless you have something substantial to build with, what you write will collapse just as the London Bridge of the nursery rhyme does. Substance in writing comes from content support. Support comes through general and explanatory statements backed by examples, anecdotes, quotations, and analysis. The support will do its job only if every point can be directly or indirectly linked to the thesis. Say you build your bridge of wood but halfway through you stick in a couple of boulders. Do you think anyone would notice? Of course they would. It's the same when you include support that doesn't relate to the content's main idea: It sticks out like a pimple on the tip of your nose. If the support doesn't blend into the face of the material, it doesn't belong.

Examples help make your material believable as well as understandable, and they should be as concrete as possible. When I say "concrete," think of that gritty, rock-strong substance. Think of things that are tangible, that you can touch, and then write as specifically, visually, and vividly as you can without using four hundred words when ten will do.

My natural, personal, and great enthusiasm and my exuberant friendliness were achingly suppressed in the early days of high school. For example, there were long atrocious hours of lost feelings and emptiness.

The sentences above were written to show what high school was like in a student's first year. The writer has used empty adjectives that don't provide specific details about the situation, and the result is so vague that you learn little about the writer or the situation beyond the obvious sense of displeasure. In other words, after you read the sentences, you still can't picture the scene and therefore don't connect to the idea. Filling in the details and tying them to one or more of the senses instead of relying on adjectives would make the example real and meaningful (and the theme clearer in the process). So, too, can actual examples make even the most abstract ideas manageable. The bridge metaphor that I am using throughout this book is an example of a solid object's being used to describe something not at all solid—writing.

A maze of gray, musty-smelling lockers greeted me each day in the high school. The trials of working a combination lock, wedging one pile of books in and hauling another out, and sidestepping what seemed like a herd of elephants stampeding from one class to another kept me too dazed even to say hello to anyone for several months.

Here are some more examples of vague versus specific support. By the way, making your material specific can make it either longer or shorter. You can't necessarily judge effectiveness by word count.

VAGUE	SPECIFIC
She deals with certain inert materials and turns them into bugs.	She cuts figures of dogs out of steel. These are then welded together into butterfly shapes.
Virginia Beach has more miles of beaches than any other city in the country.	Virginia Beach has 38 miles of beaches—more than any other American city.

His musical tastes are much broader than mine.	His musical tastes include rap, pop, jazz, and bluegrass, while I like only classical.
I am the right person for this job because I'm super experienced, and I've worked with lots of people and done lots of different things. I not only have all the necessary qualifications for the job, I also have all the qualities an employer is looking for in an employee.	During my five years as manager of the Clothes Tree, I supervised five employees, opened and closed the shop daily, managed payroll, and controlled inventory. Moreover, I won bonuses every year for increased sales and exemplary customer service.

If specific, a supporting example can provide relevant information that can clarify your point. You can also support an idea by mentioning similar occurrences that show that your point of view is not limited to your own experience or opinion. For example, the statement, "Genocide is thought by many to be an act of atrocity belonging only to the Nazis in World War II, but this is not so," might be backed up by the statement, "The slaughter of humans because they are not of a certain race, ethnic or economic background, or religion is found throughout history, going as far back as Biblical times, with the murder of all babies in Jerusalem by Herod, or as far forward as current times, with the massacres of Tutsis by Hutus in Rwanda."

You can also pull your examples from other written materials, providing textual support. The previous discussion of genocide might include the following somewhere in the development: "A more careful look at genocide has some scholars redefining the role various 'heroes' have played in this sordid history. In Stephan Thernstrom's article on Columbus in the *American Educator*, he discusses the 1992 statement by The National Council of Churches which proclaimed that Columbus was as guilty of genocide as Hitler." In a less formal paper such as a personal narrative, you might use a textual reference to illuminate your feelings. For instance, you might describe your parents' distrust of your boyfriend or girlfriend by alluding to Shakespeare's *Romeo and Juliet*: "They understand my love as well as Juliet's parents did when they forbade her to see Romeo anymore. Look how badly that situation turned out, and yet that's the attitude my parents have."

Either one of these ideas, formal or informal, could be supported and developed in yet another way, through an anecdote. An anecdote is a short story told to liven up the material while also supporting it. In the piece about genocide for instance, the writer might include a relevant personal story.

> For my grandfather, a Jew growing up in Russia after World War I, genocide was his expected fate. His parents gave the authorities a different name than his true one when he was born, and a few years later claimed that he had died. Both ploys were to circumvent his being a victim of a pogrom. When he was but fourteen, they smuggled him aboard a freighter heading west, to America, to keep him safe from the genocide that soon took their own lives under the reign of Stalin.

The narrative about parents would be more likely to include an anecdote relating an incident experienced by the writer rather than someone else, as that would provide greater support in a personal account than would a story about someone else. Used sparingly, anecdotes are an antidote to tedium, in addition to excellent content support if well chosen. In nonfiction, the anecdote must *always* be *entirely* true.

Additional support can come from a quotation, as long as it is pertinent, not overly long, and taken from a reliable and credited source. The source could be a person who has spoken to you, a book, magazine, newspaper, movie, television program, or any number of other things. A quotation gives your words credibility (believability) by showing that your statements do not represent merely your opinion. "Unless there is a good reason for its being there, do not inject opinion into a piece of writing," says the master of editing, E. B. White. Support yourself with a quotation, as I just did, or as the writer of the following paper did when writing about Mick's crisis of adolescence as depicted in Carson McCullers' *The Heart Is a Lonely Hunter*.

> Music functions as both stimulus and catharsis for Mick, who dreams of becoming a concert pianist. Mick always has a song in her head and heart, and she is transformed by merely listening to music. In one scene Mick is lying alone on the grass in front of her house, and it comes to Mick "Like God strutting in the night...This music was her—the real plain her." Bewitched by the music, Mick pounds her thighs with her fists, at first in time to the rhythm, then wildly, beating herself until she is crying and then scraping rocks on one hand until she is bleeding. At the height of her fury, Mick is in agony. A moment later, she is serene.

Quotations, anecdotes, and examples can supply concrete support for your central idea. That support is worthless, however, if it doesn't in some way explain the theme. The support must *add* to the reader's understanding of the subject and therefore doesn't work if it merely repeats the main idea, as in the following paragraph. The main idea, from "How To Do Your Own Banking," is underlined. The rest is fabricated to show how *not* to develop an idea.

> <u>Money is a tool that makes it easy to convert your intelligence, labor, and talent into the things you want and need.</u> You can get what you want with money. There are lots of things money can buy. Hard work and brain power are all that you need to get life's luxuries and necessities. If you throw in talent as well, then it is really easy to turn your efforts into money and then into what you crave out of life.

Because the supporting sentences restate the thesis without adding any new information, they are not useful. The paragraph fails to communicate more than the initial idea. Now look at the same idea, transformed by new information and specific, relevant examples. Notice how the last sentence restates the first and moves the paragraph's content back to a general idea.

> <u>Money is a tool that makes it easy to convert your intelligence, labor, and talent into the things you want and need.</u> Whether those things are groceries, clothes, a new car, or college tuition, you can get them if you put your money to work for you. First, make a long-range financial plan. Second, plan a budget and follow it. Include in your budget money for short- and long-term goals. Next, revise your budget and adjust your spending habits each month to meet your obligations and your goals. Last, study the banking options available to you so that you can put your money where you can use it at the lowest possible cost and save it at the highest possible interest. Before long your hard work and sound planning will convert your dreams into reality.

As you can see, the support is effective when it helps the reader process the thesis. Otherwise, it is worthless and should be omitted or revised. Your task as writer is to add to your reader's understanding of your thesis through the unique way you link ideas, facts, and images to your main thought.

The same main idea can be developed in different ways, simply by choosing different information for support. Compare the next two examples, which share a common thesis but differ in development. Again, the thesis is underlined.

John Dickinson's standing in the shaping of the American Constitution is shamefully obscure, partly due to his health problems during the Constitutional Convention. Dickinson had never been physically strong. He was frail to the point of emaciation, and he was ill throughout that summer. No doubt this explains why many Convention members, William Pierce among them, were disappointed in him as an orator. It also explains why Dickinson did not deliver any extremely long speeches. Indeed, Dickinson twice left the Convention due to illness. Problems such as this kept him from the Convention's spotlight and, in turn, from his deserved place in history.

John Dickinson's standing in the shaping of the American Constitution is shamefully obscure, partly due to his health problems during the Constitutional Convention. Dickinson's physical weakness prevented him from speaking very often at the convention, although he was a gifted orator. Nevertheless, the longest, most impassioned, and most eloquent speech of his career was written for delivery at the Convention. A forceful stand against slavery was the topic of the paper, and he worked on it feverishly, to the point of exhaustion. But he did not deliver it. Debilitated by the heat and severely ill, he was forced to return home for rest, thereby missing a larger place in history.

Both paragraphs analyse, develop, and support the thesis without simply repeating it. Because both have substance, both are effective.

WHAT IF YOU BUILT A BRIDGE AND NOBODY CAME?

Once you understand how to provide support for your content within one paragraph, you can expand on that practice to include many paragraphs. Each one will analyse, develop, and support the thesis by exploring related ideas. The main idea, all the related ideas, and the supporting information together make up the content of a longer work. But the content is more than just its parts or components. It is a body of thought with a purpose. Why build a bridge for no reason? A bridge is not typically for decoration; it is for transportation. If it is a bridge for hikers over a canyon, it will be built a certain way. If it is a bridge for trains, though it might be over the same canyon, it must be built a different way. So it is with writing; your content must reflect both your purpose and your audience.

The purpose might be to test what you have learned or to accomplish a specific task, such as persuading someone to do something (examples: to hire you for a job, to accept you in a training program or at a university, or to make a change in an institutional or governmental policy, such as mandatory testing for homeschoolers or a company's restrictions on dating co-workers). The purpose might be to express your feelings, concerns, or complaints. Whatever it is, you must have more reason for writing than just that you were told to do so. But that's not all you need to know to get started. You must also know for whom you write. Just as there are all sorts of reasons for writing, there are also all sorts of audiences for your writing—teachers now; employers, friends, and clients in the future. Both the audience and the purpose for which you write are vital in determining what the content will include and how it will be shaped.

Your focus can't crystallize until you pin down your purpose and audience. With purpose and audience in mind, you can start processing the information about which you will write, whether that information comes from research, your own history, or from the writing and teaching of others. Focus the information into a single, general idea; make sure that you can support that idea with particular and concrete examples, references, quotations, anecdotes, and ideas.

Once you have pulled together the ideas that will make up your content, you can write your thesis and primary supporting points as sentences. This done, you can put the sentences together, one by one, like building blocks. Then you can take sections of blocks—or clusters of ideas—and cement them together. As you do so, you give shape to them. You arrange them to stretch across space without collapsing, to touch down on the other side, and to hold up while the audience crosses from beginning to end.

Getting to the other side, to another person's mind, requires more than just well-considered ideas, however. You must have a blueprint for building, a way of putting your ideas together. That blueprint is organization, the structure that holds your thoughts together.

SUM UP
1. What is the subject of this chapter?
2. What is the focus of this chapter?
3. In one sentence using your own words, state the thesis of this chapter.
4. State the major supporting points for the thesis, writing one sentence for each point.

5. After class discussion add any new points, and if necessary, rewrite the thesis in a sentence that concurs with the view of the teacher or class.

REACT
1. Briefly note what in this chapter is significant to you, and why. Give an example that demonstrates your main point.
2. In your own words say why focus is important to content.
3. Look back at the list of thesis statements. Write down the statements that you think are substantial enough to develop.
4. Why is support important to content? Give an example.
5. How are focus, purpose, and audience linked? Think of examples besides those in the chapter.

ACT
1. Develop the following general ideas into focused thesis statements, finding for each a slant suitable for development.

> •Cruelty to animals is unfair.
> •Communication is important to everyone.
> •Euthanasia is the practice of deliberately putting to death those suffering from terminal illnesses.
> •Immigrants do not always know how to read or speak English when they first arrive in America.
> •Relationships can be stressful.

2. Write two or more supportive ideas (not examples, but points that could be further developed) for each of your focused thesis statements. For example:

> •Thesis statement: An effective conclusion satisfies the reader that all has been said that needs to be said.
> •Supportive points: 1) One way to conclude is to refer to the introductory remarks without repeating them verbatim.
> 2) A summary that recapitulates the chief points but frames them in different language gives them greater credibility.

Each of these supportive points could be expanded further. Make sure that yours could be also.
3. Rewrite the following vague sentences, making them more specific and visual. If necessary, use more than one sentence.

•Nature is a marvelous, special, bounteous world that offers new vision to careful viewers.
•Sports are meaningful because they are both cool and hard.
•I have kept a certain item, which is beautiful, for years because of its importance.
•Littering has a definite impact on the planet.

4. Give examples for each of the following statements.

•Through several acts I let go of my childhood and accepted the responsibilities of my adulthood.
•Many readers are easily distracted.
•Temptation confronts everyone, but morality must prevail.
•There are many ways to say, "No."

5. Develop the following statement into a focused, supported paragraph. Use two different types of examples (anecdote, textual reference, etc.). Write a second paragraph developing the same statement in a different way with new examples.

Opponents of censorship point to the First Amendment for support: "Congress shall make no law...abridging the freedom of speech, or of the press."

"Writing...is like driving a car at night. You only see as far as your headlights go, but you can make the whole trip that way."

E. L. Doctorow

SECTION 2: HOW TO BUILD A BRIDGE

Chapter 4, Organization: The Blueprint

Chapter 5, Other Approaches to Organization

Chapter 6, Rewriting: Analysis

Chapter 7, Rewriting: Style

"In some cases the best design is no design, as with a love letter, which is simply an outpouring, or with a casual essay, which is a ramble. But in most cases planning must be a deliberate prelude to writing. The first principle of composition, therefore, is to foresee or determine the shape of what is to come and pursue that shape....The more clearly [the writer] perceives that shape, the better are his chances for success."

William Strunk, Jr. and E. B. White

four

Organization: The Blueprint

You can't escape organization.

You and I are organized around skeletons. The shape of our bones determines the shape of the flesh that hangs on them.

A car's engine is organized. The basic framework is the flow of fuel and the principle of internal combustion.

Even a cake is organized. The baking powder and salt go with the flour; the sugar mixes with the eggs. Drop the baking powder in with the eggs and you get lumpy goo. The ingredients are assembled in a logical order, step by step from measuring cup to bowl to cake pan to oven to the dinner table.

You can't escape organization; it is natural and essential. You can surely mess it up, however, if you don't know what it is, how it functions, and how to use it. Organization is the framework underlying your writing, the backbone that determines the order and shape of your points, and the way the whole is held together.

Two processes, analysis and synthesis, beat in the heart of organization. In the first the writer breaks down the overall idea—the thesis or general proposition—into elements or parts so that a hierarchy can be figured out. That is, the writer lists points related to the thesis, decides which points are most important, which are least important, and how the points relate to one another. The second act, synthesis, puts those elements together to form a unit, arranging them in such a way that they make a pattern or structure not obvious before. The organization of the ideas helps transform them from ingredients to a finished whole; from baking powder, salt, flour, eggs, and sugar to a cake.

Picture our bridge and a bridgebuilder, who for the sake of simplifying pronouns, we'll make a male. During the process of analysis, the bridge builder gathers and sorts the materials. He picks out the rocks he might use, sorting them into related piles—turquoise ones in one pile, gray in another, gray-blue in yet another. Then he sorts each of the colored piles further: round, square, rectangular, or triangular, and so forth, until all the rocks have been categorized. Once the piles have been sorted, the builder can eliminate what is now seen as unnecessary. Perhaps, for instance, all those triangular turquoise rocks don't blend in a pleasing way and are thrown aside.

Now the builder is ready to put the rocks together—to begin the synthesis. He decides to use one rock, the gray-blue rectangle, as the dominant feature and all others as fillers and support. He builds a wooden frame to set up the bridge's backbone—the beginning, middle, and end of the bridge, as well as the size and length of the bridge. Next, he arranges the rocks so that all the rocks hold one another up. He then fills the cracks between them with mortar, although he won't need a lot if has chosen and placed the rocks for a tight fit. When the framework is removed at last, all the parts hold together, and the bridge stands. Synthesis.

Or, suppose a heavy, round boulder in the middle of the arch does not fit with the rest. The boulder drops out, and the bridge collapses.

PALATABLE PARAGRAPHS

As the rock is the basic unit of the bridge and the sentence is the basic unit of writing, so the paragraph is the basic unit of organization. It follows the same logic as the sentence and includes the same basic elements—the subject and information about the subject—but on an expanded scale. The paragraph contains a central point and supportive points; it has a clear structure in itself (a beginning, middle, and an end); its points are linked to one another and to the central point. The information, overall, moves from the general to the specific and back to the general.

Let's return to the baking analogy. You start with the general idea of baking brownies; you move to the specific idea of pulling out the needed ingredients, and to the very specific measuring of the ingredients. You get a little more general again and mix the dry ingredients, then the wet. Even more general, you mix the two together. Pour the batter in a pan, bake, and you wind up back at the broadest idea—a plate of brownies, rich, chocolatey, chewy, and ready to eat. Organization follows the same pattern, moving from the general to the specific and back to the general. We examined this process in the chapter on content, and you can see how it works in the following paragraph.

It's 11:30 p.m., and you were supposed to be home by 11. You get a flat. Beating your fist on the steering wheel hurts your hand and doesn't get you any nearer home, so you step outside and take a look at the damage. Then you open the trunk, pulling out the jack and the spare. Next you set the emergency brake, remove the hub cap, and unscrew the lug nuts, placing them in the hub cap to keep from losing them. Finally, you lift off the stupid flat. You roll it aside, replace it with the spare tire, and reverse the process, all the way to the point of driving again. (Only now it's midnight, and you're really in trouble.)

See how the paragraph follows the organizational pattern? It starts with a big idea: You have to change a flat to get home. It also ends with a big idea: You have changed the flat and can continue on your way. In between are details that relate to those big ideas. The details start on a broad level and move to the most specific, placing the lug nuts in the hub cap. Then you reverse the trend to regain the broader picture. The overall shape of the ideas and the paragraph is like an hourglass. Sound organization is based on this shape, on this one principle: The writer proceeds from the general to the particular and then reverses to proceed from the smallest point back to the broadest again—from general to specific to general.

Hourglass Illustration

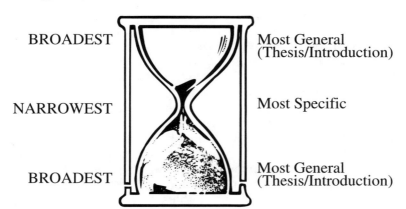

BROADEST   Most General
(Thesis/Introduction)

NARROWEST   Most Specific

BROADEST   Most General
(Thesis/Introduction)

Here's another example of the shift from the biggest idea to the smallest detail, which makes up the top half of the hourglass.

I am outside.	"Outside" is general.
I see green.	"Green" is still general but also more particular.
I see a field lined with trees.	More particular.
I walk to the edge of the field.	More particular yet.
A creek stretches between the field and the trees.	Even more particular.
The creek is dry.	Very specific.
I take off my shoes and feel the dust between my toes.	A precise detail, the smallest and most focused of all.

If these sentences were shaped into a paragraph, more sentences would be added to shift the reader back to a general idea (the widest point on the bottom half of the hourglass). This broad point could be a descriptive idea ("I am outside" is descriptive). Or, it could be an abstract, even poetic idea such as, "The outside is like my soul, green at first glance but empty as dust in reality." On the other hand, it could be practical: "The soil is so dry that the field will soon die." Regardless of the nature of the main idea, however, its development will follow the same principle and form the same hourglass pattern, even though the pattern will sometimes be spread over multiple paragraphs.

The hourglass is the general overall pattern of the paragraph. The structure within that pattern, and within the paragraph, further defines the paragraph's organization and content. The general idea at or near the start forms the beginning, or introduction, of the paragraph. (We've seen this idea labeled the thesis, theme, topic sentence, and universal. I'll use the terms interchangeably.) Once the general idea is stated, the paragraph begins the shift toward the most focused, detailed point. That section is the middle, or the body, of the paragraph. It is still considered the body as it spreads back out, shifting from specific to general. As it again reaches the most general point, it shifts into the ending, or the conclusion, of the paragraph.

Following this structure is vital. It enables you to communicate logically, and it makes it possible for the reader to follow that logic.

Compare the following two paragraphs, one of which puts the idea in structural order and one of which doesn't. The first example has a clear beginning, middle, and end; it moves from the general to the specific to the general.

At my school there is a certain room in Building Two that stirs up craziness for teachers and students alike. Everything is cockeyed in this room, which has no windows. The front half of the room is painted yellow; the back is green. The right wall is dark blue with a splash of pink in the corner; the left wall is light blue. The ceiling is partially tiled, partially covered with gypsum board. There are four clocks, one each on the front and back walls, and two on one of the side walls. All the clocks are set differently. School bells ring on the quarter hour, so each clock rings every fifteen minutes, but not in sync. This means that during a one-hour lecture, the bells ring sixteen times. No one relaxes; no one listens to the teacher, not even the teacher. We all listen for the bells. Without any windows to look out, and too many clocks and colors to look at, the occupants in the holding tank of Room 101 are driven mad until the last clock mercifully rings out a release.

The second example mixes up the beginning, middle, and ending by interchanging general and specific ideas; the result is that there is no clear progression of ideas.

In the center of our recreation room at the YMCA is a pool table with ripped felt. I always get my cue stick stuck in it. We're only allowed in there on weekends. To the left of the pool table is a chrome work-out bench. The recreation room is very big, a perfect place for parties. I like working out, but I can't press that much. To the right of the pool table is a video game. Actually, I can press 100 pounds, but a lot of kids can do more. We would like to be able to use the room more often. The cue ball is missing, so we use the eight ball instead.

It is hard to find a single, main idea in the second paragraph. Also, the information is confusing because specific and general details are jumbled together like cheese, ham, and spinach mixed into ice cream. The end product isn't palatable. Focus on one idea, put the supportive points in proper order, take out the irrelevant points, and your writing will make sense. Put the paragraph overall into proper order and structure, and it makes a point.

The recreation room at our YMCA would be a perfect place to hang out, but there are several problems related to its use. One of the main points in its favor is its large size; it's big enough to fit fifty people at once. We are only allowed to use it weekends between noon and four, however, so its large size is compromised by the mob wanting to use it in such a restricted time. The room also has some great equipment: a chrome work-out bench, a pool table, and three video games. Unfortunately, these features also all have problems. The work-out bench is just to the left of the pool table and so close that someone working out can get jabbed by a cue stick. As for the pool table, its felt is ripped, and the cue ball is missing. If the equipment were fixed and better located, more people would use the rec room. If we were allowed in at other times, the rec room would also be used more often and more efficiently. With these elements improved, the room would meet its potential as a perfect place for recreation, something sorely needed in our small town.

Now the paragraph hangs together; its parts are in order and its main point is clear and sufficiently supported. Notice that several sentences were dropped because they didn't directly support the paragraph's central idea. They kept the material from coalescing. Of course, if you're a careful reader, you'll notice that not every paragraph is developed this way. T. Rees Cheney, author of *Getting the Words Right*, points out that some writing might move the opposite way, from an opening that is specific to a global, cosmic generality, such as from whirling atoms to whirling planets. Once you learn and become an expert at "the rule," then you can play with it, so long as you maintain loyalty to a central idea.

PERPLEXING PARAGRAPHS

"As long as it holds together, a paragraph may be of any length—a single, short sentence or a passage of great duration," says William Strunk in *The Elements of Style*. Obviously, a one-sentence paragraph communicates only one aspect of one idea and must be both general and specific within itself. A multi-sentence paragraph conveys the central point and its supportive points. What holds the points together as a unit is the overall hourglass shape and the movement within that structure from beginning to middle to end, as well as the way the points are linked. They are tied by their relationship to one another and by the inherent logic of that relationship.

A paragraph about skateboarding, for instance, can't include details about aluminum unless the two topics are clearly linked.

Skateboarding is an easy but challenging sport. Lightweight aluminum wheels make the boards easy to maneuver if you are new to the sport and to do tricks well if you are already an expert. Manufacture of aluminum would lessen if recycling became mandatory.

The three sentences above, in addition to various errors, contain two unrelated major points (the first and last sentences) and one supportive point (the second sentence). The two major points are not connected, and the hierarchy of ideas is therefore skewed. Although the paragraph seems to follow the hourglass pattern—broad idea to smaller idea to broad idea—the hourglass falls apart, as the two broad ends are not linked. For a paragraph to hold together, it can have but one main idea. All the other ideas must in some way verify, prove, or explain that one idea. In the example above, the point about the aluminum wheels explains the main idea by discussing a detail about ease and expertise in skateboarding as related to the substance aluminum. The ideas are related in a context, and the link between the points comes naturally. This link is called coherence. There must be coherence among all supportive points and the paragraph's central idea.

The support must be carefully limited and selected; you use only those points which work logically together and with the thesis. Further, you include only as many points as are needed to make the main point clear. As we have seen, you also tighten the coherence between supportive points by limiting your points to those similar in topic, as well as by tinkering with the order, breadth, and depth of the ideas.

Another way to establish coherence in a paragraph is to choose a developmental focus, or order, for the points: spatial order, chronological order, the order of importance, or what might be called a "zigzag" order. Several previous examples demonstrated spatial order. The paragraph describing the recreation room uses spatial order—the objects are in physical relationship to one another. The paragraph about the outside uses spatial order to lead the reader to the creek. In this method of organizing, one item leads to the next tangential one until the overall picture is drawn. In chronological order, mentioned in Chapter Three, one point follows another according to the clock or calendar.

Stating your support in order of importance is another plan for coherence, one often used in persuasive writing. Usually the order in presenting the points is from the least important to the most important, or from a minor statistic to a major statistic. In the paragraph below, from Forrest McDonald's *The Phaeton Ride: The Crisis of American Success*, the most important supportive point serves as the conclusion.

Thus was born what is sometimes called the welfare mess. It has been widely publicized that in our proudest city, New York, more than one person in five collects welfare payments of one sort or another; less publicized is the fact that by 1971 welfare expenditures constituted nearly that proportion of the entire economy. In that year, the combined federal and state governmental expenditure for social welfare was in excess of $170 billion, out of a gross national product of just over a trillion dollars and a gross national income of $850 billion. In other words, nearly one American dollar in five was used to pay people to do nothing at all—not merely to do something useless, such as sorting papers for people who themselves do nothing except sort papers, but to do *nothing at all*, and not aspire to rock the boat by doing something.

Lastly, switching back and forth between ideas—a zigzag order—also works to hold a paragraph together, providing the ideas are closely linked by subject. This pattern can be used to set up a step-by-step support system. Or, the action of switching might be to contrast ideas:

The dog bit my brother.
But my brother bit him first.

My brother needed two stitches.
The dog needed five.

More seriously:

Mary Beth Carter opens her refrigerator door.
Freon leaks into the atmosphere.
She clicks on the air conditioning.
A puff of Freon drifts into the air.
She sprays her kitchen counter for bugs.
The aerosol wends its way outside.
For Mary Beth Carter, it's another day in her kitchen.
For the planet, it's another chink in the ozone layer.

Zigzag order can be used for comparison as well as for contrast. Using this method, you might give one view and then the opposing view, or you might state two or three similarities in a group, then two or three differences.

•One view, then the opposing view:
My parents say that I must be home by midnight.
I think that I am old enough to stay out as late as I wish.

•Several similar points together, followed by a group of contrasting points:
Colleges that have separate dormitories for males and females say that they are safer and cause fewer problems overall. Separation prevents both sexes from embarrassing encounters. It is also easier to supervise parties. On the other hand, colleges which have established mixed dormitories report few problems. The participants seem to be socially at ease with one another, and they claim that there are no more parties in mixed dorms than in separated ones.

You can also go back and forth between supportive sections, first making a broad supportive statement and then providing a specific support or detail for that statement. The pattern then repeats.

I don't like Wally.	(Thesis)
He is a nerd.	(Broad supportive statement)
He wears black glasses taped together at the nose.	(Specific supportive point)
He is mean.	(Broad supportive statement)
He mashed wet chewing gum into my hairbrush.	(Specific supportive point)
He is unprincipled.	(Broad supportive statement)
He stole money from the church collection plate.	(Specific supportive point)

In addition to these methods, you can include transitional (or linking) words or phrases to fasten the points and parts together. Saying "In addition" in the first sentence of this paragraph tied this paragraph to the previous one. Furthermore, you can use the same technique inside a paragraph, as I just did by saying "Furthermore." Repeating words or pronouns which refer to words or ideas in previous sentences also ties the points together, as in these examples:

•If an *applicant* cannot take the time to look up a word in the dictionary, what does that say about the kind of work *he or she* will do here? If the *applicant* cannot create a professional looking résumé, that *person* is not qualified to work here.

•Thousands of people are *writing* today about the space shuttle. Little kids are *writing* stories to take home to their mothers, who will pack the papers in drawers until they are yellow and brittle. High school students are *writing* papers due on Friday. Film *writers* are frantically *penning* scripts about space travel, and reporters are *writing* articles for the morning, afternoon, and evening editions. Everywhere in the world, but especially America, people are *writing* about both the personal and the practical appeal of space flight, a dream that has reached beyond previous human boundaries.

In sum, there are many ways to make a paragraph stick together, and it is essential that it does hold fast, for the paragraph is the building block for larger units of writing. If the building blocks are not glued together among themselves, the larger work will come apart.

PACKAGING PARAGRAPHS

To form a longer work is simple: Write two or more paragraphs about the same general point. In doing so, you are putting into effect on a larger scale the same organizational principles that create a paragraph, a scale that can be expanded from a two-paragraph essay to a ten-volume history. Regardless of length, only one central idea remains.

In practice each paragraph in a longer work will be a unit unto itself with its own central and supporting ideas, but the central idea is a lesser point than the principal one guiding the overall composition. Each paragraph will also have its own hourglass shape and its own structure, with an introduction, body, mini-conclusion, and its own coherence. Its topic sentence must relate not only to the primary generality but also to the lesser generalities in the preceding and succeeding paragraphs. It must combine with the other paragraphs in such a way that overall they form an hourglass shape, moving from the general to the specific to the general. In addition, the paragraphs in combination must have a clear structure, with a definite introduction, body, and conclusion. Finally, the structure underlying the whole must be well balanced. That is, the introduction or conclusion shouldn't be longer than the body, but the three areas should be proportionate to one another and appropriately short or long, according to the complexity of the central idea.

Wow. That's a lot to master, and that's one reason why organization is the biggest nightmare facing the novice and professional writer alike. Fortunately, a tool exists for figuring out what the parts are and putting them together, and that tool is the outline. The outline is a set of directions, a map for proceeding. It is a flexible map, however, because as you draw it you learn from it. Thus, the plan you end up with may not be what you set out with. Like an adventurer, you may set off to discover the ruins of an ancient civilization and find only the corner drugstore, or you may think you're on the way to the drugstore and end up in Atlantis. The outline does your exploring; it helps you discover how big or little your ideas are, and how long or short your material must be to encompass and develop those ideas fully.

A lot of people eschew outlines as being too old-fashioned, rigid, or labor-intensive. You may find, with practice, that you can get by without one. A few scrawled notes in logical order may suffice. But you're not at that point yet, and you won't get there until you've practiced outlining many, many papers. I have made my living as a professional writer for more than twenty years, but I don't begin the smallest project without an outline.

Several outlining methods exist and work well. All have the same aim—to provide order for your material. Some are formal, some less so. Some are more intuitive. Try them all. Which one you choose will depend on which works best for you; what works best might vary according to the length and complexity of the writing task. A single descriptive paragraph, for instance, doesn't need—and couldn't even be framed into—a formal outline. A quick listing of key words, each word signaling an idea or its support, would be ample. On the other hand, a narrative for a college essay could benefit from a more formal outline, such as one listing ideas in full sentences, because the act of outlining would help the writer determine what to say.

A formal outline uses a form like the following:

Thesis statement: _____
I. First major point
   A. Supportive point for I
      1. Support for the support, subtopic of A
      2. Further support, related to the support in A
         a. Lesser support, related to the support in 2
         b. Lesser support, related to the support in 2
   B. Different supportive point for I
   (and so forth...)
II. Another major point
   (and so forth...)

Note that Roman numerals are used for the main points. In order of development and importance, the subtopics are given capital letters, Arabic numerals, then small letters. The main points are topics or subtopics that support the primary thesis. For development each subtopic must have at least two subdivisions or none at all. Typically, the points are written as single words or as a brief heading, but they could be full sentences. Either way, the format remains the same. (The advantage of the full-sentence outline is that it gives the writer a firmer grasp of content and of intent, as the writer must clarify both to write a complete sentence.)

Your outline might consist simply of a list of topics numbered for order and clustered for similarity. The writer of the following list jotted down ideas as they came and then labeled them to fit an organizational plan. Then, to see how the information fit into the overall organizational pattern (the hourglass), and to see whether there were any gaps in the development, the writer recopied them in the proposed order.

Thesis: Because wrestling as a sport requires great discipline on and off the mat, dedicated participants find that all areas of life improve.

I. Important qualities
IA. Discipline
IA1.   Hours
IA2.   Patience
IA3.   Respect for self and others
IA4.   Following strict set of rules in competition
IB. Dedication
IB1.   Hard work
IB2.   Time involvement
IC. Will to win
ID. Mental fitness
IE. Physical fitness—physical discipline
II. Benefits—other areas where qualities apply (second part of theme)
IIA.   Confident
IIB.   Thinking fast
IIB1.   Education
IIB2.   Other competitions
IIB3.   Life in general
IIC.   Being fit physically increases mental alertness
IIC1.   Studies improve
IIC2.   Concentration for other activities improves
IID.   Learn to rely on wits
IIE.   Stamina increases
III. Willpower to win a tough match applies to all activities

After reconsidering the points, the writer arranged them as follows and reshaped the last point into a concluding statement. Notice that several points have been deleted because they were too similar to others.

> Introduction/Thesis: Because wrestling as a sport requires great discipline on and off the mat, dedicated participants find that all areas of life improve.
>
> I. Important qualities
> IA. Discipline
>   IA1. Patience, respect for self and others, following strict set of rules in competition
>   IA2. Physical fitness—physical discipline
> IB. Dedication
>   IB1. Hard work
>   IB2. Time involvement
> IC. Will to win
> II. Benefits—other areas where qualities apply (second part of theme)
> IIA. Thinking fast—education, other competitions, life in general
> IIB. Being fit physically increases mental alertness
>   IIB1. Studies improve
>   IIB2. Concentration for other activities improves
>   IIB3. Learn to rely on wits
>   IIB4. Develop stamina
>
> Conclusion: All these qualities and their applications enable the wrestler to tackle and master new challenges with confidence.

PATTERNING PARAGRAPHS

The previous outlines demonstrate how you can use this organizational tool to sort out information to see which points are relevant and which should be deleted; which are most important and which are of lesser importance; which are general and which specific; which go with what ideas; which needlessly repeat other ideas; and finally, what order it should all go in. But you might at this point be looking at this summary and the examples and thinking one of several things, all discouraging.

"Yeah, right," you might be saying. "Who's got time to write an outline this long?" I won't kid you. The process does take a long time. It sometimes takes me longer to write an outline than it does a draft, but then the draft flows smoothly because I've answered my toughest questions about content and organization before I even began "writing." What's really discouraging is to write a whole draft that has no direction and that requires massive rewriting just to find out what the real subject matter is or should be. A well-developed outline won't eliminate revision, but it will shorten the time it takes to write a draft, and each draft will be infinitely clearer than it would have been otherwise, because you will be refining rather than defining points. Read that again: refining rather than defining. The difference is enormous.

You might also be grumbling, "This is too hard. I don't know how to write an outline to begin with, never mind to rewrite it." This, too, is probably true. So I'm going to give you directions. Whether you want to or have to write the most formal of outlines or are left to your own devices and allowed to create the most casual of outlines, you should still do the following:

1. Form a general thesis; write it in a full sentence.
2. Write supportive ideas.
3. Cluster ideas to group those that are related.
4. Decide which idea in each cluster is the most important. For a multi-paragraph work, write those major supporting ideas as sentences. These major supporting ideas are your sub-theses.
5. Number the principal supporting sub-theses (whether written as sentences, headings, or single words) in logical order. Logical order means that, overall, the order will move from the general to the specific and back to the general, and that each paragraph as well as the whole will have a clear beginning, middle, and ending.
6. Number and order the lesser supportive ideas relating to major ones, following the same directives as in Step 5.
7. If you are applying a specific order to your outline, that is, spatial, chronological, hierarchical, or comparison/contrast, arrange your ideas accordingly.
8. Put the entire list together, writing your main idea sentence (the opening generality) at the top. Identify the three structural sections and note them somehow, such as by putting brackets around them. Your page should look something like this:

Opening Generality	(Introduction)
Major Supporting Generality	(Body)
Major Supporting Generality	(Body)
Closing Generality	(Conclusion)

Of course, the number of major supporting ideas you list will vary from point to point and from one piece of writing to the next.

9.   Reread the whole list. Cross out any ideas that don't add something relevant or that repeat a point without enlarging upon it.

Once you have completed these steps, you are ready to begin writing. Your major supporting ideas will become paragraphs; you will fill out those paragraphs by using the information from the appropriate cluster, in the logical order which you have already established. You have a skeleton; now flesh it out.

Organization is active evaluation. First you take your ideas apart to see what they really are—that is the analysis. Then you put them together to make something new—that is the synthesis. Analysis includes sorting through your thoughts to find a focus, writing that focus as a principal generalization, and determining support for that generalization. Deciding which points are most important, what the order of points should be, and which points work together in idea clusters is part analysis, part synthesis. Assembling your information to form a clear structure involves synthesis, as does the act of writing a list, a rough or formal outline, or casual working "directions." At each stage you evaluate your intent and the way your ideas match or don't match that intent. The goal is to make what you say the same as what you mean to say.

The first tool for meeting that goal is learning about syntax and structure. The second is understanding how topics become ideas—the content. The third is how to transform those ideas into a complete, tightly woven unit of thought—the organization. You, the reader, now have all three tools and the basics for building your own bridges. You are ready to be both engineer and architect. You are ready to build a working model—the first draft.

SUM UP
1.   Write a paragraph summary of this chapter's thesis and its major supporting points. Use the hourglass principle to structure the paragraph.
2.   Using those points, write a broad outline of the chapter to see its structure and development.

REACT
1.   Define analysis and synthesis. Describe the process by which a writer analyses and synthesizes.
2.   Why are both processes necessary for sound organization?

3. Why is the paragraph the basic unit of organization? How does its structure duplicate the structure of a longer piece?

4. Why is it important to follow the "hourglass pattern"?

5. Think about conversations you have had during the past few days. Which were "coherent" and which not? Could you repeat those that were *not* coherent to a third party, or would you need to reorganize them to do so? You don't need to write your answers (unless your teacher asks you to), but be prepared to discuss these questions.

6. What is an outline? How does making an outline help you organize? Do you have good organizational skills? Be honest in self-evaluation. How would greater self-discipline and organization benefit you? How could you introduce more order into your life and your thinking?

ACT

1. Write a series of sentences (at least six) that shift from the biggest idea to the smallest detail and back again. Start with the general idea, "Body language often speaks louder than words."

2. Rewrite the following paragraph so that it has a sound structure (a beginning, middle, and end) and a logical organizational pattern (from general to specific to general).

> Instead of my slender, strong fingers, I imagine my grandfather's gnarled, arthritic fingers tracing the cover pattern of geese in flight. By that point, I have settled down, and I can carry myself as I should, with my grandfather's composure. I pull out the watch whenever I feel tempted to yell at someone, to be hasty, or to ignore my responsibilities. The watch's three-inch diameter is too big to fit comfortably in my jean pockets, but it nestles in my hand, the worn gold smooth against my palm. My only heirloom, my grandfather's watch, reminds me to be courteous, as he was. I rarely notice the time but just think while the second hand methodically clicks. I close the cover gently and slowly wedge the watch into my pocket. The contrast slows me down: my impatience compared to his patience, my restlessness next to his sturdy will. I see him fumble with both hands for the catch as I flick it open with my thumb.

3. Using spatial order, in one paragraph describe a room that your best friend would hate.

4. Write a paragraph on one of the following topics. Before you begin, think about your focus, and write a thesis statement. Develop the paragraph in either chronological order, order of importance, or a zigzag order.

Family secrets
Life without television
Life without books
A personal memento
Something that irritates you
Why your dog needs disciplining
A sports event
Something you feel guilty about
Your worst habit
An embarrassing incident

5. Rewrite the paragraph using a different developmental order.

6. Practice outlining by making one for a hypothetical paper. Write a thesis statement for a topic of your choice. Jot down your major supporting and minor supporting points. Sift through the ideas and eliminate irrelevant points. Cluster related points. Number the ideas so that they fit into the overall organizational pattern (the hourglass). Fit the ideas into outline form with opening and closing thesis statements. Refer to "Packaging Paragraphs" and "Patterning Paragraphs" for guidance.

"You can't wait for inspiration. You have to go after it with a club."

Jack London

five

Other Approaches to Organization

When I am trying to write the first draft of a piece, I find myself thinking of anything and everything else I could be doing. Suddenly I remember the phone calls I need to make, the pants that need hemming, a book I want to finish reading. And if I'm really having trouble, I don't even mind doing the dishes. Now that's desperation. Like a cold engine on a snowy day, I need jumpstarting.

Fortunately, there are numerous ways to run jumper cables to your writing brain. Prewriting activities can rev up even the deadest of engines. What activities you use, whether you employ one or several or the same methods all the time, depends on you. In this chapter I offer you some alternatives to the formal outlining procedure discussed in the previous chapter. Maybe they will suit your temperament better.

WAKE UP, BRAIN

Reading is one way of beginning. You read before writing to learn more about a subject. You also read to alert the brain to the way other people are using words. To get myself started writing this chapter, for instance, I read some general thoughts about making the most of my day. I read a chapter from a book about writing, and I scanned a few other books for ideas about prewriting exercises. Most of what I read can't be applied directly here; reading it, however, fixed my thoughts on the right track.

You don't have to read a slew of books or even one book before you write. But take the time to read some material relevant to your subject, even if only a few paragraphs or a few lines. If you are writing something personal, such as a narrative for a college application, you could read some sample narratives and essays. If you are writing a description, you could skim a few descriptions of the type you are writing, as well as some that are different. Contrast can heighten your understanding of what kind of style you need to employ or avoid. For instance, if you have to write a concise report of an event, you might read newspaper articles to get a feel for their tight, impersonal style; you might also read a description by Mark Twain to understand the difference between objective reporting and vivid prose. Note the dissimilarity, for example, in the language and feel of the following two quotations, which say essentially the same thing. The first is from a speech by Twain.

> There is a sumptuous variety about the New England weather that compels the stranger's admiration—and regret. The weather is always doing something there; always attending strictly to business; always getting up new designs and trying them on people to see how they will go. But it gets through more business in spring than in any other season. In the spring I have counted one hundred and thirty-six different kinds of weather inside of twenty-four hours.

> The weather in New England is unpredictable and, for a newcomer, surprising in its variety.

Reading quotations may alert your mind to the extent that word choice, details, and sentence style affect the impact of a composition. This, in turn, might influence how and what you write.

As you read, you may want to take notes of how a piece is written. For a report or research paper, you need to keep a record of key statistics and quotations. Such notes are useful for a letter of opinion as well. You might copy a line that amuses you, a phrase that inspires you, or a passage that seems to click with a feeling deep inside. Whether you make notes at all isn't important. What is important is that reading before writing can start the current flowing in your brain.

TRY A BRAINSTORM

Another way to get the current going is brainstorming, a process of examining a subject or idea by putting your mind on wheels and letting one idea roll to another as you talk or write. In a sense, you are traveling with your ideas to see where they'll take you. The road you're on is your general purpose, idea, or image. The original idea may be vague; you give it direction by writing or talking about it, dredging up everything you imagine about it, and mixing each new thought with the idea. You write or talk about questions and ideas that arise as you brainstorm; this action leads to new ideas and questions. The more you travel over an idea, the clearer it gets—the firmer the ground beneath your wheels. Before long you have a great deal to write about and will forget that you were having a hard time starting.

You can brainstorm alone, with a partner, or in a group. If you are writing as you brainstorm, use marks such as underlines, arrows, and circles to signify strong or interesting or confusing points. When brainstorming with a partner, you and your partner jot down notes whenever an idea strikes; compare notes when you're done and then discuss the new ideas. In a group brainstorming session, you usually need one or two persons to keep a record of key ideas, and another to keep the traffic moving on the appropriate roadway—the principal cluster of ideas. Don't be inflexible, however; sometimes the side trips are more valuable than the main route. The purpose of brainstorming, after all, is to come up with some ideas—and then some ideas about those ideas—so that you have something to write about.

Look at the process, step by step. Below is the initial stage of brainstorming—writing down everything that comes to mind about a topic. In this example a writer looking for a way into the topic "credit card usage" began by writing an anecdote about a friend.

> My friend Georgia got a credit card in the mail when she went to college. She didn't have a job, any credit history, or any information about how credit works or how to budget her money. To her it was free money, and she spent it on everything from nights on the town to books to clothing to weekends at the beach. She ran it up so high she couldn't pay the bill and had to drop out of school to go to work to pay it off.

Now the writer begins the brainstorming list. Note that some ideas are more complete than others, and many are irrelevant. Note, too, that grammar and punctuation aren't important; getting the ideas down fast is.

- whole thing unfair, no one explained it to her
- credit cards = high debt/banks push them to make money off kids
- college freshmen, high school seniors, me. Would I be able to handle it?
- Mom said Georgia needed a budget. budgets for old ladies
- hidden costs of interest; how interest works; how much money costs
- borrowing—pretend money almost, not real-seeming; "free" money—not really free, but seems like it, until the bills come in

•irresponsible use; books, travel home, emergencies, okay; even sales when it's something you need and have planned for. But nights out, dates, limos—that's stupid. she should have known better. or should she?
•Whose responsibility is it? Kids are capable if well informed. It's up to the banks.
•she wasn't even working; I work, but no one's offered me a card. Do you have to owe money to get credit? After Georgia dropped out, she got two more credit card offers in the mail. Big problem for a lot of people.
•some people work, like me, can't get credit. discrimination?

A brainstorming session ends when you can think of nothing more to say. You then read your scribbles, marking the points that seem most likely to work. Say, for instance, that the aim of the previous brainstorming session was to write an editorial letter questioning the credit card push on college freshmen and graduating high school seniors. Read through the above list with this purpose in mind. What material would be dropped? Which points would the writer keep to work from? The writer might mark the brainstorming notes as follows, crossing out obviously irrelevant points, grouping a few points with letters (A, B, and so forth), and adding a few more ideas as they occur to the writer after reading the notes. This writer found a few points (in italics) that needed to be examined in a future brainstorming session.

•whole thing unfair, no one explained it to her
•credit cards = high debt/banks push them to make money off kids
(A)•college freshmen, high school seniors, me. Would I be able to handle it? *(Is this relevant or not?)* It really is ultimately the responsibility of the cardholder.
(B)•She charged nights out, dates, limos—that's stupid. she should have known better. Or should she?
•~~Makes me angry, her and the banks~~
•~~Mom said Georgia needed a budget. budgets for old ladies~~
(C)•hidden costs of interest; how interests works; how much money costs
(C)•borrowing—pretend money almost, not real-seeming; "free" money—not really free, but seems like it, until the bills come in. *(Both points deal with a larger point: Responsibility is knowing how it all works, knowing that credit is real—real debt.)*
(B)•irresponsible use; books, travel home, emergencies, okay; even sales when it's something special you need and it's a great deal

(A)•Whose responsibility is it? Kids are capable if well informed. It's up to the banks. *(These two points both deal with responsibility but contradict. Now what?)*
•she wasn't even working; ~~I work, but no one's offered me a card. Do you have to owe money to get credit?~~ After Georgia dropped out, she got two more credit card offers in the mail. ~~Big problem for a lot of people.~~
•~~some people work, like me, can't get credit. discrimination?~~
New points: Informing customers is the bank's job. Make sure kids, especially, are informed and capable of paying off debts.

What gives direction when you are brainstorming is your purpose. If, for instance, the writer above was composing a humorous spoof rather than a serious essay, the emphasis would be entirely different, and other ideas would be circled for development. The focus would shift from responsibility to crazy credit card use or "old ladies budgeting." Regardless of the purpose of the writing, brainstorming can get you going on a project of any length, from a single paragraph to a book.

PUT YOUR BRAIN ON AUTOMATIC PILOT

Still another method for getting started is "automatic" or "timed" writing. This process wears out your hand but energizes your thinking. Write non-stop for a predetermined amount of time, say ten, fifteen, or thirty minutes. You can write on a subject or an idea, or you can write whatever you are thinking at the time. No matter what you write, you cannot stop writing until the time is up, even if you just write, "I don't know what to write" fifty times. Eventually you'll get bored and write something real.

Although the result of such writing may contain gems of thought and expression, its purpose is not to be a final product but to awaken your mind and gain confidence in your writing. It is the warm-up for the "real thing." And why not warm up? Athletes and dancers stretch their muscles before using them. Musicians warm up fingers and tune up ears by playing scales; an actress tests her voice and shakes out her fears. A writer, too, can stretch the muscles, warm up the fingers, tune up the senses, and shake out fears— simply by writing for the sole purpose of warming up.

Have plenty of paper and several sharp pencils or a smooth-flowing pen on hand for this exercise. Decide how long you will write (at least ten minutes). Pick a topic or an idea or just start writing. Whatever you do, DON'T STOP WRITING. Don't lift the pencil or pen off the page. Don't erase or cross out or fix spelling mistakes. Don't worry about grammar or punctuation or sentence structure. No one can grade you on practice, and if you worry about the rules while you write, you won't write. Just keep your hand moving until the time is up.

This activity is like a non-stop brainstorming session, but looser. The advantage is that it can lead you deeper into inner thoughts, past your first ideas to your second, third, or fourth. It can help you write more creatively, because you are not worrying about the end product and not stopping to think too hard about the "right" way to say something. You sidestep the critical editor that peers over your shoulder and keeps you from writing. It builds a bridge despite your worries that you might not be up for the job.

After you stop writing, take a few minutes to relax. Then read what you've written. Search for the strongest thoughts and the freshest expressions and mark them. Save them for use in an outline or your first draft, or put them in your journal for later use.

GOING IN CIRCLES YET?

Forming a spiral pattern from your ideas is a fourth jumpstarting technique. In the center of your page, write a word or phrase that identifies your topic concisely. Starting on the outside edge, write whatever you can think of about the topic. Work your way around the edge of the paper, turning the paper as you write. At first you will write broad ideas. As you circle toward the middle of the page, try to pin down the more specific ideas by mentioning precise details. When you reach the middle, you will have formed a spiral of words. Again, the technique loosens you up and lets you have a little fun while you unleash ideas. As with other prewriting exercises, you now read what you've written. Sort, choose, and eliminate thoughts. Make a list of the main points. If these lead to a different idea than the one you began with, write a new main idea and make a new spiral of thoughts.

Be adventurous about trying prewriting activities. Each time you begin writing, you're exploring a new territory, one without maps; you enter the uncharted realms of your brain.

Throughout any prewriting exercise—and there are many others that allow you to collect, discover, and observe your impressions before writing a draft—you concentrate on finding and filtering ideas rather than on refining them. The same is true with the whole first draft. Whether you're writing five lines or 50,000, your aim is first to get your thoughts down in a quick form, then to organize them, next to fill in the details, and finally to write a closing. Polishing these thoughts and correcting the technical parts will come later.

PUT ON YOUR TRAVELING SHOES

Warmed up? Know which road you're traveling and where you're going? Good. You are ready to assemble a model of the ideas you gleaned from your prewriting exercises. The model is your first draft, and this is how you build it. For now we will focus on the essay, as it is the springboard for so many forms of writing.

However you begin the writing process and generate your ideas, at this stage you have a page or more of notes before you. Read those notes carefully and critically. Which best suit the purpose of your writing? What *is* your purpose? Write it down. Now ask yourself: Which ideas relate to my purpose? Which ideas are the strongest? Which are the weakest? Mark them with stars and study them.

Next, link your ideas and your purpose to one main idea (your generalization) bigger than the rest but not too big to develop. It may be that one of the ideas in your list is already large enough to be the main idea, or it may be that you'll discern yet a larger idea when you read the list. However you come to the idea, write it out as a whole sentence at the top of a fresh page and, if possible, pin or tape a copy of it to your desk or the wall above your desk to refer to during the writing process.

Now, concentrating on your generalization, write down everything, large or small, that relates to it. Read the list; scan your notes. Some of the points will be the same as in your prewriting exercises, but because you have thought them through a bit more, they will be more defined. Others will be new. Ask yourself: Which ideas are major ideas, providing broad support for your thesis, and which are minor? A minor idea helps substantiate a major idea, and the connection between them must be clear.

Can any of the minor ideas fit with the major ones? Sift through the ideas and identify their relationships to one another. For instance, you could label the major ideas with capital letters, the minor ones with small letters or numbers, and then match them up—A, A-1, A-1-a; A-2, A-2-b; B, and so on—to see which ideas cluster together. Eliminate any ideas that don't fit in a cluster or aren't significant enough to stand on their own. This process is similar to outlining, but more loosely constructed. Here's how your page might look before clustering ideas.

Before clustering ideas:
Thesis: *Intense is the adjective that best describes me.*
Concentrate hard
Never stop job until done
Carry on many activities
Work extra time if needed
No halfway efforts
Volunteer at Red Cross, learned CPR & infant CPR
Volunteer at art museum
Volunteer tutor; help teach younger siblings
Assistant coach Little League
Babysitting: took YMCA babysitting class, took child development course through college extension program, bring the kids books from library, plan activities ahead of time for them, clean house if kids are sleeping, write list for parents of what we did
Like to travel
Study area first
Like to ride trains, you see more
Traveled across Canada once on a train

Study your major ideas. Decide in what order these should be and number them accordingly. Here is how the author numbered the above example:

After clustering ideas:
Thesis: *Intense is the adjective that best describes me.*
A: Traits: A-1: Concentrate hard
A-2: Never stop job until done (perseverance)
B: Carry on many activities
A-3: Work extra time if needed (industrious)
A-4: No halfway efforts (thorough)
B-1: Volunteer at Red Cross, learned CPR & infant CPR
B-2: Volunteer at art museum
B-3: Volunteer tutor
B-4: Help teach younger siblings
B-4-a: Check math homework for fifth-grade sister
B-4-b: Read to and discuss books with 4th & 5th grade brother and sister
B-5: Assistant coach Little League
A-3-a: Babysitting—took YMCA babysitting class, took child development course through college extension program, bring the kids books from library, plan activities ahead of time for them, clean

house if kids are sleeping, write list for parents of what we did (all show working "extra time")
~~like to travel~~
C (or A-4-a?): Study area first
~~like to ride trains, you see more~~
~~traveled across Canada once on a train~~
C (or A-4-b?): Organized a group of peers to travel and report on travels to my homeschool website

The comments about travel and train rides were irrelevant to the main idea—"my intensity"—and were therefore crossed off. Also, although the writer found a group of related ideas and clustered them under the larger idea of "traits," only two of those, A-2 and A-4, have supporting ideas. In addition, some of the ideas, those labeled *C* (or *A-4-B*), aren't clearly connected to the main idea. On the other hand, details about tutoring and teaching could be combined under another heading, such as "Share enthusiasm with others." This person needs to rethink the generalization and to look for some more supporting ideas, and to eliminate some of the ideas competing for dominance.

REMODELING THE MODEL

On the next page is the example after the writer has brainstormed and clustered ideas. Notice that the generalization has been revised to match the content; what the writer actually had in mind wasn't clear until it was written on paper.

Enthusiastic is the adjective that best describes me.
A: Work extra time if needed and always do activities to the fullest
    A-1: Babysitting
        A-1-a: Took YMCA babysitting class
        A-1-b: Took child development course through college
            extension program
        A-1-c: Bring the kids books from library
        A-1-d: Plan their activities ahead of time
        A-1-e: Clean house if kids are sleeping
        A-1-f: Write list for parents of what we did
    A-2: Organized a group of peers to travel and report on travels
        to website
B: Carry on many activities (put enthusiasm to positive use)
    B-1: Volunteer at Red Cross, learned CPR & infant CPR
    B-2: Volunteer at art museum
    B-3: Assistant coach Little League
C: Share enthusiasm with others
    C-1: Volunteer tutor
    C-2: Teach younger siblings
        C-2-a: Math
        C-2-b: Reading
    C-3: Created and maintain homeschooling website (could go
        under B also)

As you give order to your ideas, remember that they can be arranged chronologically, thematically (as in the above example), contrastingly, or conceptually. As we saw in Chapter 4, the broadest ideas will be first and last, and the most narrow (the most detailed) will be in the middle, so that the points form an hourglass pattern. If you are writing one paragraph, you are ready to fill in the gaps, tying your points together quickly and loosely in the first draft. If you are writing a multi-paragraph paper, you have several steps ahead.

NEXT STOP, FIRST DRAFT

First, write a sentence for each major supporting idea. You will shape a paragraph around each one and its cluster of minor ideas. As with the previous steps, the information to be included is not rigid, and the writer learns more about the message of the paper by trying to write ideas as full sentences. The first sentence in your list will be your theme. Add, at the bottom of the list, a sentence which states that central idea in another way, a way that takes into account the information and ideas which you will apply to it. This final statement is your conclusion, here called the "closing universal." Watch how this process works with our example, as the writer does the job of writing the main ideas in sentences. Notice that the ideas continue to crystallize with each step of the process.

> •Opening (theme): Enthusiastic is the adjective that best describes me.
> •A natural outgrowth of my enthusiasm is my willingness to involve myself to the fullest in everything I do.
> •A passion for helping others, a key aspect of my enthusiasm, has led me to volunteer for many causes.
> •Closing universal (theme restated): The opposite of enthusiastic is indifferent, an adjective that couldn't be applied to any moment of any day in my life.

What you have before you now is a working outline. You may make it more formal if you choose or are so required, but what you have—call it a skeleton, a foundation, or a model—contains all you need to begin writing. You merely need to flesh it out, to fill in the gaps between major and minor thoughts.

After you write your ideas as sentences and put them in order, you create a paragraph from each major sentence, using the sentence itself as the starting point and your related ideas as support. (The actual sentence may change once you get writing.) As you form each paragraph, remember that it can contain only the one main idea. The sentence stating that idea need not be the first in the paragraph, but it typically comes in the first two.

The following example includes the opening two paragraphs of the first draft of our model. Notice how the writer built up the main idea in the introduction and used examples from the brainstorming list to support the second paragraph. The last sentence of the first paragraph lays out the direction which the development will take, because now the writer must answer the implied question, "How exactly do you share your enthusiasm with others?"

> *Enthusiastic is the adjective that best describes me.* I embrace life fully and passionately, and this passion shows in all aspects of my life. I cannot do anything halfway but must always learn and do everything I can about whatever involves me. I can't keep still when there is so much to do, in and out of school. Sharing my enthusiasm with others is an important way by which I express myself and fulfill myself.

In everything from work to recreation, *a natural outgrowth of my enthusiasm is my willingness to involve myself to the fullest in everything I do.* For instance, I have been working as a babysitter for the last four years. As soon as I was old enough, I took the YMCA babysitting class to help me on the job. I soon felt limited, however, by the minimal amount of information in that class; I wanted to know more. Recently I satisfied this need by taking a child development course through a local college extension program. As for the other side of the coin, my own recreation, I love to travel and prepare for traveling by reading everything I can about the area. Last summer I organized a travel club to cross Canada by train. As a group we wrote reports on our travels, and I e-mailed them to my homeschool website.

Look again at the process, step by step. The writer built the opening paragraph around the broadest point in the hourglass, a generalization that introduces the theme ("Enthusiastic is...."). Around the first of the major supporting sentences, the writer built an hourglass-shaped paragraph, fleshing out the core idea with details and supporting evidence. The next paragraph in the essay would develop the specific ways that helping others reflects enthusiasm, and the final one would build a conclusion that was a reshaped statement of the theme.

As you the writer fill in, you add substance to your ideas so that the organizational skeleton includes all its working. You bring in supportive details, transitions, coherence, major and minor ideas, and a heart—a central idea that makes it all tick. The product is a working draft. It may be rough, but it'll do its job. It will show you what you're thinking so that you can say what you mean—in the way *you* want to say it.

SUM UP

Write a short summary paragraph of this chapter. Include a brief explanation of the various prewriting exercises.

REACT

1. In the past what have you found most difficult about writing?
2. What advantages are there in having more than one option for getting started writing?
3. Which prewriting exercise appeals to you the most and which the least? Why? Can you think of other exercises that might be effective? Make up one

and describe it so that someone else could try it. If you can't think of one, look one up in another writing book (*Getting the Words Right* or *The Courage to Write*, for example) and explain it briefly.

4. After class discussion add any ideas generated in class for other prewriting exercises.

ACT

1. Start a quotation section in this part of your journal. Go to the last page of the section (so it will be easy to find in the future), and working backwards, title several pages with the heading "Notable Quotations." For entries in this section (unless otherwise noted), the quotations can be as short as a phrase or as long as a paragraph. Find and record some strong or stirring quotations (and their sources) to begin the section. Include one about writing (not from this book), one that is funny, and one that is personally meaningful.

2. Using the guidelines in the section, "Try a Brainstorm," pick one of the following topics and brainstorm about it alone or with a partner. Remember as you write and while you review your brainstorming list that you are looking for two things—a focus for your topic and support for your focus. Your aim is toward a general essay written for an audience of your peers.

> Creativity
> State lotteries
> Censorship
> "Workfare" vs. "Welfare"
> Girl or Boy Scouts
> Cameras in courtrooms
> Teenage curfews
> Sports

3. Do a ten-minute timed writing, using one of your quotations as a catalyst. Do not lift your pencil or pen from the page, and do not worry about grammar. Just write everything you think; begin with thoughts that relate to one of the quotations you have selected, and let your mind rove freely from there. This exercise is less focused than the brainstorming one. You are trying to summon forth ideas pulsing deep in your subconscious mind. When you're done, put the writing aside for a while. Later read what you've written, and mark any expressions or thoughts that appeal to you.

4. Reread "Going in Circles Yet?" Beginning with the topic of your choice, form a circle pattern from your ideas. Read what you've written, and highlight the main points. If these lead to a different idea, form a second

spiral of thoughts with the new idea at the center. Again, select and list the main points.

5.   Follow the steps in the sections, "A Model of Your Ideas" and "Remodeling the Model," and build a working outline, using a sentence for each major supporting point, from one of your prewriting exercises (#2, 3, or 4).

6. Write a first draft from your working outline.

"The difference between the right word and the almost right word is the difference between lightning and the lightning bug."

Mark Twain

six

Rewriting: Analysis

Okay, you've built a bridge—at least it *looks* like a bridge—but it's still rough. The foundation seems solid, but the boards which form the span are rickety, splintered, and weak in spots. Big spaces yawn between them. The way across looks shaky. It's a long, long way to the bottom, with nothing to catch you if you fall. You're stuck on your side while you make repairs.

Once in while, a first draft happens easily, and the writer builds a bridge as solid as the earth on the first try. When that happens, it's a joy like no other. Most of the time, however, that miracle happens only in a few sections; sometimes it doesn't happen anywhere. Fortunately, you aren't relying on luck, and you do have a safety net, after all: You can rewrite.

Rewriting is not merely reprinting or recopying. Rewriting is the opportunity to revise. It has been said many times that to revise literally means to "see again." In my experience, however, revision is actually seeing for the first time. What you are seeing is what you have really said, as well as what you didn't say, and you can't discern either one until you have copy in front of you. Do you ever find, for instance, that you've said something altogether different on the paper than what you set out to say? I do. You may find that what your words say is better (or worse!) than what you set out to relate. Regardless of what you discover when you reread your first draft, if you rewrite, you can pin down your points more precisely. You can try again to say what you mean.

You start rewriting by evaluating: reading, carefully and critically, what you have said and how you have said it. Evaluating leads to rewriting; rewriting leads to re-evaluating.

Reviewing (which mostly examines content and organization), revising for style, and editing (a clean-up process) are the three phases of rewriting, and all three overlap. As you review your content, for example, you may notice wording problems. Wording problems, in turn, may alert you to stylistic problems. Likewise, a grammatical error may influence clarity and, therefore, content. In time you will become so familiar and comfortable with all three aspects that you can revise for all three at once, but first you must understand the nature and workings of each. We'll begin with the process of analysing your writing.

Reading, rewriting, and rereading are the essentials of that analysis. It is easier than you might think to perform these steps so that you can learn what to change and how to change it. Start big and work down. The pattern of the rewriting parallels the hourglass pattern of your organization. You scan the writing for the broadest information; you zoom in on smaller and smaller details; you back off and look at the general information again.

DID I SAY THAT?

Start with instinct. Just as you wrote your draft quickly and intuitively, so will you read it. At first look only at the big picture. Scan the paper for glaring problems. Mark the weak areas or make brief notes as you read. Practice with the following paragraph. Read the following swiftly and see if you detect any obvious problems.

> Adolescence is by far the most difficult obstacle you have to overcome. They don't know what it's like. I am having trouble with feeling too much. That is, I'm feeling confused and blue a lot. Adolescence is probably the most complicated time in a person's life. It affects our lives from the time we are twelve to the time we rest eternally. Sometimes I just want to sleep or listen to music for hours. Leaving home to go see friends or work or just hang out doesn't help.

You probably noticed several big problems right away, such as the changes in point of view (you, they, our, I), the unclear reference in the second sentence (who are "they"?), and the vagueness of the subject matter. The paragraph doesn't have a definite theme, and it isn't organized. This much is apparent even with a swift reading of the material. What exactly is wrong with the organization and content, and how to fix it, are questions answered during a second reading.

After you've scanned your paper the first time (and marked or noted troubled areas), read it again. You will still be reading broadly and intuitively, but you will begin the focusing process by asking yourself content and organization questions such as the ones which follow. Make notes on another piece of paper or on the draft itself as you answer the questions.

CONTENT
1. Is the information clear? If not, mark passages that are muddled.
2. Are the facts organized, supported, and developed, or are they merely listed?
3. Is there one principal theme? What is it? Write it down without looking at the original, and then compare the two. If they're different, decide which one you want to aim for.
4. Have you interpreted and transformed the material or spit it out without digesting it?
5. Does the material have substance? Is the support relevant?
6. Are opinions clearly distinguished from facts?

ORGANIZATION
1. Is the overall structure clear?
2. Is there a definite beginning, middle, and ending?
3. Does the structure overall follow the hourglass principle, moving from general to specific to general again? If you're not sure, draw an hourglass on a piece of scratch paper. Label the sections with your introductory and closing sentences at the top and bottom and your most specific details in the center. Fill in the space in between with the major supporting points in the order you've given them. Do they really fit?
4. Is the overall order logical? (Does each point relate to the one before it and after it?)
5. Is the support logical?
6. Is the support sufficient. Do you provide enough information to make the points believable and clear?

As you ask these questions, your notepad will fill with comments, and your first draft will become an incredible mess. Great. You're doing it right.

If, at this stage, you find that your paper has major problems, such as more than one main idea, insufficient support, or no introduction, work on correcting them. These large questions must be answered positively before you can work on the details. Bear in mind these first two stages of rewriting as you read the following essay, looking first for glaring problems and then for answers to the content and organization questions.

Water, not gold, is our most precious element. If Americans can't monitor their water usage and control water pollution, the country may not have enough water for future generations. Cities are battling over water rights, and California in 1990 restricted water usage due to its drought. The average household annually flushes enough water down the toilet to supply a family of four with water for six and a half months.

Controlling water usage is important. Don't leave it to the politicians; don't make it a matter of legislation before you act. Parts of Virginia enacted water restriction laws in 1991.

If every American household used ultra-low-volume toilets, up to 108 gallons of water would be saved daily per household. If everyone used a dishwasher instead of handwashing dishes, 5.8 gallons of water would be saved with each load. These measures, which are just a few of the possibilities, would add years to the life span of our finite water resources. If everyone turned off the tap instead of running it when brushing teeth, up to two gallons of water would be saved each time, saving 2,214 gallons a year.

If every lawn were planted with ground covers instead of grass, an average of about 2,500 gallons a month, or enough to supply the needs of a family of four for ten days, would be saved. If Americans recycled their paper, innumerable trees would be saved. Every day Americans throw away enough paper to stretch in a line from Los Angeles to New York City.

The whole thing is scary. I visited Haiti once, where water was turned on in the city only twice a day for an hour at a time, and the people fought to fill their buckets. I don't want that to happen here.

A quick scan shows that there is a clear organizational pattern to the essay, but the pattern is one that is not working well. While the overall sense of the essay is clear—water shouldn't be wasted—the points don't add up to a strong conclusion. The scan also shows that there are many details about water usage that provide good support but that are nevertheless out of place; where they should be located isn't evident at first glance, however.

The content and organization questions reveal the sources of the problems and direct the way toward resolving them. For example, organization question #3 shows that the second paragraph must be rewritten in the hourglass pattern, as right now it moves ineffectively from a large point to a yet larger point and then closes with a small point. The content questions show that there are no horribly unclear points, but question # 5 leads us to question the inclusion of information about trees and paper. The organization questions show that the facts are just listed, as opposed to being put together in a way that would make the larger point clear. Also, there isn't a clear beginning, middle, and end, and there's no conclusion at all. The overall pattern is not that of an hourglass, but that of an accordion—big, small, big, small. Together, the questions reveal that the content itself isn't bad, but the organization is keeping the writer (and the reader) from reaching a clear, dominant point.

The content and organization questions together show that most of the points must be regrouped. A few points need more support, such as "pollution is another factor" and the opening statement claiming that water resources are at risk. These points must either be developed or dropped altogether. Some points need to be clustered around a major point because they are too small to stand alone (details about water restriction in some areas, for instance). Lastly, the writer has ended the paper with a narrowly focused anecdote instead of a conclusion.

The quick scan gave the writer a sense of what to look for when asking the content and organization questions; the questions themselves show what areas need work. Before the writer of the above essay performs any detailed revision, the essay's structure must be straightened out.

MAKING IT SAY WHAT I MEANT TO SAY

First the writer must write a more definite introduction. The next step could be to write a firm conclusion, and the third might be to regroup the points so that all related points come together. Because there are a few holes in the content, the writer may have to brainstorm a bit or do some research to come up with more support for the key points. The writer would revise for these larger concerns before moving on to the next phase of revision.

Yes, this is a lot of work. Yes, it's worth it, and yes, it gets easier the more you do it. With practice more problems are caught at the first glance; with yet more practice, there are simply fewer problems. So don't give up.

Following is a revised version of the above essay, with the major organizational problems corrected.

Water, not gold, is our most precious element. If Americans can't limit their water use and control water pollution, the country may not have enough water for future generations. The key to changing what looks like a bleak future is to become aware of the facts about water usage and then to take individual steps to correct the situation.

Controlling water usage is important. Drought in various areas over the country has continued to deplete the amount of water available in reservoirs and major rivers. The result is that farmers don't have enough rain for crops or water to irrigate, and major cities are battling over water rights. Yet prominent scientists say that there is enough water, if we use it wisely.

This effort can take place on every scale and must do so if it is to have impact. On the grandest scale the government could enact further legislation to protect water in the same way it protects endangered species. Pollution of inland waterways by companies or individuals is illegal, and the laws should be enforced. Parts of Virginia and Pennsylvania enacted water restriction laws in 1991, and California in 1990 restricted water usage due to its drought. Actions such as these may point the way for other states.

Governmental action, however, won't have enough of an impact if individuals don't take up the battle. Don't leave it to the politicians; don't make it a matter of legislation before you act. Every reader of this can make a difference. If every American household used ultra-low-volume toilets, up to 108 gallons of water would be saved daily per household. If everyone turned off the tap instead of running it when brushing teeth, up to two gallons of water would be saved each time, at a savings of 2,214 gallons a year. If every lawn were planted with ground covers instead of grass, an average of about 2,500 gallons a month per family, or enough to supply the needs of a family of four for ten days, would be saved. These individual measures, which are just a few of the possibilities, would add years to the life span of our water resources.

We can't live without water. Does America want to become a country of people fighting among themselves to have enough water for drinking, cooking, and washing? Since our resources are limited, it makes sense to take a rational approach by painlessly decreasing our water usage now, on all levels, while we still have a water supply to protect.

To correct the organizational problems, the writer rebuilt the introduction so that the thesis was presented as fact, not just opinion, and included mention of the major areas the essay would discuss. This gave the writer a natural pathway for development and organization throughout the paper. The writer then expanded the support for the main idea in the second paragraph, then the third, and so on. As for other support problems, the writer either built up the weak ideas or moved them to where they could tie into other points. The idea about pollution, for instance, was too big a subject to tackle in a brief essay, but the writer successfully worked in mention of one aspect of the idea by tying it to a more relevant point. Lastly, the writer added a definite conclusion, changing the original anecdote into a broad restatement of the thesis.

Your content and structure must fall in line overall, between paragraphs, and within paragraphs. Once you accomplish that, you are ready to examine your material sentence by sentence, using more focused questions. Since you would have worked out the biggest organizational problems by now, most of the questions pertain to content. Don't forget about organization even though you've checked it over already. Rewriting can sometimes cause new problems.

Here are some more questions you can ask to help identify problems one sentence at a time.

CONTENT
1. Is each sentence clear?
2. Are any sentences vague or confusing?
3. Does each sentence contribute to the whole?
4. Can I take out any sentences without losing something of importance?
5. Are there any inconsistencies?
6. Is anything repeated unnecessarily?
7. Would some sentences go better elsewhere? (Often the best place for some is in the wastebasket.)
8. Does *each* and *every* point relate to the principal generalization?
9. Does each sentence suit your intended purpose and audience?

ORGANIZATION
1. Does each sentence match the order of development promised in the introduction?
2. Does each sentence relate to the main theme, either directly or indirectly? If it refers to information elsewhere, is that other information actually included?
3. Is the closing sentence of each paragraph tied to the opening sentence of the one that follows? If not, is the shift in content made smooth with a transition?
4. Is each sentence linked conceptually to the preceding one and to the following one?

PICKING WORDS TO SAY IT

Each sentence, even each word, is a bridge in itself. Naturally, then, word-by-word examination is the next step. A single word precisely chosen is as important as a single block in a bridge. If the bridge is built of marble, it'll glisten. If it is built of salt, it'll melt in the rain.

In this phase the writer must ask, "Does each word add to the content?" Try cutting out words. Is the meaning of the sentence much the same even without the deleted words? If so, what, if anything, were the words adding to the content or the organization? Is each word the best one for the job? Are some words rhinestones, there for the show? Leave in the diamonds, take out the paste.

Compare the two paragraphs in the following example, one stuck together with an excessive number of words, one trimmed to the diamonds.

> When I was a little, young child, my father took me on peaceful, very long, rambling walks through the forests and countryside in the most serene atmosphere. The long walks became and grew to be a very thriving and sensitive part of my heart. Talking on subjects that were irrelevant to the world, but not to us, singing songs that were unknown to man, and laughing like hot storming thunder were the moments that my father and I shared. On one of our walks, my father gave me a very special acorn, an acorn upon which he made a face with gleaming eyes and a very wistful smile using a twig to complete the acorn's visage. Then tears began to roll down my father's face and onto his lips as he said, "This is the way I always want to remember you."

> When I was seven, my father often took me on long, peaceful walks in the forest near our home. I relished the walks because I loved nature, but mostly because I loved being with my father. The talk, songs, and laughter were ours alone. On one walk, my father picked up an acorn. With a twig he scratched a happy face on the side and then pressed the acorn into my hand. "This is the way I always want to remember you," he said, and he burst into tears.

The second version saved fifty-five words, yet it was more to the point, more visual, and more dramatic.

Pass each word under your magnifying glass and improve upon what you see. Then, take ten giant steps back. Look again at the piece as a whole. Sometimes detailed changes interrupt the overall flow of a piece, and you must cement the parts together again. Other times, you lose sight of your writing's larger purpose and its audience after examining and rewriting it so closely. Go back to the initial content and organization questions and ask them again. Also ask the following:

1. What am I learning as I write this?
2. Do I feel uneasy with any part of this? Do I sense that something is wrong?
3. Have I chosen the most significant aspects of the topic?
4. Do I still think this is an important topic? Have I treated it as if it were important?
5. Will my audience understand what I've written?
6. How else could I have done this? Would some other way, such as a different organizational pattern or different support, have been better?

And you can never ask this too often: What is the one most important thing I am trying to convey?

SAY IT 'TIL YOU SAY IT RIGHT

One of the hardest things about rewriting is that it is tough to be objective about your own words. In other words, it's hard to answer the above questions honestly. Reading your piece aloud to yourself or to someone else can help. Or, try writing a new outline from your revised draft without looking at the original. Do they match? What areas have changed for the better? For the worse? Ask someone else to read your material. Have that person write a one-sentence condensation of the piece. Does it parallel your thesis sentence? The phrasing won't be exactly the same, but the idea should match yours. If it doesn't, ask the reader to point out the sections that support a different idea. Try anything that will help you learn from what you've written.

Remember, neither the words nor the material on which they are written is sacred. Throw out what doesn't work. If it saves time, "cut and paste": physically cut out the bad sections and tape the good parts together. Instead of rewriting a whole page just to add one paragraph, use an additional sheet for the new paragraph. Then mark the place where it will be inserted in your next draft. If you're working on the computer, mark your print-out and then make corrections on your disk or hard drive.

Revision can mean restructuring your design, your aim, or even your ideas. There is always more than one solution to the problems you encounter. Your challenge is to find the one that works best for your purpose and audience. When you recognize your choices, you realize your power as a writer.

These choices begin with rewriting. The process of rewriting works from the broadest view (an instinctive scanning) to the smallest detail (the impact of a single word) and back again, to the effectiveness of the piece as a whole. As you revise, you're a detective seeking clues for better communication or an athlete flexing and strengthening your muscles. You're a chef trimming the fat from a hunk of meat or an artist adding color to a black-and-white picture. You're a brain surgeon, examining your own brain under a microscope.

You investigate, examine, rewrite, and re-examine repeatedly throughout the process of writing. As you ask and answer questions, revise and ask again, your focus is on content and organization. You will, however, notice and improve your style—how you're expressing your ideas—as you rewrite. Once the basic points have been sorted out, you can give more attention to this area, scanning and rewriting specifically for style.

Your aim is to reflect your own individuality by making your writing vivid yet concise, active but not busy, smooth but not flat. Style is the architecture, and you are the architect, building a bridge that not only works, but works magnificently. Style is you, at your clearest, most brilliant best.

SUM UP
1. In a brief paragraph sum up the chapter's main points, and briefly describe the rewriting process.
2. After class discussion, review your summary to see whether you stated clearly enough the importance of rewriting.

REACT
1. What role does analysis play in rewriting?
2. How do you feel about rewriting a paper? Why is rewriting so important a phase? What does the maxim "Hard writing makes easy reading" mean?
3. In what ways can revisions make a difference in the quality of your writing and thinking? (Address both points.)
4. What do you find the easiest to improve when rewriting? The hardest?
5. After class discussion add any suggestions which might help you revise more effectively.

ACT

1. Add three strong quotations to the "Notable Quotations" section. One quotation should refer to an issue of national concern, one to an issue of international concern, and one to a personal issue. Credit the sources. Here is one by James Joyce that I like: "Errors are the portals of discovery." Discuss its meaning and see how it relates to your life.

2. You should have a first draft from the exercises in Chapter 5. Apply the first set of "Content and Organization Questions" to it. Write down your responses. If the answers show problems in these areas, revise the essay's content and/or structure before going on to Exercise 3. Date your revisions. (It may help to work with a writing partner or group.)

3. After you have examined content and organization and rewritten to satisfaction, examine the essay in more detail. Ask and answer the second set of "Content and Organization Questions." Rewrite again to correct any problems you find. (It may help to work with a writing partner or group.)

4. Count and record the number of words in your essay, and review each word for clarity, preciseness, and vividness. Then rewrite, cutting at least twenty-five percent of the words from the essay. That means you'll cut one of every four words. At least.

5. In one sentence answer the question, "What is the one most important thing I am trying to convey?"

6. Show the essay to a writing partner who has not previously read your essay. Without revealing your answer to #5, have your partner read your essay and answer the question. Do the answers match? Discuss ways to improve the essay.

7. Photocopy an article from an encyclopedia (usually tightly written and well organized), and try to rewrite it, reducing the number the number of words by one quarter, without omitting any facts. (The "Booker T. Washington" sketch in *The Dictionary of American Biography* is a good one to try.)

"Revising is part of writing. Few writers are so expert that they can produce what they are after on the first try....Remember, it is no sign of weakness or defeat that your manuscript ends up in need of major surgery. This is a common occurrence in all writing, and among the best writers."

William Strunk Jr. and E. B. White

"Ever tried? Ever failed? No matter. Try again. Fail again. Fail better."

Samuel Beckett

seven

Rewriting: Style

If it weren't for style, all bridges with the same function would look the same. A highway bridge in Italy would look the same as a highway bridge in Japan; a foot bridge in Somalia would look the same as one in Scotland. In reality that is not the case. One bridge does not look exactly like another. Each has a style all its own, a style shaped by the mind and experience of its designer. Every piece of writing, too, has a style all its own, a style shaped by the mind and experience of its author.

Most people think of style as the clothing they wear. Pop singer Michael Jackson, for instance, started clothing fads with his style of dressing. In 1988 hundreds of thousands of teens imitated his style, wearing his signature white socks, black shoes, ankle length pants, and single white glove on the left hand. Only Michael wore the outfit naturally so the clothes moved as he moved, sang as he sang. He selected clothes that matched his personality and experience—brilliant by some accounts, eccentric by others, but certainly individualistic. Your individuality might not be as iconoclastic as his, yet it appears in your writing as you, without consciously thinking about it, select words and phrases that reflect your personality and interests. Your style is as unique to you as Jackson's is to him.

Style relies on two senses: sight and sound. Do the words create pictures? Are the images fresh and vivid? Can you see what the writer describes? How do the words sound? Read aloud, does one word meet another with a kiss or with a slap? Do the punctuation, voice, and sentence structure mesh together or strain apart? Does one idea melt into the next, or do the ideas seem disconnected? When the elements of sight and hearing work smoothly, the reader cruises through them; it is an effortless ride in a limousine. When they jostle one another, the reader bumps into the words. It is a rough ride in a jalopy with a driver who can't shift.

Although your aim is to write naturally, an effortless ride comes only with conscious effort. You must work at employing the stylistic elements—

coherence, conciseness, smoothness, and sound—which together give vividness to your writing. You must work, too, at avoiding stylistic pitfalls. In time that work will become subconscious. There will be less tinkering in the rewriting process and more style flowing naturally in the first draft. Eventually, your writing will be crisp and vivid. Right now, however, you need to understand the elements of style and learn how to make, as Arthur Plotnik put it in *The Elements of Editing*, "just the right improvement to create light, joy, song, aptness, grace, beauty, or excitement where it wasn't quite happening."

By the way, there is no point in using a stylistic device for its own sake. The reader will recognize it as such after tripping over it. By all means experiment, but be willing to toss out the experiment if it doesn't improve your writing. Reading aloud is the best test.

PUT IT TOGETHER

Holding your piece together overall, between paragraphs, and sentence to sentence is called *coherence*, and it is the first element to consider. You have already worked with organizational unity. The parts that make up the content of a draft should stick together like gum to a shoe before you begin this phase of rewriting. If you haven't kept the content unified, all the transitions in the world won't hold your writing together. But if your content is already unified, transitions are the quickest way to sew one sentence to the next, one idea to another. Here is a standard list of transitional words and phrases. Some link ideas chronologically while others link them according to their inherent relationship.

above	further	on the other hand
accordingly	furthermore	on the contrary
again	hence	opposite to
also	here	otherwise
although	however	presently
another	if this be true	second
as a matter of course	in addition	similarly
as a result	inasmuch as	such
as well as	in contrast	then
at last	in fact	then too
at the same time	in order to do so	thereby
besides	in short	therefore
beyond	insofar as	third
consequently	in sum	thus

doubtless	in the distance	together with
equally important	in the long run	too
even so	lastly	to sum up
finally	likewise	to this effect
first	moreover	to wit
for example	nevertheless	whereas
for instance	next	whereby
for the same reason	no less than	whether

The list includes both formal and informal transitions, and the choices are abundant, yet many a budding writer forgets to choose any. Read the following paragraph, which has no transitions. Note which points seem to begin or end abruptly.

An individual often feels the pressure to belong to and be admitted into social cliques. One might have to fulfill certain requirements. These requirements might be to wear a particular make of clothing, talk in a special jargon, or do certain activities. I would rather act independently and do what is best for me. I feel no such pressure and am not intimidated by any group.

Now read the same paragraph with transitions. See how the sentences have been stitched together

An individual often feels the pressure to belong to and be admitted into social cliques. To be admitted, *however*, one might have to fulfill various requirements. These requirements might be to wear a particular make of clothing, talk in a special jargon, or do certain activities. *As for me*, I would rather act independently and do what is best for me. *Thus*, I feel no such pressure and am not intimidated by any group.

At this stage of rewriting, you would scan your draft for transitions, as we just did for the above example. Are there any? Are there enough? Do the ideas flow together? You don't need a transitional word or phrase at the start or end of every sentence. The example above needed but a few. Content and organization, remember, should link the ideas naturally. You add transitions so that the flow of the language also sounds natural.

Many writers use the same transition repeatedly, even when another transition would make more sense. The repetition is boring and the inaccuracy confusing. Bear in mind, too, that some transitions are particular about placement. *However*, for instance, means "in whatever way" or "to whatever extent" when placed at the beginning of an independent clause, but it means "nevertheless" when placed internally or at the end. Be sure you know the meaning of a transition before you use it.

Also is one of the most overused transitions. Count the number of times it appears in the following paragraph.

> The preacher turned away from the grave and rested his hands on my shoulders. For the first time since I had learned of my friend's death, I was comforted. I also felt as if tomorrow would not be as painful as I had been expecting. However, I also remained very empty, as if a mole had burrowed through my insides and also left a hollow shell. I was also infuriated at the thought of my friend's senseless death.

Also appears four times, which is three or four times too often. Did you notice, too, that the writer put *however* in the wrong place? What other transitions in the above example could be changed? How would you change them? Where could the writer omit transitions and instead improve content? Here is a revised version, using transitions less self-consciously. When style is unobtrusive, the reader can concentrate on the writer's content instead of the delivery.

> The preacher turned away from the grave and rested his hands on my shoulders. For the first time since I had learned of my friend's death, I was comforted. Tomorrow, I felt with relief, would not be as painful as I had been expecting. The respite was momentary, however. His hands lifted from my shoulders, and the emptiness returned. Anger came too. Why did she have to die?

Besides transitional words and phrases, the simple repetition of key words, used sparingly, will link ideas effectively and offer variety to your writing style. Observe how the repetition helps build an analogy in the following passage.

> Suppose you don't like soup. Maybe you tried it as a child, and it seemed vile and wretched stuff. But I want you to try it again, because I like it so much. To entice you, I won't give you store-bought soup or instant soup. I will search for the best recipes and make the most delicious soup I can for you, knowing that as you try it, each taste will be better, and those tastes will linger on your palate.

For a Westerner, an introduction to Asian poetry is too often like the child's initial taste of soup. Having been spoiled by preconceived notions, the adult is tempted to avoid it and to leave the inspection of another culture to someone else. To overcome such reluctance, the reader must try the best translations, just as the diner must try the best recipes. One would assume that the best translations are readily available. This is, alas, not the case. Instead, much of the poetry has been diluted and made palatably bland, the translations Anglicized so much that they have lost the content and power of the originals. Homemade soup has given way to generic, canned soup.

For additional spice and coherence, use phrase variations (key words or phrases slightly changed). In the following excerpt concerning black migration to Canada in the mid-1800s, the writer uses phrase variations (underlined) to link the paragraphs to one another and to tighten each paragraph. The original phrase has a double line beneath it.

William Brown, a fugitive slave, was an effective anti-slavery speaker who preached a doctrine of self-respect, hard work, and self-improvement. He advised blacks to emigrate to the North as a first step towards their growth. His goal was full equality, and his aims and teachings can best be summed up by his own words: "Black men, don't be ashamed to show your colors, and to own them."

Austin Seward was another black who was not ashamed to show his colors. A dedicated abolitionist, Seward sought to overcome prejudice and become an integral part of a predominantly white society. With the aid of sympathetic white friends, he succeeded, becoming a prosperous grocer in New York. Yet Seward found that he owned more than his own colors, he owned an obligation to his kind. In the 1830s he sacrificed the security that he had gained to organize and direct a settlement of fugitive American blacks in the wilderness of Canada.

Try inserting a few phrase variations into your drafts. Read the changed sections aloud. Are they smoother? If so, keep the changes. If not, try again or restore the original version. Be careful not to overdo this technique.

Pronouns that refer to words or ideas in preceding sentences are another valuable transitional tool, both within and between paragraphs. As with so many transitional devices, moderation is the key to successful use. With pronouns you must also be sure that your reference is clear and that the point to which you refer exists on the paper, not just in your mind.

> •Unclear reference: During the day he watched the children, and at night he cleaned the house, ate ice cream, and read magazines. *This* had not always been the case.

> •Clear reference: He had assumed the role of homemaker almost too completely. During the day he watched the children, and at night he cleaned the house, ate ice cream, and read magazines. *This role reversal* had not always been the case.

Too few or too many transitions, no transitions between paragraphs, and too many of the same transitions are the chief problems interfering with stylistic coherence. Be on the lookout for them as you revise. Well-considered transitions will pull your material together and help you omit needless words.

KEEP IT SHORT

Omitting needless words is the art of conciseness, a second element of style. As William Strunk put it in *The Elements of Style*:

> Vigorous writing is concise. A sentence should contain no unnecessary words....This requires not that the writer make all his sentences short, or that he avoid all detail and treat his subjects only in outline, but that every word tell.

That every word should tell is the aim of writing; that every word *can* tell is its power. Words pack a wallop if you let them. You "let" them by choosing them precisely, by modifying them only when necessary, and by using no more words than necessary.

What is precision, really? When a machinist makes a part, there is what is called a "tolerance" of error: The part has to be of such-and-such a size and cannot stray from that size more than a fraction. A hole in a machine part, for instance, might have a 1/64-inch tolerance—or about as wide as this line: ____. A microchip has a tolerance in the thousandths of an inch, and gage blocks have a tolerance of a few millionths of an inch; these tolerances are smaller than you can see without a microscope. That is precision. Words should be so precise that there is no room for guessing the author's intent.

Look for the subtle shades of meaning in words, the nuances which tell the reader more than just meaning. "Today I learned something new about getting a job" says something different from, "Today I figured out something new about getting a job." *Learned*, in the first sentence, implies that the speaker received the information from an outside source, perhaps read a tip in a magazine or book, or was told something by a potential employer. *Figured out* implies action; the speaker put 2 + 2 together through experience and observation. Some words are clearly and unarguably one shade—black or white. Others fall between—shades of gray. Strive for the shade that suits your meaning, mood, audience, and purpose. Examine your writing by asking, "Is every word the best one for the job?" Then check each word to see that it is.

Thoughtfully chosen, most of your verbs and nouns won't need modifiers. Adjectives and adverbs tend to sap the life from the words they modify, as do qualifiers. Qualifiers modify or limit your words. As a teacher of mine used to say: *"Very* never adds very much." Read the list below.

apparently	somewhat	sort of
essentially	basically	especially
ultimately	inevitably	definitely
seem to	slightly	kind of
really	totally	literally
very	practically	actually

If you find these words occurring in your writing, cross them out. Nine times out of ten you are using them out of habit or to compensate for a weak and imprecise word choice. Compare the effectiveness of the following pairs of sentences. The first of each set relies heavily on modifiers, while the second is precisely built.

•Effusive, overflowing ingenious actions that don't have true, actual substance are just empty, prettily painted clouds of fluff.
•*Creativity without substance is sweet-smelling fluff.*

•Freud apparently believed that fantastic mental images, like the succession of images occurring in sleep, came from the functioning of the id and were controlled by the ego.
•*Freud thought that fantasy, like dreams, came from the id and was controlled by the ego.*

•Would a lottery really solve the state's drastic budget problems or just kind of move the problems to other places?
•*Would a lottery solve the state's budget problems or merely shift the problems elsewhere?*

•The drive was so long, drawn out, and tortuous that literally every bone and muscle in my body really ached, including my brain.
•*The twelve-hour drive numbed my rear and brain alike.*

Wordy material either uses too many words or uses "big" or "fancy" words when small ones would do (*parsimonious* instead of *stingy*, *obfuscate* instead of *confuse*, for example). If your writing is verbose, condense it.

•Wordy: The fact that he had no money for dating never stopped him from trying to get a girl to go out on a date with him. (26 words)
•Concise: He didn't have any money for dating, but that didn't stop him from trying. (14 words)

•Wordy: In June I matriculated after a quadrennial residence at my family's homeschool and commenced college shortly before the autumnal equinox. (20 words)
•Concise: I entered college in the fall. (6 words)

•Wordy: The reason why he went back east, traveling away from his farm, is because he hated and abhorred the west coast and especially pistachios after working diligently and slaving away as a disenchanted pistachio farmer in California for twelve years. (40 words)
•Concise: Twelve years of working with the red-dyed pistachios had stained not only his fingers but his perception of the west. He fled his California farm and headed east. (29 words)

Reread the last example. The revision is shorter and more vivid. Dividing one sentence into two has also given the style more snap.

As you revise your own work, challenge yourself. Can you make the same points in fewer words? Could you remove at least five adjectives or adverbs? Could you condense at least five sentences by choosing more precise words? Your final draft will be more vigorous if you can meet any of these challenges.

PLAY IT SMOOTH

Smoothness is a third vital element of style. Smooth writing sails the reader across the ocean with a steady wind and a gentle swell of sea; nothing exists but the adventure. Choppy writing is a sail in gale force wind and crushing waves; it can sink the vessel. What makes for smooth writing is consistency, fluid phrasing, and a flowing sentence structure.

Consistency of voice is essential. Voice can mean verbal voice—active or passive. Use the active voice of a verb rather than the passive to add vigor. When a verb performs the subject's action ("He sucked a lollipop"), the verb is active. When the verb expresses an action done to or acted upon its subject, the verb is passive ("The lollipop was sucked by him"). A writer might choose to slow the action by using the passive voice, but a lively pace demands the active voice. For that reason the active is preferable.

Voice can also mean point of view—who is speaking and who is being addressed. Formal writing typically has an objective or third person "speaker" (he, she, it, or they). The subjective, or first person, point of view (I or we) is found more often in informal writing. Whichever voice you choose must be appropriate for your audience. You would not, for instance, write a research paper in the first person voice. Similarly, addressing the audience directly by using the second person *you* is appropriate for casual writing or when the voice applies to a specific audience, as it does in this book. Using *you* to mean people in general (the indefinite use of the pronoun) can be confusing, and it invariably halts the flow of a composition. Likewise, the indefinite use of *it* and *they* interrupts the stylistic rhythm. Look at the confusion and awkwardness caused by indefinite use in the following examples.

•Indefinite: You feel sad when you first leave home, but you become excited later.
•Clear: Many young adults feel sad when first leaving home, but most become excited later.

•Indefinite: I can spend as much as three hours tuning up the car. You just never know how long it will take you.
•Clear: I can spend as much as three hours tuning up the car. I just never know how long it will take me.

•Indefinite: In this poem it reflects despair.
•Clear: This poem reflects despair.
•Clear: In this poem the author reflects despair.
•Clear: Despair is the subject of this poem.

•Indefinite: In rural areas they relieve tension by engaging in outdoor activities.
•Clear: In rural areas teens relieve tension by engaging in outdoor activities.

Consistency in voice keeps the reader from having to ask who is speaking and to whom the writer is referring. If you switch speakers mid-sentence, mid-paragraph, or mid-composition, your writing will be choppy and unclear, as is the following paragraph.

Don't underrate the importance of your appearance when you apply for a job. When people apply for a job, their first impressions are the only impressions. They should wear your best clothing, and they shouldn't have holes or wrinkles in your clothes. If you do, they won't hire you.

If your material mixes speakers, revise it; choose one voice and stick to it. If you have trouble catching voice problems, try circling the pronoun representing the "speaker" in every sentence. Then read all the circled words. Do they match? If not, correct the ones that are inconsistent. Here is the above example revised to contain a single voice.

Don't underrate the importance of your appearance when you apply for a job. First impressions are the most important impressions. You should wear your best clothing, and you shouldn't have holes or wrinkles in your clothes. If you do, the employer won't hire you.

OR:
The importance of the job applicant's appearance shouldn't be underrated. The first impressions that the applicant makes are the most important. The applicant should wear the best clothing, without holes or wrinkles, or the employer will hire someone else.

Consistency in tense, another vital aspect of smoothness, also keeps the reader from losing track of the action. Only shift to a different tense when it is needed to express a change in time. See how confusing the tense shifts are in the following examples.

•Unnecessary tense shift: If possible, *look* for work a week or two before classes begin so that you *could beat* the fall rush.
•Consistent tense: If possible, *look* for work a week or two before classes begin so that you *can beat* the fall rush.

•Unnecessary tense shift: Let the manager *know* when you are available; you *will call* regularly to ask for assignments or before you *will have* a big chunk of time for working.
•Consistent tense: Let the manager *know* when you are available; *call* regularly to ask for assignments or before you *have* a big chunk of time for working.

•Unnecessary tense shift: *Try* unusual outlets for temporary assignments. If you *had contacted* publishing firms, direct marketing firms, or research outfits in town, you *could offer* your services.
•Consistent tense: *Try* unusual outlets for temporary assignments. If you *contact* publishing firms, direct marketing firms, or research outfits in town, you *can offer* your services.

Think through the time sequence before and as you write. If an event is happening now, use the present: "I am writing with a broken pencil. I am sharpening the pencil." If it happened in the near past, put it in the past tense: "I *wrote* poorly with a broken pencil, so I *sharpened* it." If it happened regularly in the past, use the present perfect: "I *have written* with a broken pencil, but I *have not done* so successfully." If part of the action occurred before the rest of the action, use the past perfect first and the simple past next: "At first I *had written* with a broken pencil, but then I *sharpened* it." Don't forget the future tense: "From now on I *shall sharpen* all my pencils before writing." Above all, don't mix tenses if there is no reason to. "I have sharpened my pencil because its point will be dull" makes no sense; the tenses are inconsistent. Instead, you would say, "I sharpened my pencil because the point was dull." Simply checking tense and making it consistent will improve style.

(Some people are put off when they see the names of the tenses because they never got around to learning them. Even if you can't remember the name of the tense you are using, you can still check your verbs to make sure they reflect when the action is happening and that any changes in the verb form make sense with the action. On the other hand, learning about and understanding the tenses will make the job of writing easier and give you more control over it, so I recommend that you do so.)

Another aspect of smoothness is the fluidity of the phrases and individual words that you use. Read aloud. Listen carefully to the sound of your words. Small glitches and big stumbling blocks alike will slow or stop your speech. Wherever your voice stumbles is probably a spot that needs smoothing. Work on it, and then read aloud again. With time and practice you will hear mentally as you read, but the audible test will always be the keenest one.

Repetition of sounds can lend smoothness, but be wary of excessive alliteration. When you see the same letter begin several words in a row, you can count on catching chiding comments coming from corrective counselors. Unless deliberately chosen for a special effect, the repetition is awkward.

Grammatical errors such as incorrect verb formation, word omission, and syntactical mistakes also impede the flow of a sentence. Pay particular attention to syntax when you revise; be sure your sentences are logically constructed.

- •Awkward and incorrect: I would not of had a date if I hadn't of asked.
- •Smooth and correct: I would not have had a date if I hadn't asked.

- •Awkward and incorrect: We could go his house and play pinball.
- •Smooth and correct: We could go to his house and play pinball.

- •Awkward and incorrect: My biggest worry after graduation is what am I going to do then.
- •Smooth and correct: My biggest worry is what I am going to do after graduation.

- •Awkward syntax: Being uncomfortable is an unreasonable condition to expect people to have to work in.
- •Smoother: It is unreasonable to expect people to work in uncomfortable conditions.

Smoothness is marred by stiffness. Rigid words and phrases, some of which are standard fillers even in professional writing, will march through your style like wooden soldiers in a ballet.

•It is evident that we deserve a smoking lounge.
We deserve a smoking lounge.
•I am writing you because it would appear that the lavatories in Chessler Hall are filled with smoke and littered with cigarette butts.
The lavatories in Chessler Hall are smoky and littered with cigarette butts.

•The reason why I would choose a V.C.R. to represent America in the 1980s is because people in our country in that decade cared more about self-entertainment than the state of the world.
The V.C.R. symbolizes Americans in the 1980s, for self-entertainment was more important to them than the state of the world.

MAKE IT TALK

You have to make your writing talk, and to do that, you have to listen to it. The beat, the pauses and stops, the accents, and the cadence can make sentences sound musical. Or off-key. (Cadence is the rhythmic measure of a sequence of words.) Your natural musical voice will reveal itself if you listen, write, listen, and rewrite.

When you study poetry, you learn how important beat is to each line and stanza. Beat moves the reader through the words. Likewise, whole sentences have a rhythm and a pace. Some move quickly. Other sentences move more slowly, as they travel through the mind's ear. Paragraphs, too, move according to the inner measure of their sentences. This measure creates a pace which you can vary to create a mood. For example, long sentences give weight to the subject matter, and thus, in a persuasive essay, you might use lengthy sentences to build a slow, deliberate argument. To add punch to your point, you might change the pace abruptly by switching to a short, feisty sentence to conclude: "Illegal dumping must stop."

Occasionally an author makes a deliberate error for the sake of impact or pacing, such as writing a sentence fragment. A fragment can add zing to your writing if done consciously and appropriately (a fragment can work in a short story or an ad, for instance, even in a writing textbook if informal, but it has no place in a business letter). Used arbitrarily, accidentally, or repeatedly, fragments are nuisances.

Be alert to other aspects of pacing such as punctuation. Punctuation does two things: It provides basic information about how to read a sentence, and it directs the flow of the reading. You might consider punctuation as traffic signals for your reader. No punctuation is a green light to go and keep going. A comma is a pause, a yellow light. A period is a stop. A red light. Dashes are an interruption, not quite a complete stop—a blinking yellow. Parentheses are an aside (a detour). A semi-colon is a lengthy pause; it is comparable to a blinking red light. Colons are open pauses, bare hesitation: lights turning green as you approach. Used correctly, punctuation keeps the traffic of your writing running smoothly.

Read the following paragraph aloud. As it has no punctuation, you must read it without taking a breath.

Creating interesting parttime work is often a matter of looking at what other people need and then doing it at a fair price first ask yourself what your own special strengths and skills are for instance are you knowledgeable about any area or are you handy with tools can you type or run a computer then ask yourself what other people need is there a need for tutoring or examcramming services or do people need cheap car tuneups and basic engine maintenance you could offer weekend fixit specials through local weeklies or flyers are people up in arms about recycling but too lazy or busy to do anything about it start your own recycling business and collect double profits customers pay you to haul their goods and the recycling company pays you for the goods if you are inventive and analytical you can match your skills and energy to the needs of those around you with hustle and chutzpah you can earn the money you need even in a tight economy and do so on your own schedule

Now, read the paragraph with the correct traffic signals.

Creating interesting part-time work is often a matter of looking at what other people need and then doing it at a fair price. First ask yourself what your own special strengths and skills are. For instance, are you knowledgeable about any area, or are you handy with tools? Can you type or run a computer? Then ask yourself what other people need. Is there a need for tutoring or exam-cramming services, or do people need cheap car tune-ups and basic engine maintenance? You could offer weekend fix-it specials through local weeklies or flyers. Are people up in arms about recycling but too lazy or busy to do anything about it? Start your own recycling business, and collect double profits: Customers pay you to haul their goods, and the recycling company pays you for the goods. If you are inventive and analytical, you can match your skills and energy to the needs of those around you. With hustle and chutzpah, you can earn the money you need even in a tight economy—and do so on your own schedule.

The paragraph above, now punctuated, flows smoothly. Partner to punctuation is sentence variation. Varying (or deliberately repeating) your structure can create a particular rhythm and mood. A series of sentences structured the same way (parallel structure), for instance, can create a slow pace and a calm mood, as in this example:

> Late summer afternoons, we gathered on the porch to rest, too tired even to chatter. Still wearing her apron, Ma poured us fresh-squeezed lemonade, then sat beside Pa on the swing. At that hour, our giant oaks cast deep shadows, stretched lazily beyond us and into the pasture. Invariably, the wind held its breath, held under the same spell of stillness. For a few moments, nature, adults, and children sat in quiet accord, aware only of life's beauty. A cow mooed. One of us giggled. Noise resumed.

But be warned: too much of the same sentence structure—indeed, too much of any one tactic—and the reader will soon be snoring. The change in sentence structure at the close of the above paragraph woke up the reader and, by contrast, accentuated the soothing tone of the first five sentences.

You can vary sentences and rhythm further by using adverbial, adjectival, and subordinate clauses in different positions within the sentence. Don't let the grammatical terms keep you from using these tools. Look them up, write examples of each, and post them on your desk as a reminder to try them out. Test your experiments on a reader. Can that person read them aloud without stumbling? If the experiments sound awkward or forced, the style is not natural to you or your reader. Revise your sentences until you are comfortable with them and they sound good.

All in all, when you write for sound and flow, you are writing as a musician composes, on the one hand seeking harmony, and on the other seeking contrasts which accentuate that harmony. You listen for a beat that propels the writing forward or deliberately slows it, and you adjust the notes and rhythms, points and counterpoints, for balance and clarity of tone. It is often easy to hear the fumbles in these obvious examples, but it can be hard to find them in your own prose. Learn to listen to and read carefully your own writing as well as that of others. Awareness is the key to mastering style.

To sum up, style is you, writing with your senses tuned to your own experience and voice and to the way your words, phrasing, sentence structure, and punctuation reflect that experience and voice. It is the sound of your mind, recorded in words. You can improve your style by consciously applying techniques for greater smoothness. But mostly you improve style by being alert to it in your own writing and that of others. Between your first draft and your last draft, your own voice must step forward and speak. You are the writer, and it is your voice the reader wants to hear—not Ralph Ellison's or Eudora Welty's, not your mother's or father's, not your English teacher's, and not mine either. Yours.

SUM UP

1. Write a two-paragraph summary of the chapter. In the first paragraph state the chapter's thesis and major supporting points, and show their relationship. In the second paragraph give a brief explanation of and example for each stylistic element.
2. After class discussion review your examples and add any others which seem more to the point.

REACT

1. What is your own definition of style?
2. How is it possible to write in your own voice and still improve and change your style?
3. Your style is uniquely you; what characteristics do you think your style shows? What aspects of your personality do you want to shine through?
4. What is meant by the "rhythm and pace" of a sentence or paragraph? Give examples. Read aloud to yourself samples of your writing. Are you pleased with the rhythm and pace? On a scale of one to ten, how would you rate your beat?

ACT

1. Add at least three quotations to your "Notable Quotations" (crediting the sources) that demonstrate distinctly different styles. Read them aloud and try to figure out which most appeal to you, and why.
2. Rephrase one of the quotations in your own words, as though you were telling a friend what the author said and meant.
3. Rewrite the following paragraph so that it is coherent and concise. Even though you will be adding transitions, the paragraph should be shorter after revision.

In Taiwan one day we visited the local elementary school where the children in first grade to sixth grade got their education from 9 to 3 each weekday, Monday-Friday. The door was open; we went inside because it was not closed, and we assumed that its being opened meant that we could. The classrooms were big. Also, they were roomy. They were airy also. Fresh air flowed through the windows and doors, as all the windows and doors, not just the outside doors but those into the classrooms, were open. The rooms had dirt on the cement floors but were tidy, and all the desks were neatly lined in rows. There were forty desks in each room. There was one teacher for every forty students, and the teacher had a big desk at the front of the room. Each classroom had a portrait of Sun Yat Sen on the front wall, and there was beside it a list of orders for the children to obey. The school was the pride of the community.

4. On a blank page list the following categories, leaving four to five spaces between each one.

Smelly Words	Morning Words	Vexing Words
Chilling Words	Soft Words	Ugly Words
Dark Words	Sunny Words	Creepy Words

Write at least four words under each category. Be original. Include nouns and verbs as well as adjectives. Get in the habit of consulting the dictionary and *Roget's Thesaurus*. Practice using them in this exercise.

5. In as few additional words as possible, resuscitate the following lifeless paragraph by making it smooth and coherent, by appealing to the senses, and by giving it your voice. Add or change punctuation as needed, correct problems with consistency of voice or tense, and change the passive voice to the active. Replace stiff wording and vague ideas with vivid phrasing and examples. Try to make the piece not only livelier but shorter.

In the student lounge lists of required textbooks were carried about by lost freshmen who didn't know where they were going owing to the fact that it was the first week of classes at college. You feel lost at first and they did. One student stood out from the rest. He carried all his textbooks already in spite of the fact that he had the whole week to buy his books. The reason why is he admired books. There is no doubt that a new book was special to him because it contained a world in itself. A book to him had importance for several reasons, and this was his feeling in being at college with his new books. All his books were new, and not one had been used before. And it was with feelings that they were carried.

6. Go back to your draft from Chapter 6. Make these revisions.

1. Rewrite one sentence so that it sparkles. Add the sentence to your collection of "Notable Quotations" for this chapter.
2. Delete any useless qualifiers.
3. Rewrite two sentences so that the sentence structure varies from other sentences in the paragraph.
4. Change two passive verbs into active verbs. If you don't have any passive verbs, fantastic. Skip to #5.
5. Look for indefinite use of the pronouns *you*, *it*, or *they*. Rewrite so that all references are clear and the voice is consistent.
6. Date your revisions.

"Find a subject you care about and which you in your heart feel others should care about. It is this genuine caring, not your games with language, which will be the most compelling and seductive element in your style."

Kurt Vonnegut

SECTION 3: WHY BUILD A BRIDGE?

Chapter 8, Purpose: Reasons to Build

Chapter 9, Another Reason to Build

Chapter 10, Putting Reasons and Purpose Into Practice

Chapter 11, Tone and Attitude: Building for an Audience

"Take out another notebook, pick up another pen, and just write, just write, just write. In the middle of the world, make one positive step. In the center of chaos, make one definitive act. Just write. Say yes, stay alive, be awake. Just write. Just write. Just write."

Natalie Goldberg

eight

Purpose: Reasons to Build

Many years ago I spent the summer in Scotland. One day I journeyed to the Orkney Islands, a small and fiercely beautiful cluster of islands to the north. To get to the main island, I had to travel a bridge of some sort. But the North Sea (specifically, the Pentland Firth) is too rough and deep, and the distance between the mainland and the island too far for a span of bridge. The only "bridge" that could serve was a boat—a ferry to carry passengers, cars, and small trucks. In this case, the way from one point to another was shaped by a particular group of needs. The task wasn't just to get across, but to get across in a way that met those needs. The purpose, as it were, shaped the bridge, and the bridge became a ferry.

At this point in the book, you have much of the information necessary to build a bridge. You have learned how to clear a building site (prewrite) and collect some building materials (content). You know that you must give order to what you build (organize) and that you will have to improve what you build (rewrite). You have even practiced all these elements. So are you ready to build? Not yet. Like the designer of the "bridge" across the Pentland Firth, you must first know your purpose or purposes in building. Further, you must understand how to use that knowledge as a decision-making tool.

Whoa, you say. Isn't the reason to build to communicate? Yes, of course, that is the reason in its essence, but purpose also asks: "What do you want to communicate?" There are four basic answers to this question and thus four basic reasons to write. Everything you write aims to meet one or more of these purposes, or writing tasks. One, you write to describe something—*descriptive writing*. Two, you write to tell a story—*narrative writing*. Three, you write to explain something—*expository writing*. Four, you write to express opinions and ideas logically—*reasoning*, or *persuasive writing*. Everything you write meets one or more of these purposes first. It can also meet a variety of other purposes, such as to analyse a book, compose a memo, get into college, or write a research paper. What is more, these reasons for writing will and should shape content, just as the conditions for traveling from mainland Scotland to Orkney shaped the method for getting there.

This chapter covers descriptive, narrative, and expository writing. The next will cover persuasive writing. While we'll isolate the tasks to understand them better, the elements of each often cross over. Even though the chapter itself is expository, I use descriptive, narrative, and persuasive techniques to show you how purpose influences writing.

DESCRIPTION: SAY WHAT YOU SENSE

Imagine, for a moment, that you are a newborn. All your experiences, from hunger to wetness to frustration, are sensory. Your eyes rove constantly, as you visually classify the sights in front of you, and your fingers reach out, searching for meaning by touching. You sniff and breathe in clues to your environment, identifying your mother by her smell, your father by his, and strangers as unrecognizable. You hear voices without recognizing them as such; soft sounds and vibrations attract you, adding pleasing dimensions to your experiences. Your ability to taste and to feel objects with your mouth is your tool for relating to them. Without your senses—seeing, touching, smelling, hearing, and tasting—the world would be incomprehensible to you.

Think about what you just read. Did you at any time picture a baby? Did you visualize any of the ways a baby explores the world? Getting you to see the world from a baby's perspective was one reason for the description. The deeper purpose was to point out that even as an adult you process the world through your senses. So do your readers. Put sight, sound, touch, and taste into your descriptive writing, and you'll create a direct passage to their nerve centers.

How else can you connect with your readers? Use details and figurative language to convey the feel of a scene, a person or persons, a situation, an object, or an idea. You must do more than look at a scene or recall a memory, reporting at random. You must analyse the subject and its impression on you, asking yourself, "What is this really like? What words conjure up these images?" You must recognize the distinguishing characteristics of your subject and then classify and categorize those characteristics in a striking, yet logical, manner.

ARE MY DESCRIPTIONS DESCRIPTIVE?

Description is simple in purpose but challenging in execution. Ask the following of any descriptive writing, your own and that of others, to test the effectiveness of the delivery.

1. Is the description clear?
2. Is there enough information to give the reader a complete picture, but not so much detail as to overload the senses and blow a descriptive fuse?
3. Are the details organized into groups so that the reader can see both the whole picture and the component details?
4. Are the ideas compelling?
5. Does the syntax reflect the complexity of the material? Are sentences varied with modifying phrases, appositives, adjectival clauses, and the like?
6. Is the wording precise, colorful, and appropriately rich? Or is it flat, familiar, and clichéd?

These questions present the criteria you must meet when you write descriptively. With them in mind, look again at the opening paragraph of this section, reprinted below. Does it succeed as well as you thought previously, now that you're aware of what it *should* do?

Imagine, for a moment, that you are a newborn. Your world is defined by your senses. All your experiences, from hunger to wetness to frustration, are sensory. Your eyes rove constantly, as you *visually classify the sights* in front of you, and your fingers reach out, *searching for meaning by touching.* You sniff and breathe in clues to your environment, *identifying your mother by her smell, your father by his*, and strangers as unrecognizable. You hear voices without recognizing them as such; soft sounds and vibrations attract you, adding pleasing dimensions to your experiences. Your ability to taste and to feel objects with your mouth is your tool for relating to them. Without your senses—seeing, touching, smelling, hearing, and tasting—the world would be inaccessible to you.

When you analyse the paragraph, you see that the description works organizationally: the ideas are logically grouped, the points tie together to make a whole, and the structure follows the hourglass pattern. As for style, the sentences are varied. All the criteria but one are well met. The reader gets a picture, but it is a general one, relying on ideas more than senses to convey the image. The first two underlined phrases must go; they are redundant and vague. The paragraph also needs a few more telling details to come to life. Adding smells to the third underlined phrase will awaken that sentence. Here is the revised paragraph.

> Imagine, for a moment, that you are a newborn. Your world is defined by your senses. All your experiences, from hunger to wetness to frustration, are sensory. Your eyes rove constantly from fuzzy blob to blurry mass, as your fingers reach out restlessly. You sniff and breathe in clues to your environment, identifying your mother by her milky smell, your father by his sweat. Strangers remain unrecognizable. You hear voices without recognizing them as such; soft sounds and vibrations attract you, adding pleasing dimensions to your experiences. Your ability to taste and to feel objects with your mouth is your tool for relating to them—fingers and pacifiers, for example, mean suck, relax, and be comforted. Without your senses—seeing, touching, smelling, hearing, and tasting—the world would be inaccessible to you.

You could go on and on, beefing this up with details, but it's not necessary. And you must be careful not to overdo. A few choice images satisfy; more is not necessarily better. The paragraph now fulfills its purpose, describing a scene in a way that appeals to the senses.

WHICH WAY IS UP FROM HERE?

In descriptive writing the development can be intuitive, unfolding according to your own sense of how things fit, as in the description of the baby. Alternatively, it can be spatial or chronological. Spatial development moves the reader from one point to the next in a logical physical pattern by using references that are visual and contiguous (going from one adjacent spot to the next), such as from left to right, right to left, near to far, far to near, up to down, and so forth. You might use spatial organization, as in the example below, to describe how a room looks, how a garden is laid out, or what you see when you lift the hood of a car. Notice that the writer focuses on spatial references to help the reader see the shape of the room and what it contains. The description wouldn't be nearly so successful, however, it the writer didn't also include many sensory impressions of the room.

The house had two rooms. I walked quickly through the first, which was bedroom and sitting room combined, to the second, which was kitchen, storeroom, bathing room, and dining room in one. I leaned against the peeling paint of the doorway and looked to the right. I wrinkled my nose at the smell of mold and body odor that assaulted me as I poked my head through the door. A long counter ran the length of the wall. The nearest section was covered with dirty plates, cups, and utensils; past them stood an open jar topped with two flies in jelly heaven. Beyond that was a warped metal basin, filled with scum-covered water. Beginning about the middle of the counter, on the other side of the basin, were piles of machine parts, most of them broken. The collection stretched to the end of the wall and cascaded onto the floor, running all along that wall to the next corner. An old-fashioned wringer washer interrupted the line-up, which petered out between its feet. Above the washer, on a ten-penny nail hanging in the corner diagonally from me, hung a blackened wash tub. I hoped I wasn't expected to bath in it.

The writer carefully marked a visual path around the room with well-connected reference points. The counter, walls, and the corners are shown in relationship to the original vantage point, the spot where the narrator stands. If a spatial description is clear, you should be able to draw a rough but accurate sketch of the area described.

Instead of moving the reader through physical space, chronological development moves the reader through time. The development might follow events in the exact order they occurred, or it might shift back and forth through time. A chronological plan might work well in relating a series of events, recapturing a memory, explaining how time has changed a scene, and so forth. A flashback, a shift to a scene from a previous time, is one tool of chronological development. The following scene uses a flashback, chronological description within the flashback, and some spatial development to describe a period in the writer's youth.

I parked the car in our old driveway. I hadn't been driving when I lived here as a child, of course, but as I pulled in, I recognized the crunch of the gravel as the same sound that used to roll beneath my dad's 1960 red convertible. Once out of the car, I looked around. My forty-year-old eyes took in the changes the years had wrought. There was smooth lawn where the rhubarb patch had once been, but I could still remember the broad, rangy leaves and the red-green stalks of the plants, like sunburnt sticks of celery, the patch filling up the corner of the yard. My mouth puckered recalling the sourness of their raw taste. That was when I was six and new to the neighborhood. By the next year I was everybody's friend, and the surroundings were toys of my imagination. The weather-beaten chestnut tree next door had smooth brown nuts perfect for slingshots. It had been knocked to a forty-five-degree angle during Hurricane Donna, and then it became a rocket ship. My playmates and I climbed it, straddled it, and shot to Jupiter in it. We were Flash Gordon and Dale battling Zarkof in the stars. When we came back to earth, we jumped down to our own planet, drew circles in the dust of good old Earth, and shot marbles. Now a plum tree, tender with soft lavender blossoms, was staked in its place.

Description invites the reader to forget his own world and enter the world you, the author, create. It enables you to share a potent image or make an abstract point clear by relating something concrete that mirrors your idea. There are many reasons to describe. The only one that isn't valid is to picture something just for the sake of describing it, to list details without creating a whole impression. A description needs a thesis, as do all the writing tasks.

NARRATION: SAY WHAT HAPPENED

Whereas description tells something to provide a picture of it, narration tells about something to show what happened with it. At the purest level, you narrate to tell a story. Most often there are secondary reasons for narrating. Your secondary purpose might be to share the impact of a scene or to explain something about the narrator. It might be to illustrate a point, as in an anecdote. Or, it might be to develop a broad theme or moral through a story (an allegory). A personal narrative might have a secondary purpose of persuading the reader that the writer is an interesting person who is qualified for college or work. But secondary purposes are just that: secondary. First comes the process of story telling.

Let's define narrative further. A narrative is a story with a beginning, middle, and an end. Sounds easy, doesn't it? Yet knowing when to start is a significant challenge for most writers. So is knowing where to end. A narrative is not a flat tale; the action rises and falls, the turning point being a climax of some sort. (The climax could be an action, such as sinking the winning basket with one second on the clock, or it could be a revelation, such as, "Suddenly I saw these daily chores as an homage to life." All the features of a story are not of equal importance; they have greater and lesser significance. These features should be connected logically with one another in relationship, time, and sequence. To put this another way, the narration must include all the points essential to knowing what happened, when it happened, and in what order it happened. (If the order, for the sake of style, is given out of sequence, the reader must still at some point be able to piece the order together.) The writer must use the appropriate tense for the sequence to be clear in time and logic. In essence, narrative writing is descriptive writing, but instead of describing something static, narrative writing describes something in motion through time and/or space.

SO WHAT'S YOUR STORY?

Here are two examples from letters to me from my youngest brother when, as a recent college graduate, he was traveling through Asia. The first is a straightforward account of a day, and the second reviews a series of events leading to one event. Notice that the first uses only the past tense, while the second must use more than one tense to show the passage of time. These narratives differ in complexity but share common characteristics. They describe an event or series of events in time, with definite starting and ending points. Nothing extraneous is included.

Pay particular attention to the tense choices (subject and verb are underlined) and the use of phrases and transitions (italicized) which help identify the sequence of events. It sounds simple enough to pick the right tense for the job, yet many writers have difficulty handling this task in complex narratives.

In the morning, I went into Taichung City and walked around *a bit*. I met a Taiwanese college sophomore who studies engineering. He led me to a place where I could buy postcards, and *then* he showed me the Taichung Park, an exhibit of traditional Chinese fans, and a cultural arts display with old paintings and artifacts. *On this trek* I noticed air-raid loudspeakers atop some of the buildings. I lunched alone, *having left* my guide at the arts display. *In the afternoon* I met my friend Charlie at the house of his Chinese language teacher, a Miss Chang. She was *sometimes* called Mrs. Tsai, for the women in Taiwan used their maiden names or their husbands' name or both. We spent *the rest of the day* in Miss Chang's small living room and looked at my pictures from mainland China, Japan, and Korea.

One day we attended a rat festival. Chainat had been losing about 30% of its rice crop to rats. *So* the government offered 3 baht (about 15 cents) for each big rat caught and 5 baht for every 20 small rats. The festival we attended marked *the last week* of the campaign. The provincial governor made a speech. The farmers *then* displayed their rats, or, *in some cases*, just the rat tails. *Next*, all of us (1,000 people) went into a rice field with sticks and beat up little rats. *Next week* we will attend the closing ceremonies. The government will award cash prizes, and we shall all feast on rats. Fried rat on a stick, *coming up*. I can hardly wait.

A TELLING STRATEGY

How did my brother know where to start his narrations? The saying goes, "Begin at the beginning," but this advice is hardly useful when you are struggling to establish the framework of an event. One way to start is to try the following brainstorming strategy before you write your outline or first draft. Create a list of all the episodes that come to mind. For instance, my brother might have written: Taiwan, capturing rats, eating rats. When you think of an event, give it a number to indicate when in the story it occurred. Beside each episode write a code of one or two words that clearly identifies it in your mind. Next, draw a horizontal line across a blank page. You are going to "draw" the sequence of events as a time line. Write the code words under the line, in order from left to right, as numbered. Place a short vertical line across the horizontal one to signify each episode. If there is an episode pivotal to the story, forming a climax or clarifying a secondary purpose or thesis, star it or make that line more prominent.

Read the words in order. Have you left out any points essential to the sequence? If so, add them in their proper places. Reread the first few points and then cover them with your hand. A new order is created. Do you need some of the covered points? Uncover the points one by one. Are all the points essential to understanding the sequence, or could some be deleted? For instance, in the first narrative above, the writer could have begun by telling where he had spent the night, and this might have appeared logical to him, since night precedes day. But that detail, placed on a time line, shows up as part of another sequence, one irrelevant to recording a specific day in Taiwan. Covered up, it makes no difference to the narrative.

Examine your last few points the same way. Are all needed to explain your main point? Do all fit into the primary sequence? Often you'll find unneeded details on this side of the time line as well. Circle the first point deemed absolutely necessary to the story and across the last point also absolutely necessary to the story, without which the story wouldn't be clear. Start and end your story at these points. As you write and rewrite for narration, you will accomplish your basic purpose if you can distinguish the significant features of the story and put them in order through time and space.

After the first draft, try asking the following questions. Together they form the criteria for successful narration. If you can't answer the questions well or at all, you know you need to rewrite.

1. Is the sequence logical, with all parts clear in time, order of execution, and relationship?
2. Are the references clear and distinguishable? Can you tell who did what when?
3. Is the overall story comprehensible?
4. Are all the ideas relevant to explaining character(s), motive, and action?
5. Are the details graphic and important?
6. Is the organizational pattern clear? If the writer uses devices such as flashbacks, simultaneity (looking at different actions at the same time), or suspense, are they clear? Do they aid or impede the telling of the story?

EXPLANATION: SAY HOW YOU DO IT

For some writers I know (including myself), strenuous physical activity provides a needed break from intellectual labor. It clears the mind, gets the oxygen flowing, and circulates the blood to some place other than the rear. When I can, I swim laps. The last time I went to the pool, however, two things went awry. I forgot my goggles, and I jumped into the shallow end of the pool. Since I'm used to swimming with goggles and from the deep end, I was disoriented. I couldn't stand the chlorine with my eyes open, had to swim with my eyes closed, and consequently bumped into the walls. Without my usual reminder that the deep end signaled a full lap, I lost count of my lengths. Needless to say, I soon gave up and went home, mission impossible.

During the short time I did swim, I was thinking about expository writing—writing that informs, provides an explanation, or both. It is description that explains a process. This type of writing can be easier than narrative writing because the focus is obvious. Also, you usually deal with only one character, one set of activities, or one goal. The aim is to discern the relationships among events, sequence, and cause and effect. Then you must explain those relationships to your readers in order of importance, chronologically, or by comparison and/or contrast. (Comparison shows how things are alike, while contrast shows how things are different.)

Back to swimming. As I churned through the water, I realized that many factors go into an explanation of something, and these factors must take into account quirky, personal details (such as beginning a lap from the deep end) and no-nonsense, practical details (such as why you need goggles). One must appraise the quirky details to decide whether to include or eliminate them. If I were telling you how to swim laps, I'd be inclined to tell you to start from the deep end, just because I do. But that isn't a significant detail. It's a non-essential detail that would give the reader a false idea of what steps are necessary to swim laps. If I included the point, I would have to qualify it, explaining that it was a habit, not a necessity. On the other hand, I *would* have to tell you to wear goggles. That point is essential to lap swimming, because otherwise you would burn your eyes, bump into walls, and get so frustrated you would stop swimming.

As a writer tackling expository writing, you must sort through all the details that come to mind in the same way I just demonstrated. You must ask which details are essential, which clarify the process you're trying to explain, and which get in the way. You start by saying, "How do you actually do this? How would someone else do this?" (As I've already pointed out, it might not be the same way.) Keep asking questions: "What are the required materials and steps? In what order do you proceed?"

Once you've figured out the details, you must list them in order. One step must lead to another, and all steps must lead to the desired goal. When you've assembled the points in order, you can write a draft, bearing in mind that your sentence structure must reflect the needs of the description. For example, you must be able to show simultaneity ("Hold the window glass steady with one hand while with the other hand you slowly edge it out of the molding trim."); proximity ("Set your printer within four feet of the computer so that your lines will reach, enabling you to pull out copies without leaving your chair."); lapse of time ("Wait thirty minutes for the glue to set."); and the consequences of various steps ("If the trees are not transplanted when dormant, you will have to water more often, and the plants may go into shock.").

Listed below are the criteria for writing to explain. They reflect the primary challenges (sometimes called "problems") of writing for this purpose.

1. Are any instructions clear and complete?
2. Could the reader complete the task with these directions?
3. Are any directions superfluous (unnecessary)?

4. Is the goal presented at the onset of the piece?
5. Is the process broken into distinct steps?
6. Do transitions smooth the shift from one instruction to the next?
7. Are the steps presented in the most logical order?
8. Is each cause-and-effect relationship clear?
9. Do the steps lead to the desired goal?
10. Is the goal restated in a conclusion, or does the piece end abruptly after the last direction?

Think of these challenges while you read the expository example, a newsletter column I wrote about preventing roof leaks. The content had to include all the essential steps, from beginning to finish. In addition, I had to define any terms that might be unfamiliar to the reader and give examples for clarification. When points came up that were relevant enough to mention but would have been a digression to explain or to discuss, I referred the reader to another source for more information instead of explaining it. The goal was to enable any reader of the column to go out and perform the task. Notice that the article, while not exciting, is successful in meeting its purpose. It does presume, by the way, that the audience is already familiar with tools and home improvement.

In the last issue I talked about the importance of winterizing your home BEFORE the weather changes. Although the temperature has already dropped, it is not too late for one more pre-winter task: an annual roof check-up to prevent leakage. Water damage is one of the most common problems in a home and one of the costliest. Yet an afternoon of easy work can forestall a lot of problems.

Arm yourself with a caulk gun, several tubes of a brand of acrylic caulk (I like Dap® or White Lightning®), an old paintbrush, an old chisel or screwdriver, and a sturdy ladder. Now go up on the roof. (A warning: If your roof is slate, wear soft-soled shoes with a good grip and only go up if the slope is minimal. Slate roofs are hard to climb, easy to damage, and best left to a professional to examine.)

First, check the flashing (the shiny metal) around the chimney. With your screwdriver or chisel, scrape out old, loose caulking and any loose cement where the flashing meets the brick. Then brush the area clean with your paintbrush. Lay a 1/4" bead (line) of caulk in the flashing seams (where one piece of flashing overlaps another), along the edges of the flashing, and on top of the chimney where the flue liners come out. If the cement is cracked or flaking, call a contractor to repair it (unless you are handy with concrete).

Next, take a look at the roof as a whole. Look for popped nails and hammer them down. Caulk cracked seams on asphalt shingles. If any shingles are missing or broken, you need to replace them or have a contractor do so (patching with roofing cement will work only temporarily). If you have a tin roof, patch any cracks in the seams with roofing cement (any brand). Likewise, a tar roof should be patched now. Typically the back of the roofing-cement can will carry instructions for patching.

Before coming down, check all gutter seams. Caulk any that are cracked or separated. Finally, on the ground again, check the downspouts. Make sure they'll carry water at least two feet from the house. If they won't, add 4" flexible tubing onto the ends. (You can partially bury these and plant liriope or some other ground-cover around them so they're less noticeable; or install cement splash guards. Both are available at hardware stores.)

Of course, you'll need to call a roofer if you have found any major leaks. In general, however, an ounce or two of caulk is worth a pound of cure.

What transitions did I use to indicate a shift in action? Can you identify syntactic structures that indicate proximity, sequence, or other complex ideas vital to an explanation? Were any of the points personal or quirky? If so, did I somehow identify them as such? The writing was organized according to sequence. Could it have been organized any other way? Some explanations have a narrow potential for order; if the details aren't stated in a particular way, the instructions can't be followed, or they won't lead to the desired result. I sometimes try several types of order in an outline to see which is the most effective.

Expository writing challenges your logic and your ability to apply descriptive and narrative skills. If you practice expositions, however, and visualize yourself following the course of action—as though you were running a movie in your head of yourself doing each step—you'll find it the easiest form of writing.

SUM UP

1. Write a short summary paragraph of the chapter. Include a list of the four basic writing tasks and the purposes of each.
2. After class discussion add any new points and clarity your original thoughts.

REACT

1. How does purpose direct your writing? Give examples from outside the text.
2. What are the problems you often experience with each of the writing tasks? Give examples.
3. Each writing task has a basic purpose. How does the purpose differ from the thesis?
4. Why does each writing task have its own criteria? Are any of the criteria the same for the different tasks?
5. After class discussion add any new points and clarity your original thoughts.

ACT

1. Add a pair of quotations to "Notable Quotations." Both should be descriptive, but choose one quotation that is rich and lush and a second one that is sparse yet telling. Both should convey a point that moves you emotionally, but in different ways (for example, one makes you feel sentimental and the other angry). Be sure to credit your sources.
2. Add two more words to each category in ACT, Chapter 7, #4.
3. Imagine that you're blind. (If you *are* blind, you have an advantage here.) Describe a room that you know well. Appeal to all senses but sight, and use tangible details and figurative language to make your reader "feel" the character of the room—and be able to walk through it without tripping over something. Use one word from your word lists (Exercise #2).

    Remember, a prewriting exercise may help you get started and find your focus. A timed writing exercise with a focus on touch, for instance, would be a good jumping-off point for this exercise.
4. Brainstorm about an event in the last year which you consider a personal "rite of passage." Review your ideas, and write your thesis statement. Pin down the points at which the action starts and ends. If you have trouble determining what those points are, create a timeline. Refer to "A Telling Strategy" for guidelines. Then write a narrative that clearly and evocatively tells the story of your "passage."
5. Explain one of the following:

    •How to plan a budget
    •How to play defense or offense effectively when the other team is better (any relevant sport)
    •How to fix something of your choice (must involve more than seven steps)
    •How to sew a dress, blouse, or pair of pants
    •How to tune up a car

•How the solar system works
•How to apply and remove full make-up

Use whatever pattern of order will work best for your subject. Remember that your aim (to explain) must be narrowed to a focus, that is, to explain for a certain reason (for instance, why you should plan for a budget). As always, you need a central idea in the form of a thesis statement.

6. Review the products of Exercises 3, 4, and 5, asking the appropriate criteria questions. Make revisions as necessary to meet the criteria.

"Whatever you can do or dream you can, begin it;
Boldness has genius and power in it."

Johann Wolfgang von Goethe

nine

Another Reason to Build

Persuasion is reasoning's battleground; reasoning is persuasion's soldier. Persuasion is the art of inducing someone to believe a certain position and, often, to act on that belief. Reasoning is the logic that makes your argument meaningful to the reader; it is the rationale you use to persuade someone. Without a rationale, an argument is only an opinion. Opinions are not persuasive; they are merely personal statements of belief. When it comes to conquering an opposing view and winning someone to your side, reasoning is your best strategy; pertinent facts and figures, examples, and comparisons are your best tactics. To write for the purpose of persuasion, then, you must first arm yourself with the principles of reasoning.

Dictionaries typically define *reasoning* as the process of forming conclusions, judgments, or inferences from facts and premises. The reasons, arguments, and proofs resulting from this process are also considered reasoning. When you reason, you must examine the available information, weigh the comparative effectiveness of one point over another in obtaining a desired conclusion, and choose a format that will enable you to reach your conclusion. There are three standard formats: *reasoning from example*, *reasoning from axiom*, and *reasoning from cause (causal reasoning)*. These formats are what you use to build a persuasive argument. A complex argument might use all three, but an effective argument can be built with just one.

PERSUASIVE EXAMPLES

When you infer (derive from reasoning) a general rule from an example or a group of examples, you are reasoning from example. In practice this means that you state your position (your thesis) and then support it through examples that make your position viable and credible (workable and believable). The premise is that if your position holds true in other situations, as demonstrated through the examples, it holds true in the situation you are proposing. Since you're drawing a conclusion from the examples, you must use more than one or two examples. Otherwise, your reader will doubt the validity of your argument and wonder about exceptions to the rule. For the purpose of reasoning, your examples do not simply flesh out the content; they are the muscle that pounds it home.

Besides using ample examples, you must use telling examples. This is when you exercise your judgment in weighing the information. Some examples are strong enough to make the point firmly, while others make the point only marginally. You must decide which ones are weak and eliminate them. The following paragraph includes one strong and one weak example. See if you can spot them as you read.

> A numerical grading scale would be fairer to students. The majority of our state's schools use such a scale. Our five-letter grading scale puts us at a competitive disadvantage. When our students apply to state colleges, the imprecision in grading often makes our students look worse than other students, even though they may actually have better records. Also, students with a 96.0 average feel cheated when they receive the same A as someone with a 93.0 average.

The third sentence makes a strong point because it brings a larger scale to the argument and thus adds credibility. The last sentence, at least as stated, is a weak point, as it refers to a minority of students and draws attention to a feeling, not a fact. It should be deleted or rephrased. Rewritten, the sentence could make a broader point about the impact of motivation on grades.

Any examples that don't tie directly to your thesis will undermine your argument. The reader's reaction to irrelevant or only loosely relevant examples is this: "Ah-hah! The writer can't think of valid points; this example doesn't even relate to the position."

> Furthermore, with a numerical scale students whose parents reward them with dollars for grades might get more money. *[You may see the importance of this, but a school board won't.]*

Your examples should show both sides of the argument. When all your points are one-sided, you appear biased. Bias equals opinion, and opinion isn't persuasive. Pointing out the opposing view and then refuting it through examples can strengthen your position considerably.

Some students oppose a numerical grading scale on the ground that students have to work harder to get good grades and therefore have less time for extracurricular activities, part-time jobs, and social life. Yet a state-wide survey last year showed that the attainment of good grades inspired students to work harder and that those students who did well in school also did well outside of school.

Similarly, you must point out any notable exceptions to the rule you are proving. If you know an outstanding example of an instance when the rule doesn't hold true, state it. If you avoid mentioning it, you lose credibility because your reader will see that your argument conveniently ignores a major point. You must address it, show why it is an exception, and note why your view still holds true despite it, as in the following paragraph.

Children under three typically need twelve or thirteen hours of sleep. They must take part of this rest during a mid-day nap, or they become too tired to function well. Some active children prove the exception to this rule, and they begin skipping naps around two years of age. Nevertheless, this group is decidedly in the minority. Also, many active toddlers compensate for their long days by going to bed early and getting their twelve hours in a longer, night-time sleep.

In sum, choose examples which show directly or indirectly why your view should dominate and why the opposing view is invalid or limited.

PERSUASIVE PRINCIPLES

Reasoning from axiom is reasoning from principles as distinct from examples. Instead of saying that a premise is true because it works in the specific situations you have mentioned, you say that because a general rule is true, it is therefore true in the situation which you are discussing. For this method to work, the axiom, or generalization, must be verifiably true. For example, if your operating principle was, "All college students are party animals," your argument would fail, because the operating principle is false. Only some college students are party animals. Always test the validity of your axiom before using it as the basis for your argument.

In addition, the axiom must apply to the specific situation in question. If I were talking about enforcing dormitory regulations, the premise, "College students who break dorm rules make trouble for all dorm students" is a workable one. If I were talking about no-smoking rules in high schools, I could say, "High school students who break the no-smoking rules make trouble for all the students." Each of these statements is appropriate for the specific situation, but neither could be applied to the other. I could make a broader statement that would cover both situations: "When students break established rules, other students pay the consequences in stricter regulations and restricted privileges." Or, broader yet, "Lawbreakers affect all society." Your task is to shape a principle that covers the points you wish to make in as specific a way as possible. Thus, the last tenet (statement of belief) would cover the college and high school situations, but only loosely so; the argument hinges on the elements of law and society. While school situations parallel these elements, they are not identical, thereby making the axiom difficult to maintain in an argument. An axiom is ineffective as a method of reasoning when it is too loose, vague, or applied incorrectly.

PERSUASIVE CAUSES

Causal reasoning says that certain elements have an impact on one another, and that from this you can assume that general principles are true (inductive reasoning) or that specific conditions or events will occur (deductive reasoning). Inductive reasoning moves from the specific to the general; information is collected and then a generalization is formed. If this causes this, and this leads to that, then this broad effect will happen. Deductive reasoning works the opposite way. It moves from the general to the specific, saying that if a broad element is true or occurs, then this will cause that, and ultimately a certain other thing will happen.

The formulas for causal reasoning are simple:

1. If A happens, B will happen.
2. If A happens, B happens.
3. Because A happened, B will happen.
4. B happened because A happened.

Here are four statements that match the formulas and demonstrate cause-and-effect relationships.

1. Deductive reasoning: If I study for a test, I will do better on the test.
2. Deductive reasoning: If students study over a period of several days for tests, test scores are higher.
3. Deductive reasoning: Because the student stayed up all night reading, he will have a hard time paying attention during today's classes.
4. Inductive reasoning: Drug use declined in the 1990s during a period of aggressive advertising campaigns addressed toward potential users. Therefore, aggressive advertising campaigns reduce drug use.

Cause-and-effect arguments have some particular challenges. Chief among them is faulty logic. Test your logic by asking yourself these questions in the brainstorming stage and again after writing a draft.

1. Which came first, the chicken or the egg? When it comes to cause and effect, this isn't a silly question. *Which is the cause, and which is the effect?* Are you confusing the two? For example, does excessive drinking cause alcoholism, or does alcoholism cause uncontrollable drinking? Some questions are difficult to answer, and might be answered legitimately more than one way, so be sure you have plenty of support for whichever way you respond. Also, be sure that you use a form of reasoning that will work for your subject.
2. *Could the cause produce the effect in question?* In the following statement, for example, the cause would not necessarily produce the effect: *"If a school dictates how students must dress, students will lose the willingness to learn."* The students might be annoyed, and a few might use that annoyance as an excuse for not studying, but there isn't enough power in a dress code to destroy the will of an entire student body. The logic of the statement is faulty; the cause could not produce the effect as claimed.
3. *Is the writer telling only part of the story?* The effectiveness of all types of reasoning pivots on a full disclosure of pertinent details. Consider this sentence: "Mr. Jackson was fired on December 12 and is filing a sexual harassment suit. He claims that Miss Howell, his supervisor, fired him after he refused to date her." This story relates only part of the details.
    Revised to include all the relevant facts, the argument differs greatly. "While it is true that Miss Howell had asked Mr. Jackson for a date the previous day, that detail is circumstantial. Mr. Jackson

had had several warnings previously about his job performance and had been told that one more problem would result in dismissal. On the day he was fired, Mr. Jackson was forty minutes late to work and took a three-hour lunch break, thereby breaking two company rules."

4. *Is this the only cause that could produce this effect?* Again, if other causes are not mentioned, the argument is weakened, as in the case above.

5. *Are there any conditions that prevented the cause from operating as usual?* If so, account for them. "When there is a good speaker for commemoration exercises, more people attend. Mr. Elijah Washington Jones spoke at the ceremony last night, and only a few people attended." The reader would deduce that the speaker was a poor one. This is an unfair deduction if other "causes" were present, such as the following: "There was a tornado warning all evening, and residents were advised to stay at home."

6. *Does a cause-effect relationship really exist?* Coincidence is no ground for argument. Just because two things occur that are related to the same idea or that happened in sequence does not mean that one produces the other. A conclusion that can't logically be inferred from the premises is called a *non sequitur*, such as this: "Because it was raining when the band played, the electricity went out." The conclusion is illogical; there is no causal relationship between the two points.

6. *Is the cause-effect relationship important?* Just because two things occur that are related does not mean that a consequence is strong enough to support an argument. Always look for your strongest argument. For example, the following argument mentions a causal relationship, but the point is so much a given that it has no persuasive impact: "If the grading scale were abolished, no student would receive a poor grade." The point is true, but it's so obvious, it's meaningless.

REASONING REASONABLY

Starting with an invalid position is as worthless as writing with carrots. Test your viewpoint in the brainstorming/prewriting stage. If you cannot list at least three to five ideas as support, then you probably have an insupportable position or one that you need to research more before tackling it. It will help if you classify your findings into types of reasoning—by example, axiom, or cause and effect. Then you can determine whether there is enough support to build a strong case. If you're having trouble coming up with support but still hold your viewpoint, try brainstorming with a partner or a group. Ask for support for the opposing view or views; writing a counterpoint for each point will give you the material you need and help you refute contrary views. What is more, you can often find a new facet of your own side by examining the strengths and weaknesses of the other. Or, you may discover as you listen and talk that you lean toward the other side. If the situation permits, change your thesis to match your feelings. After all, writing is a process of self-understanding.

Continue to test your viewpoint as you write, read, and rewrite your drafts. Because you learn what you think as you write, you may find after a few drafts that you no longer believe in or agree with your original proposition. Support for your new position will have crept into your writing. Use it in the revised draft. Again, a reading/writing partner can help you find discrepancies in your content and organization.

Understanding what reasoning is and how to use it requires practice and observation. Read a great variety of material, and read it specifically to dissect the reasoning at work. Underline successful tactics; make notes. You can further test your reasoning and your persuasion by asking yourself the following questions as you read either outline or draft:

1. Is the position valid and convincing?
2. Is there enough support to show that the position is significant (worthy of writing and reading about)?
3. Is the organization sound?
4. Do the ideas build logically on one another?
5. Are any points ambiguous?
6. Are all claims supported?
7. Does the argument conclude soon after the key points and the most forceful ideas have been presented, or does it ramble on?
8. Is there a definite summary and conclusion? If the writing is persuasive, is there a call for action or a directive to rethink a previous position?

IF YOU CAN REASON, YOU CAN PERSUADE

Persuasion enlists emotional appeal while marching forth with muscular assertions; the strategy is to entice the reader into embracing your position. It is the machismo conviction that what you say should be done, should be done; that what you say is desirable, is really desirable. It is the lure of a cunning mind that uses brain, not brawn, to persuade someone to a certain view or course of action, to make the reader *want* to believe or do something.

The goals of persuasion are belief and action, although sometimes the action is only changing or affirming a belief. These goals turn around the *proposal*: the claim or claims you are trying to establish in conjunction with the action that you are seeking. Claims are assertions that something—an idea, a plan, a fact, or a value—is due and fitting. According to Annette T. Rottenberg in *Elements of Argument*, the three types of claims are claims of policy, claims of fact, and claims of value.

Claims of policy assert that a particular course of action should or should not be followed. For example: "Recycling of aluminum, plastics, and paper should be handled by the city sanitation department in weekly collections." Or: "Recycling of aluminum, plastics, and paper is an individual matter and should be handled through independent agencies."

A proposal related to a claim of policy must prove a need for a change (or to retain the status quo, that is, to let things remain as they are). The proposed policy or plan must also be workable. For instance, if the first claim above asserted that collections should be twice daily, the claim would not be workable. If the city is bankrupt and has been canceling programs right and left, there may not be money even for weekly collections; the claim would still be unworkable. If, in the second case, no independent agencies handle recycling, then this proposal would be unworkable.

The plan or proposal must also be free of major disadvantages. If the city would profit from recycling, then it would be a major disadvantage to the city to let independent agencies handle it. If providing recycling would be a drain on the city's revenues, independent agencies might provide an answer. Thorough research into all aspects of a plan should reveal the disadvantages which you must then weigh against the advantages.

Lastly, the proposal must be better than other plans or policies, and the argument must demonstrate why.

> Weekly collections would increase the amount of material being recycled, thus easing the strain on our landfills and our natural resources. While it would cost the city $500,000 for the initial investment in trucks, the plan would generate $100,000 a year in money earned for recycled materials. A program based on individual contribution would have limited involvement and would scarcely ease the landfill crisis; in addition, it would raise no revenue for our failing city coffers.

Notice that the argument uses specific details and facts as proof for the claim. To be effective, you must document your claim.

Claims of fact differ in that you are not examining a course of action but an assertion about a certain situation. You might think that this means you have to prove a fact, and how would you do that? But in a claim of fact what you are actually trying to prove is not that the fact is true but that your fact(s) proves your assertion to be true. Your argument is created by marshalling the best information available to support your claim. This information consists of reasoning, proven facts, proven axioms, statistics, examples, and quotations, all organized to persuade the reader of the veracity of your assertion. Here are some examples of claims of fact.

•Infants require the stimulation of touch to survive.
•Watching more than one hour of tv a day increases violence in adolescents.
•Weatherproofing a house can save thousands on heating bills.
•Exercise helps alleviate stress.

Obviously, a claim of fact is insupportable with insufficient proof. The claim must be realistic. "Blondes have more fun" is a claim that pretends to be fact but which is not supportable. (I am a brunette, and I have a lot more fun than some blondes I know.)

Unlike a claim of fact, which takes a general view and looks at it unemotionally, a *claim of value* is a stance on an issue, emotional, spiritual, intellectual, or otherwise. It asserts that something is worthy or unworthy, admirable or despicable, right or wrong, or generally with or without merit. It is a judgment. As such, it teeters on being an opinion, and, as I said earlier, opinions are not persuasive. Therefore, you have to take extra care that you provide sufficient and logical support. You must also give the reader the criteria for judging the claim. For instance, if you said, "A pass-fail system is unfair," you should not just rail against the system. You would have to describe the system, describe any other systems available, and compare the merits and demerits of all (or all the major ones). You would also have to ask and answer the questions, "What's fair? What's unfair?" Depending on how long your essay or letter was, you might skim over the criteria in a few sentences or analyse them fully in a few pages. Then you would have to use reasoning and support to show the relative strength of your stance and why it was important for your audience to care about it.

Here are some sample thesis statements that indicate claims of value.

•A grading curve hurts most the students who work the hardest. (The writer would have to define "hurts," "most," and "hardest.")

•The Senate's process of intensive confirmation hearings for Supreme Court Justices is out of control. (The writer would have to define what was meant by "out of control.")

•Machiavelli was the most influential political theorist of all times. (The writer would have to compare him to other theorists and discuss their influence as compared to his.)

•I am the best candidate for the position of research assistant. (The writer must prove the claim by defining "best" and by addressing issues of skill, experience, aptitude, and attitude.)

PERSUASION IN ACTION

As with claims of policy and fact, you employ a claim of value in a variety of uses, including general essays, letters to the editor, personal narratives for college, and application letters for jobs. All these require persuasion, and all are framed organizationally around four basic steps.

1. Introduce the thesis in an attention-getting way. Make the reader aware of your topic.
2. Once the reader is aware, keep the reader interested by showing why the reader needs to pay attention. If you're discussing a problem, you must show the nature and scope of the problem in what is known as the *problem statement*. For example: "The writing assessment showed that a problem in persuasive writing is use of appropriate language and tone. Students have trouble conveying a strong feeling in a tone that is forceful and evocative, not slangy or whiny."
3. You must lead the reader through all the information needed to weigh the merits of your position. You must defend your position, supporting it fully.
4. You must satisfy the reader by proposing a solution or point of view, and in closing, request action, belief, or approval of the idea at the heart of the thesis. Tell the reader what you want the reader to do or believe. For example:

•Write a letter today to your school board protesting censorship in the school libraries.
•Give a contribution today to help research on multiple sclerosis.
•Make it a daily habit to do something helpful for someone else without telling anyone about it.
•Revoke the curfew for dorm residents.
•Change the grading system effective next semester.

The conclusion may be a summarizing comment, instead of a call to action per se, especially when your writing has mixed purposes, such as to persuade but also to apply for a job or to analyse an idea. "I look forward to an interview." Or, "As applied, Machiavelli's *Prince of Politics* was the book of treachery, not politics." The idea is not to follow a formula, but to understand the principles behind what you are doing.

You now have a sound basis for understanding the principles not only of persuasive writing, but descriptive, narrative, and expository writing. You are well armed to conquer the subtler aspects of purpose.

SUM UP
1. In as many paragraphs as needed, write a summary of this chapter's main points. Highlight the chapter's thesis statement.
2. Write any questions you may have about the chapter.
3. After class discussion add any new points and clarify your original thoughts. In addition, answer any questions you listed in #2.

REACT
1. What are the differences in the way examples are used when reasoning from example and when supporting a general essay?
2. Describe the elements of a strong argument. Think about what kinds of argument are likely to persuade you of something. Try ranking them in order of persuasiveness.
3. Recall a piece of persuasive writing that caused you to change your mind or to do something you wouldn't otherwise have done. (Ads are designed to persuade, and sometimes they do. If you're stymied, you might remember a particularly good ad that impelled you to buy a particular product.) Analyse the piece and try to figure out why the argument was effective. What kind or kinds of argument does the writer use?

ACT

1. Add to "Notable Quotations" one demonstrating solid logic and one demonstrating persuasion based on emotional appeal. (Hint: Speeches are a good source for persuasive quotations. Look in the library for daily or weekly speech tabloids.)

2. Read through speeches or the editorial section in newspapers and magazines. Check the logic used in the writing, looking for non sequiturs. Find at least two and explain why the logic is faulty. Rewrite them to make the argument logical.

3. Write a paragraph aimed at convincing traditionally schooled students to homeschool. (If you are in a traditional school, aim your paragraph toward convincing homeschoolers of the merits of a public or private education.)

4. Write a persuasive paragraph using reasoning from example. Conclude with a proposal that is a claim of policy, fact, or value. The paragraph should respond to the following problem.

> Two men put a roof on a new house. Each does half. One is an experienced roof-builder; the other has no experience. They each work the same amount of time. The half of the roof that the experienced man built does not leak; the other half does. Do both men get paid? Do both get paid equally? Does effort count as much as result? Does an experienced person have an obligation to correct, educate, or compensate for an inexperienced person?

5. Rewrite your paragraph using reasoning from axiom. Conclude with a proposal using a different type of claim.

6. Rewrite your paragraph using causal reasoning, either deductive or inductive (or both). Conclude with a proposal using the remaining type of claim.

7. Test your logic, reasoning, and persuasion in your three paragraphs by asking yourself the questions in the "Persuasive Causes" and "Reasoning Reasonably" sections. Rate your three arguments as effective, mildly effective, or ineffective. Exchange papers with a writing partner, and rate each other's arguments. Discuss the results and ways to improve each paragraph.

"I see but one rule: *to be clear*."

Voltaire

ten

Putting Reasons and Purpose Into Practice

There is usually more than one reason for writing; purposes overlap. You may need description to bring your narration to life or explanation to clarify how your proposal will work. Nevertheless, whether isolated or enmeshed in a dozen goals, purpose shapes content. *All* reasons for writing, primary and secondary, shape content. Specifically, purpose influences what information you choose to include and what you choose to exclude; it helps you clarify what your content must be. Imagine all the information about a given subject; that information, written down, is a list without shape. It is a sprawling amoeba, slobbering around without definition. Try to fit an amoeba into a pattern of organization. The content spills over the edges because the organism does not have a rigid perimeter; its shape is undefined. Purpose gives your information and ideas form by giving you boundaries.

Purpose helps you make decisions about content and about how to organize that content. A letter of application, for instance, has a clear purpose: to persuade someone to hire you for a specific job. The information you include must relate only to that purpose; you select information that demonstrates that you have the requisite skills and attributes needed for the job. You must organize that information so that it fits the structure of such a letter. That is, you must state the purpose of the letter immediately, without fanfare, and you must make it clear which job you are seeking, before you say anything at all about what a great person you are. Your options regarding both content and organization are thus limited by purpose.

Okay. Purpose shapes content and organization, but how do you, the writer, put this into practice? You do it by clarifying your primary and secondary purposes before you begin a draft. You can do this mentally, you can use some of the earlier writing exercises, or you can try the following method.

In a column down one side of a page, list your reasons for writing, from the most basic reason ("to describe a room") to the generally relevant ("to describe a room so that a person could walk through it in the dark") to the loosely relevant ("to satisfy a writing assignment"). Now brainstorm about your content, thinking about all these reasons as you do so. Write your thoughts in a column beside the reasons. When you are finished, draw a line from every thought to every reason with which it can connect. If you have any thoughts left over, those not connected to a purpose, they are probably irrelevant and may be crossed off. If you have any purposes that have no ideas connected to them, you need to re-examine the purpose to make sure it fits with your primary purpose. If it does (or if it *is* your primary purpose), you need to brainstorm again, or perhaps do some research and take some notes to ensure that you have sufficient relevant content. You need not follow this practice every time you write, but it helps to try it a few times with each of the four writing tasks (description, narration, explanation, persuasion) so that you get a feeling for how purpose affects content.

Here is another way of looking at how this works. Here is an amoeba-like list of random thoughts about hot chocolate. Again, the writer doesn't worry about grammar at this stage.

- instant, Swiss Miss; pour and stir
- a Charlie Brown character melted a brown crayon in water to make it
- whipped cream—canned, fresh, frozen
- chocolate curls on top of melting cream
- superior taste of made-from-scratch cocoa
- kids like any type, as long as it's chocolatey
- memories are made from distinct tastes
- Nestle's Quik in the winter as a kid, sitting in the furnace room
- cocoa in summer in Banff, Alberta, Canada, at age 17
- mocha—coffee and cocoa
- microwave or stovetop preparation
- steamy hot, chocolatey water out of the coffee/chocolate machine at the ice rink, when I was 8
- caffeine in chocolate; a "pick-me-up"; good or bad for kids?

Think about the four writing tasks. If your aim were to describe, would you have enough material to work with? No. You have only a few details, such as "chocolate curls on top of melting cream." How about narration; is there enough here to put together a story? No, although there are hints of a story. What events led up to sitting in a furnace room, drinking cocoa in

Canada, or ice skating? More brainstorming with the intent of narration is necessary before you could write about hot chocolate in this context. Similarly, there are a few points related to explanation (how to make hot chocolate) but not enough information yet. As for persuasion, you could argue only the question of whether caffeine is good or bad for kids or whether home-made cocoa is better than instant. At any rate, the list lacks the focus that purpose would give it.

Purpose in Action: Brainstorming

Observe in the following lists how considering the topic within the boundaries of each writing task has directed the brainstorming. Some thoughts from the original list have been deleted, and some have been included in all the lists. I've added new points for each, as now I have guidelines for choosing the material.

TO DESCRIBE
Whipped cream, canned, freshly made, or frozen
Chocolate curls on top of melting cream
Nestle's Quik, sweet and milky; left a milk mustache
Instant cocoa is sugar water; real cocoa is bittersweet chocolate
Steamy hot, chocolatey water out of machine
Marshmallows—sticky, white puddles
Little vs. big marshmallows
Chocolate mud at bottom of cup
Good memories

TO NARRATE
Cocoa as a memory
Summer in Banff, Alberta, Canada, at the Banff School of Fine Arts
The restaurant served cocoa, the mountains out the window
Coming of age; first time away from home, first real cocoa, first real whipping cream, first chocolate curls on top
Impact of sights and tastes on senses
Memories are made from distinct tastes

TO EXPLAIN
Methods of making cocoa and hot chocolate
Shave a bar of chocolate, melt in a small pan, beat in milk from a bottle thick with cream
Microwave or stovetop, milk or water
Swiss Miss instant; add hot water, stir
Nestle's Quik, Ovaltine, and other mixes; use hot milk and stir
Cocoa from scratch; cook powder with sugar, cinnamon, vanilla, and hot milk
Add whipping cream or marshmallows

TO REASON/PERSUADE
Superior taste of made-from-scratch cocoa
Memories are made from distinct tastes
Rich chocolate curls
Real whipped cream
Watery, sugary taste of instant mixes; not memorable
Milk chocolate rather than dark; dark richer, memory lingers
Create special combos such as mocha
Pleasure of ritual
Rituals summon memories; doing something "instantly" doesn't leave time for reminiscing

See how the content had to change once purpose was a factor? As I made up these lists, I mentally checked every thought against the goals for each writing task. Because I know what is expected from each task, I could add or drop ideas according to whether they would help me reach those goals (and whether they match my thesis statement, of course).

Now look at the process one step further, in draft form. As you read the four essays below, observe the way the same points are redirected and reorganized from one piece to another to accomplish different aims. Also notice how some points serve the same contextual capacity in all four essays but may have been rewritten for greater impact. In addition, notice that the purpose affects the complexity and, correspondingly, the length of each piece. This will frequently be the case. Be alert to how many details from the brainstorming lists appear in the essays. (The thesis statement in each essay has a double underline.)

1. Description/Hot Chocolate

Say the words, "hot chocolate," and delicious images spring to mind within moments. The picture starts above the cup and moves downward, one vision following another. First flashes the image of a stiff mountain of canned whipped cream, spiraling lopsidedly to the heavens, above steaming dark liquid. Or you picture a wobbly tower of home-made whipping cream, soft clouds spilling over the sides of a fat china cup, chocolate curls freckled atop. Or you see sticky visions of marshmallows, little ones melting together in a glob or big ones with brown-tinged edges, white puddles floating in a child's "Peter Rabbit" mug.

Remembered taste follows sight, as you recall the cool, soft flavor of the topping chased by the hot, thick taste of the chocolate. Milky Nestle's Quik, bittersweet cocoa, rich chocolate syrup, or sugar-water instant mixes—regardless of the recipe, the taste satisfies. And after the last sip, the liquid gives way to chocolate mud, that residue at the bottom of the cup that creates a mustache on your upper lip. No matter how it's made, hot chocolate is soul-satisfying, each cup a museum of memories.

2. Narration/Hot Chocolate Sends Me Places

I can see my breath this morning, and I'm wearing three sweaters to warm my outsides. To warm my insides, I've made a cup of hot chocolate and slathered it with home-made whipped cream, piled high and topped with chocolate curls. <u>Memories are made from distinct tastes</u>, and with the first creamy, chocolatey sip, I'm transported back in time thirty years.

I was seventeen and attending Banff School of Fine Arts in Alberta, Canada. It was a June day, but the air was as breathtakingly crisp as the air I breathe this morning. I sat in a restaurant during a break between classes, watching the owner chip away at a bar of chocolate, melt it in a small pan, and beat in milk from a bottle thick with cream. When it was hot, he poured it into a tall mug and topped the brew with an enormous mound of home-made whipped cream. Then he shaved the chocolate bar some more, dropping delicate curls on top of the melting cream. I had never had genuine cocoa before; I had never had real whipped cream before; I had never even imagined having chocolate on top of it all.

I looked past the cup and out the window at the Rocky Mountains, majestic and magnificent, the polar opposite of my flat midwestern home. It was a day of firsts, and whether it was the cocoa, the view, or being away from home, at the first creamy taste, I came of age. I knew I was beginning an adventure that would last a lifetime.

3. Explanation/How To Make Hot Chocolate

You can make hot chocolate several ways. You can make it from a mix or from scratch, and there are several variations for each. The instant types—Nestle's Quik, Ovaltine, Swiss Miss and the like—use the same basic method. Measure the prescribed amount of powder or syrup into a large cup or mug, or empty a premeasured packet into it. Depending on the instructions with the mix, add either hot water and stir vigorously, or add cold milk; heat in the microwave or on the stove; and then stir well.

Making hot chocolate from scratch takes a bit more time. One method uses a bar of presweetened chocolate. With a sharp knife or a grater, shave off a handful of chocolate for each cup you make. Melt it in a small pan over a low flame, stirring constantly. When it has fully melted, beat in one cup of milk with a spoon, whisk, or electric beater. Heat this slowly, again stirring constantly, until well mixed. Taste before serving, and add more chocolate according to preference. An alternative method uses powdered cocoa. To make a single cup, heat up one cup of milk in a saucepan over low heat, stirring frequently. Meanwhile, measure one heaping teaspoon of cocoa into a tall cup. Add two teaspoons of sugar, a pinch of salt, one-sixteenth teaspoon of cinnamon, one-quarter teaspoon of vanilla, and two tablespoons of cold milk. Stir until blended well. Add the hot milk, or, alternatively, fill the cup with more cold milk and heat in a microwave for one to two minutes.

Regardless of the method you use, top the hot chocolate with whipped cream of any type or marshmallows, and then drink up for a delicious taste treat.

4. Persuasion/Home-made Is Better

For adult tastes, made-from-scratch cocoa is superior in several ways to instant mixes. I say *adult* tastes because most children care little about what they drink as long as it is sweet. Adults tend to be more discriminating, and here is why they should apply their sophisticated palates to home-made hot chocolate.

First, the taste is richer and more satisfying. Compare the overly sweet, milky taste of Nestle's Quik to the dark, deep flavor of cocoa; it is the difference between margarine and butter, powdered eggs and real eggs, instant coffee and fresh brewed. The water-based mixes are laced with extra sugar to compensate for the lack of milk, so they are not only sickeningly sweet but less nutritious. Furthermore, more taste combinations are possible with home-made cocoa. Try concocting a spicy version, using cinnamon and vanilla; a chocolatey version, using chocolate curls that melt in your mouth; or blends with a kick, like mocha—coffee and cocoa. The more flavorful a drink, the more it pleases.

Second, making hot chocolate the slow way offers the pleasure of ritual, and rituals open the doors to memories—to other outstanding cups of the brew. The act of stirring the chocolate into the milk might remind one of a particular place and time, say the Rocky Mountains and a cup of hot chocolate in the summer. A taste of cool, freshly whipped cream chased by hot, bittersweet chocolate might evoke a memory of the first taste of real cocoa and whipped cream. Doing something "instantly" doesn't provide enough time for reminiscing. If you mix and swallow, the experience passes too swiftly.

Gulping down instant hot chocolate just to fill up is one approach to life. Making cocoa from scratch is another. It is an approach that satisfies the soul as well as the taste buds.

Purpose shapes content and organization, as these examples show. What details were selected, how those details were developed, and how the information was processed changed according to the guidelines of each writing task, the way Jello changes shape when poured into different molds. These same forces shape your material, too, giving you clear boundaries within which to select, eliminate, and organize information. The perimeter may expand to encompass multiple aims and intertwining tasks, but the more precisely you can define your reasons for writing, the more clearly you can write.

SUM UP

1. In as many paragraphs as needed, write a summary of the chapter's main points. Highlight the chapter's thesis statement.
2. Write any questions you may have about the chapter.
3. After class discussion add any new points and clarify your original thoughts. In addition, answer any questions you listed in #2.

REACT
1. Give two examples demonstrating how purpose shapes content and organization. Do not use examples from the text.

ACT
1. Draw four columns on a blank page. Designate one column for each of the four writing tasks. Brainstorm about the same topic for all four tasks, duplicating relevant points as you shift from one column to another. When finished, compare lists. You should see some duplicate points and many original points in each column, and the overall picture should be one demonstrating the influence of purpose on content.
2. Write a draft on the subject, using your brainstorming work in #1 and picking just one of the writing tasks as your aim.
3. Write a draft on the same topic but for a different purpose.

"The process of writing is a process of inner expansion and reduction. It's like an accordion: You open it and then you bring it back, hoping that additional sound—a new clarity—may come out. It's all for clarity."

Jerzy Kozinski

eleven

Tone and Attitude: Building for an Audience

My brother Steve once asked me, "What's the best present to give a girl you like?"

"It all depends on the girl," I answered. "For one it might be diamonds, for another a poem. You have to give her something that fits her." The same is true in writing. You have to write what fits the nature of your reader. That reader, or readers, is your audience.

Who is your reader? Right now it is a parent, school teacher, or professor, but this will not always be the case. Nevertheless, considering your teacher as a one-person audience will help demonstrate how reader expectations influence you. Suppose you're writing for a teacher whose hero is Hemingway. That teacher will prefer short sentences, a blunt style, and brief essays. A positive response could depend on your ability to adapt to that style. Suppose an assignment overlaps classes to foster multi-disciplinary writing skills. In that instance you may have to write for more than one teacher—perhaps your father teaches English and your mother science and they have different ideas about what they want from an essay. Likewise, in a traditional school or in college, the teachers might have vastly different interests. A history teacher might want copious amounts of footnoted facts and dates, a science teacher might want statistics, charts, and graphs, while your literature teacher might want lush prose—all for the same shared assignment. What you say and how you say it has to reflect their expectations.

MAY I HAVE THIS DANCE?

In a way, you are preparing to ask your reader to dance. "Can you 'slam,' 'boogie,' or 'jitterbug'?" you might ask, depending on your partner's (the reader's) age and interests. What you are really saying is,

"Who are you?" You can't dance until you know. The question is easily answered in school, but outside those walls the answer is trickier, for you have more possibilities for partners. The audience is broader. So you must ask the following questions, which will help not only to peg the reader's identity but to pick the right material for that reader.

1. Who is the reader?
2. What is the reader's background?
3. How old is the reader?
4. How much background knowledge does the reader bring to the material? How much about the topic is already understood, and how much must be explained?
5. What does the reader want to know about the material? What are the reader's interests in the material?

All readers are influenced by their surroundings and culture. The reader might be an individual or a group, a company's CEO or a newspaper's subscribers. The reader might have travelled internationally or never have been more than two miles from home. The reader might be someone who grew up in Watts or Grosse Pointe, Manhattan or Sopchoppy. While you can't read the reader's mind, the very presence of the reader necessarily limits and shapes your content, wording, and style. These boundaries are needed; without them you would have to guess, even more than you do now, what to say and how to say it for the greatest impact on your audience.

You can see the audience's impact most easily when considering age. The reader's age influences vocabulary, sentence structure, length, and complexity. These aspects of writing must match the reader's experience, maturity of thinking, and level of comprehension, yet many writers overlook these factors. In addition, you must consider that the slang and phrasing patterns familiar to one age group—your own, for instance—may not be comprehensible to another. An article for senior citizens might harken back to the slang of the 1920s, but such phrases would be meaningless to today's teenagers.

Here is an example showing the same general information written for readers of five different ages. Note that how much information can be included and how detailed it is can be affected by age. Also, the first two obviously need illustrations or must accompany a hands-on demonstration, and more explanation is needed to explain or provide vocabulary than is needed for older readers.

•Age 5: Look at the box on the screen. That's called a dialog box. I click the little boxes inside the big box to change the way the picture prints. I can make it print standing up or lying down.

•Age 8: You can choose how you want your story or picture to print. You open what's called the dialog box and use it to make your choices. Dialogue means talking, and in a way you're talking with the computer. You're telling it what you want. Look at the little boxes inside the dialog box. That's where you click to make the picture go up and down. The "up" direction is called *vertical*. The sideways direction is called *horizontal*. You can also make the printing black on the page, or if you had black paper, you could make the printing white.

•Age 14: There are options provided in what is called "the dialog box," so that you can flip the image vertically or horizontally, print in reverse (white on black instead of black on white), and print in different type styles or "fonts."

•Age 22: The options provided in the dialog box include a flipped image (vertical or horizontal), an inverted image (black and white reversed), and unlimited downloadable fonts.

The vocabulary, sentence structure, and complexity of the sentences had to be changed to suit each age. Did you recognize that the readers in this example all had one common background element: some understanding of computers? If they hadn't, the material would have had to be vastly different, the dance set to a different tune.

THE READER TAKES THE FLOOR

What input does the reader actually have? You have just seen one example of how the reader's age has an affect on writing. As hinted at above, the reader's background knowledge is also a key influence in determining the vocabulary and complexity of the material. An article for a medical journal about gene splicing would use the jargon of the medical profession, which might be lost on the readers of, say, an archaeological magazine. Yet the same topic could be addressed in both, if the language were revised and the content adjusted. Similarly, the readership of a children's magazine might not know the Latin term *parotitis* but would recognize *mumps*. Thus, while readers do not call you up and tell you what to put into your writing (it would be easier if they did), you have to try to figure out what their input might be. You have to give the reader the floor, as it were, and see what steps they know.

What the reader already knows and understands is critical to content. If I were writing this textbook for junior high school students, for instance, I would assume that the readers had far less writing experience than you. I would eliminate certain topics, such as business writing, and I would break down the explanations into more basic concepts. I would use simpler examples and require far less work in the exercises. On the other hand, if my audience consisted chiefly of other professional writers, I would skim over certain areas, such as the reasons for writing, and I would go into greater detail about rewriting and marketing. I would again change the examples, this time to make them more complex and relevant. What I say depends on what the reader already knows; it is the same with you and your reader. (When a teacher is your reader, it depends on what the teacher wants you to know, experience, or practice.)

The content, including examples and other supportive material, is further directed by what and how the reader thinks and feels. What concerns one reader or group of readers will differ from another. As an exercise, consider what the idea of safety might mean to a two-year-old, a six-year-old, a teenager, a mother of a single child, a father of twelve children, or an eighty-five-year-old retiree. These people share some concerns, but say "safety" to each, and you would probably get considerably different responses, especially if you threw in a change in environment, such as urban versus rural. The two-year-old considers safety as: no fingers in plugs; no crossing the street; standing near mommy or daddy when strangers are around. The definitions are simple. A six-year-old thinks of plugging in the TV without touching the prongs, or whether it's safe to cross a street before without an adult. The list changes with each person because each has a particular perspective. What the reader wants to know, what the reader's interests are, and what is important to the reader concern you vitally as you determine content.

A TANGO WITH THE READER

The tango, a dance long out of fashion in most circles, is a flirtatious, intimate, and daring dance. Its performance depends on the partners' moving in harmony through an intricate and intuitive series of steps, one minute cheek to cheek, the next whirling apart in a complicated pattern. Writing for an audience is like dancing a tango, trying to figure out what steps your partner knows, and trying to mesh them with your own moves and style.

Sometimes you and your reader will be simpatico—of like minds. Sometimes you won't. Readers have rhythms of their own. This is both a curse and a blessing. It makes your work harder, but if your work weren't hard, it would be boring.

The task is to know your readers so as to prepare yourself to dance with them. This task is particularly important in persuasive writing. A hostile partner won't go with the flow; an estranged reader will step on your feet. A sympathetic audience doesn't need to be convinced, but it needs to be motivated to move to the beat. An undecided audience can be swayed either way. To catch the attention of an uninterested audience, however, you have to display dazzling footwork. On the other hand, you don't want to be so dazzling that your partner, the reader, can't follow your fancy words or ideas. Think about each possibility before you take the floor.

Another consideration, again especially in persuasive writing, is, "What are the reader's needs?" A fellow named Maslow developed a hierarchy of needs that we can use here. He said that once people meet their basic needs—food, drink, shelter, and sleep, they can explore other needs. If their needs are not being met, they usually are not interested in or unable to explore. The needs run up a ladder from the basics to safety needs, to love needs, esteem needs, and self-actualization needs. Each progressive level deals less with immediate physical wants and more with fulfillment of the mind and soul. When you address an audience, you must take into account all these needs. If someone is unemployed, it will be hard to persuade that person that unemployment benefits should not be extended past their usual deadline. You have to write "for the stomach." When you write a letter of condolence, you deal with needs occasioned by loss and grief; you write for the spirit. If you write a love letter, you speak to the needs of the heart and soul. Awareness of the audience's needs will give you greater control over the direction of your writing. You can take the reader in your arms and lead across the floor in the direction *you* want to go.

MOVING TO THE INNER RHYTHM

Sometimes you hear a song and catch an underlying beat. You dance to it, following the inner rhythm. Words, too, can have an inner beat, a subtle, driving force beneath the skin that moves the reader in a different way than they would given different words about the same subject. This inner meaning could be called "tone."

Tone is a way of saying something more than the individual words themselves can. This is easier to identify in spoken words than it is, at least at first, in written words. Think of the times someone has said, "Oh, *great*." The intonation hits a note attuned to the writer's inner voice. It may not mean great at all, but "What a drag," or "How awful," or "How could you do this to me?" The way the word was spoken, its intonation, clued the listener into its real meaning. When you are writing, you clue the reader into your real meaning through tone. In my example I used italics, but most of the time you express tone by word choice and phrasing.

You need to learn to distinguish and mimic a variety of tones so that you'll have options when you write. Here are a few possibilities; doubtless you can think of others.

Formal	Casual
Polite	Sarcastic
Serious	Witty
Friendly	Impersonal
Grateful	Indignant
Seductive	Satirical
Analytical	Spiritual

Tone is a tool for keeping your audience at a distance or pulling them closer. You use tone to draw the readers into the meaning of your words, getting intimate as if to press a personal message in each reader's hand, or establishing an impressive distance to awe them with authority. In other words, the reader influences what you will say, but you can use tone to influence the reader.

Be aware of the many elements that signal a formal tone: material packed with statistics, written entirely in the third person, devoid of anecdotes, and generally impersonal. It keeps the reader at a distance. So does material that uses "big" words or Latin words or complex (not merely long) sentence structures, such as a sentence with a great deal of information up front and the main subject-verb clause at the end (a periodic sentence). You often find parallel structure in formal writing. This structure has twin clauses, frequently with the same introductory phrase and the same count (number of beats or syllables) in each, such as, "Whether the fabric of society crumbles, or whether the fabric of society holds fast...." The deliberate, studied impact of such a structure gives it a formal weight. Complex symbolism, allusions, and metaphors, as well as use of the passive voice, also indicate a tone that keeps the audience sitting in the back of an auditorium far from the speaker. Here is an example of a sentence with a formal tone. Taken from Charles Dickens' *A Tale of Two Cities*, the sentence is periodic in construction, has a complex, parallel structure, and uses passive voice—three characteristics of formal writing.

> The form that was to be doomed to be so shamefully mangled, was the sight; the immortal creature that was to be so butchered and torn asunder, yielded the interest.

Sentences without contractions also keep the reader at a distance, although this separateness may be moderated by allusions to personal matters. If the sentence structures tend to have the subject-verb clauses toward the beginning of the sentence, with the modifiers toward the ends (a "loose" sentence), the impression will also be less formal. There may be more imagery, and even, but not necessarily, an anecdote or two. The following is an example of a tone that isn't strictly formal, but that still keeps the reader at a distance—in the auditorium, but with front row seats. The excerpt, from *The Picture of Dorian Gray* by Oscar Wilde, includes two sentences, the first complex, the second simple. The variety of sentence lengths signals a less formal style, although the complexity of the first sentence is far from personal. In addition, both sentences are loosely constructed; the subject and verb come immediately in each clause. The verbs are active ("he had uttered a mad wish" versus "a mad wish had been uttered by him"), and the visual imagery is more specific.

> He had uttered a mad wish that he himself might remain young, and the portrait grow old; that his own beauty might be untarnished, and the face on the canvas bear the burden of his passions and his sins; that the painted image might be seared with the lines of suffering and thought, and that he might keep all the delicate bloom and loveliness of his then just conscious boyhood. Surely his wish had not been fulfilled.

A familiar tone puts the audience in your living room or even on the same couch as you and often has less precise information. The sentence structure is looser. Simple and complex sentences may be intermixed, possibly even with some parallel phrasing of different lengths (not the frequently equal lengths of formal writing). Most of the sentences will be in the active voice, which removes distance by making the action seem first hand and up front. A writer may use asides—casual comments to the reader that interrupt a primary thought. In general there will be more dashes, parentheses, and appositives, as the writer feels free to add thoughts as they come. Contractions are common. The formal vocabulary gives way to shorter, more common words, even slang. The tone is warmer as it comes from the second or first person point of view. The writer has more freedom to include anecdotes, even jokes. Watch how I change the tone of Oscar Wilde's sentences so that the mood becomes familiar.

> I'd wished—I know it was mad of me—that I'd stay young and the portrait get older. I'd keep my own beauty just as it was (not a bad deal, when you think about it). The canvas face would have to put up with my mistakes—my passions and my sins. The painting would be the one to suffer, not me. I'd get to keep my good looks, not to mention that glow of youth. Did my wish come true?

A tone that is even more personal, that is intimate and relaxed, pulls the reader within arm's distance or even holds hands. An intimate tone assumes an interested reader, and it is casual in language and format. Even sentence fragments work. Imagery and anecdotes are sprinkled about liberally. Face-to-face commentary includes more pronouns, often uses the first person, and might use run-ons and stream-of-consciousness phrasing to rub noses with the reader. P. G. Wodehouse, in *Carry On, Jeeves*, provides an excellent example of techniques that put the reader and speaker on familiar terms. He uses a rambling sentence followed by several fragments to give the sense of conversation. His choice of "loony-doctor" is far from the formal "psychiatrist" or "doctor of psychiatry."

> Well, you see, Old Sir Roderick, who's a loony-doctor and nothing but a loony-doctor, however much you may call him a nerve specialist, discovered that there was a modicum of insanity in my family. Nothing serious. Just one of my uncles. Used to keep rabbits in his bedroom.

Examine the following sentences for the way they control distance. Notice that the message is somewhat the same in each one. I have arranged them in order of distant to close tone. The first is most formal; the last is most casual.

> •The hazard of lead poisoning, once believed to be restricted to low-income families but now recognized as a concern for all Americans living in pre-1978 housing, has been deemed one of our country's greatest problems.

> •Lead poisoning threatens anyone living in a house built before 1978; it is not a problem just for low-income families.

•Lead poisoning's a real hazard—a threat to anyone, poor or rich—who lives in a house built before 1978.

•Lead poisoning's the pits—scares me to death—because anyone, including me, who's living in a house built before 1978, is at risk.

CAREFUL WHERE YOU STEP

When you're dancing, you have to watch that you don't step on any toes. The same is true in writing. You don't watch your feet, exactly, but you do have to watch your words. This is more than a matter of stomping on your reader's feelings (although that's a consideration); it's also a matter of ensuring that the reader understands what you mean. When you choose a word or phrase, you must be alert not only to meaning, but implication. What a word means on the street, in certain groups, under particular circumstances, or in context with other words is as essential for you to know as its primary definition. This knowledge can help you avoid a faux pas (a social blunder or indiscretion) that may lessen your credibility with your reader or destroy it altogether.

On the other hand, knowing the connotations of words can put you at a great advantage in applying tone with an audience appeal. For most people, for instance, the phrases "home-cooked breakfast," "fluffy pillows," or "freshly laundered clothes" have positive connotations, and these connotations conjure up whole images. Even single words can summon up a strong feeling. The word "home" may make the average reader think of comfort. There can be exceptions to the average reaction, however, and this is when it is important that you know your reader. Suppose you were writing an essay on "What a Home Is," and your readers were orphans; would the tone of the essay change? Of course it would. You would have to pick and choose words that would reach out to these individuals and show sensitivity.

Connotations may also be shaped by the time period in which a word was used. That is, a word or phrase written in one period may have a different meaning in another era. For example, in the early 1990s saying, "Man, she's bad," meant she's "fantastic, the best," but saying that in the 1950s meant that she was immoral. Although most of your writing assignments won't incorporate slang, being alert to the fact that the words you choose may have subtle nuances of meaning can help you choose the precise words you need. It can also help you keep slang out of writing when it doesn't belong.

DON'T CHANGE THE SONG IN THE MIDDLE OF A DANCE

You can't switch to a fast song just as your readers are getting cozy with a waltz. Their feet will get tangled. Similarly, you can't switch tone mid-sentence. Rhythm, syntactic structure, and word choice or phrasing indicate tone, but inconsistencies in any of these areas will confuse the reader. For instance, it would be disturbing to find a vivid image amidst impersonal expository writing.

> Because pressure-treated wood is saturated with water in the course of the process, and because the wood is usually air-dried, it is often as wet as a baby's diaper when it reaches the building site.

The phrase, "wet as a baby's diaper" gives a clear image, but the tone is too casual for the rest of the sentence. Simply saying "saturated" would have been less jarring.

Likewise, it diverts the reader's attention to find a lyrical passage in a technical piece.

> The SP3 is a fully automatic sample changer, holding 24 samples at a time. The samples do not need to be the same type of material or have the same viscosity. The changer offers a feature, that of automatic calibration, making calculation a gentle respite for the soul's weary effort.

Humor in the midst of something somber is equally distracting, although there are times when a writer mixes tone to make a point or to create another tone, such as a satirical or cynical one. This must be a deliberate effort, however, as it is in the following example.

> The widow was late for the funeral. Her mother-in-law tapped the black Delta dirt with a faded black umbrella, held tight with a thick rubber band. Her boys stood around the grave, their black slickers draped over their backs at their mother's command. Stiff white collars chafed their necks, and cuffs, rigid with starch, scraped their wrists. Short black rubber boots stretched over their polished black shoes. But the only drenching they got on that dark day was from sweat.

Tone is the voice you use to reach your audience. Once you decide that a tone is appropriate, stick with it. You thereby control your tone to meet both your purpose and the needs and backgrounds of the readers. Changing tone consciously while still staying true to your own natural style will take practice, but the skill you gain will give you tremendous versatility.

PLAY YOUR OWN SONG

The way you feel toward and judge yourself, your readers, a subject, person, idea, or thing is your attitude. Attitude is the feeling behind a belief about something—for it, against it, or uninterested in it. Your attitude influences your writing. For instance, you might objectively discuss the pros and cons of changing the legal drinking age to eighteen, but if you have strong feelings about the issue, it subtly affects what you say and how you say it. That, in turn, affects how readers respond. Since you want your readers to respond a certain way, you must be aware of both your attitudes and theirs. If you are to be master of your writing, you must also understand how to control and direct attitude. You can play your own song, but only if you know all the lyrics. Otherwise, attitude will be the master.

In general, your attitude will be subjective (positive or negative), objective (neutral), or some shade in between. It's those shades of gray that get you in trouble. Clarity of attitude requires keen observation of your own thoughts, for sometimes your position won't be obvious. The confusion in your own mind will lead to word choices that are ambiguous (having several possible meanings or interpretations) or contradictory, and ultimately to content that is unfocused or inconsistent.

What is your attitude on your subject? How do you figure it out if you don't know? Often, despite all prewriting exercises, your attitude becomes clear only as you write. After you write your draft, it is a worthwhile investment to doublecheck your attitude. Do this by making three columns on a page. Label one column "positive," one "negative," and one "objective." Dissect your material by reading it line by line, putting into the appropriate column any points, words, or phrases which clearly indicate attitude. When you have finished, compare the columns. Which attitude "weighs" the most? Is that the attitude you meant to present? If not, rewrite, either with the focus on the newly revealed attitude or with more emphasis on the attitude you originally intended.

SPOTLIGHT ON ATTITUDE

You might draw attention to a great dancer by turning on a spotlight. Attitude is usually, but not necessarily, more subtly lit. Just as you can clue the reader into your tone by toying with the connotations of words, so can you clue the reader into your take on things. For example, you can put words together to make a point by contrast:

> •his *enormous* brain, the size of a *pea*
> •the effort was *stupendously puny*
> •She said, "Don't be polite," so I had to be polite.

These phrases indicate attitude by posing opposite elements side by side. Such contrast can be developed into *irony*, an undercurrent of commentary that can be simple: "How were the kids?" "Oh, quiet. As quiet as the Fourth of July," (meaning that they were outrageously loud). Or, it can be subtle and sarcastic: "Last year alone, the lead-cleaning campaign managed to clear three houses of lead." As it stands, this statement seems positive. But when I add the information that "in our city there are at least 30,000 lead-contaminated houses," the *alone* becomes ironic and *managed* becomes cutting. Context is an essential component when maneuvering connotations and developing irony.

When you talk about controlling context, you are primarily talking about controlling wording, about being able to select the precise words you need. That sense of exactness comes from the willingness to explore language and the effort to remember and apply what you learn. Keeping notes of wording that is breathtaking in its precision or collecting striking quotations and their sources for future reference in a journal is useful.

By now you understand that some words are naturally more positive than others. Likewise, some words are intrinsically negative. A positive or mild way to say something that otherwise would be harsh, offensive, or even taboo is called a *euphemism*. When you phrase something in a particularly negative or disparaging way, you are using *pejorative* language. "He passed away," is a common euphemism for "he died," a blunt phraseology that is unpleasant or frightening for many people. Saying, "he went to meet his maker" is a euphemistic way of saying the pejorative, "he kicked the bucket." Here are some other examples.

EUPHEMISTIC	PEJORATIVE
Aroma	Stench
Obliging	Spineless
Strong-willed	Stubborn
Open-minded	Vacuous
Slender	Skinny
Shy	Wimp
Golden ager	Old geezer
Articulate	Loudmouthed

Controlling attitude is fun, but not necessarily easy. Or, you might say, "Controlling attitude is easy, but not necessarily fun." It depends on your attitude.

PUT ON YOUR DANCING SHOES

Fitting your writing around your reader is as fundamental an operation as putting your arms around your dancing partner, or pinning a costume on a ballet dancer. If the fit is wrong—too loose or too tight, or the material too stiff or too flimsy—the dancer can't perform properly. The dancer jumps; the costume rips. A grand jeté in the buff has an impact on the audience, but it isn't exactly the impact the dancer desired. I have seen this happen literally on the stage (by accident), and I have seen it happen figuratively in writing. If you don't fit content, organization, style, vocabulary, phrasing, tone, and level of complexity to the reader, the thesis will never leap from the page. But if you consider your audience, you can leap as high as your imagination will soar.

SUM UP
1. Write a short summary paragraph of the chapter. Highlight the chapter's thesis statement.
2. List the writing you've done in the past year and state who the audience was. See whether you can describe in a few phrases the salient (essential) characteristics of each audience.

REACT

1. What "needs" do you have? Are your basic needs met? How different are your parents' or guardian's needs? What needs are common to all people? How does one discover the needs of others?
2. What kinds of audiences are there? Give some examples besides the ones in the text.
3. Age and knowledge are but two influences in determining the reader's interests. What are some others? Give some examples demonstrating the impact of other influences.
4. How can you manipulate tone and attitude? Name some situations in your daily life when controlling tone and attitude would help you cope or communicate.
5. What is the overall tone of this book? Does it shift at all? What is the author's attitude toward the reader? Give examples that demonstrate your views.
6. Think about the writing you are going to be doing in the coming year, and try to form a picture of the audience. Answer the questions in the section, "May I Have This Dance?" for two different audiences.

ACT

1. Add to your "Notable Quotations" some especially clever euphemisms and some particularly ironic remarks. Credit your sources.
2. Write a series of sentences concerning the same subject for readers with four different sets of interests. Do this exercise again for a second topic. Almost any subject will do, but here are a few suggestions.

Prayer	Scuba Diving	Computers
Safety	Exercise	Pride
Dating	Competition	Success
Environment	Parenthood	Responsibility
Terrorism	Punctuality	Homeschooling

3. Write a sentence in the third person for each tone listed in "Moving to the Inner Rhythm," conveying its mood without saying or demonstrating it directly. Saying, "Excuse me, will you please pass the salt?" will not suffice for "polite," for example. Saying, "The recipient of an invitation is generally requested to reply, even when declining it," would do because the verb choices and sentence structure convey a formal and polite attitude. Control your tone through details, examples, and precise word choices.

4. Write four sentences: one formal, one moderately formal, one familiar, and one personal. Do the exercise twice, once with a single topic (four sentences on the same topic) and once with four different topics. Each sentence in both sets should incorporate a few of the characteristics given as indicating levels of formality.

5. Read the sentences below and note what kinds of readers might strongly agree with the position, strongly disagree, or be neutral. Where do you put yourself on each of these issues?

> 1) All athletes, from the high school to the professional level, should be tested for drug use before every game, and abusers expelled from the team.
>
> 2) "We are advocates of the abolition of war; we do not want war; but war can only be abolished through war, and in order to get rid of the gun it is necessary to take up the gun." (Mao Tse-Tung, *Quotations from Chairman Mao*)
>
> 3) "Equality for women doesn't mean that they have to occupy *the same number* of factory jobs and office positions as men, but just that all these posts should in principle be equally open to women." (Alexander Solzhenitsyn, *Letter to Soviet Leaders*)

6. List five or more euphemisms and their pejorative counterparts. Check the listings in *Roget's Thesaurus* to find other possibilities.

7. In Chapter Seven's "React" section you rated your "beat." Read aloud writing that you have done since then and rate it. Are you getting closer to a 10?

"Proofread carefully to see if you any words out."

William Safire's "Fumblerules"

SECTION 4: CLEANING UP THE CONSTRUCTION SITE

Chapter 12, Editing: A Usage Checklist

Chapter 13, Editing: Checkpoints for Wording and Spelling

Chapter 14, Editing for Punctuation, Sentence Structure, and
Capitalization

Chapter 15, Presentation: Appearances Matter

"Always dream and shoot higher than you know you can do. Don't bother just to be better than your contemporaries or predecessors. Try to be better than yourself."

William Faulkner

twelve

Editing: A Usage Checklist

EDITING AND PROOFING: THE CLEAN UP

We've taken a metaphorical break and done some dancing in the last chapter, but now we're back to laboring on the communication bridge. At this point you should have gotten your bridge to arch from one solid point to another, created some working drafts, and tested them with questions about content, organization, style, and purpose. Your achievements thus far are cause for celebration. Alas, just when you're satisfied with your work and ready to relax, another task arises. To pass final inspection, you must clean up the job, much as a cleaning crew would pick up the debris left from construction. Instead of sawed-off boards and lumps of fallen concrete, you must sweep up grammatical errors, wording, and technical problems, and spiff up overall appearance and format. The cleaning crew for your work is your teacher and, if you're lucky enough to have them, your writing partners. A red pen or a pencil will serve as a broom, and a trash can will serve as, well, your trash can. I've filled plenty.

In the writing world the maintenance workers are called the editors and the proofreaders. The editor's job is to examine and revise the material painstakingly so that the agreed-upon rules of English are consistently applied. Accuracy, correctness, precision, and crisp focus are the editor's vision for all writing; therefore, they must also be your vision for writing. The proofreader's job is to read printed copy for spelling or typographical errors. You must do that too. How words work with one another, how a word must be spelled to convey a certain definition, how punctuation guides interpretation; and how verbs, adverbs, and adjectives are used and formed—these are the types of rules you, as editor, must maintain. You enforce these rules so that your readers can follow your ideas without confusion or distraction, just as the chief engineer on a bridge makes sure no wires are poking through the tarmac.

Whether from ignorance or carelessness, most people make the same mistakes over and over again. I make mistakes myself, but I catch them (or try to) when I edit, because I have learned to scrutinize my work. Sometimes I read my work aloud, as this is one good way to root out problems. You might try this too. Another strange method—my own favorite—is to scan the material backwards, from the end of the composition to the beginning. For some reason, you pay less attention to content, organization, and style when reading backwards, but you can see problems with grammar, wording, and mechanics more easily. After you proof backwards, read from the beginning again, looking first at the manuscript as a whole, and then sentence-by-sentence the same way you did when revising your drafts.

Some writers edit the material categorically, examining once for grammatical errors, again for mechanical errors, and so forth. While this method is not quick, it is thorough. Whatever method you use, your aim is to skim the material for problems that you may have skipped over when you were concentrating on the larger issues of content and organization.

I have divided the editing section into four chapters to help you get used to editing and proofing. Each chapter describes common problems and, in some cases, tricks for avoiding them. Some of the typical mistakes will not be typical for you. Read the chapters thoroughly one time and use them as reference thereafter.

Notice that many of the examples can be revised several ways. The same is true for your writing. If you are not satisfied with one version, create another. Eventually, you will be able to edit for different types of problems simultaneously.

Tiresome as it might be, I've used standard phrases for grammatical rules to give all readers a common reference and because, like it or not, you have to learn the rules to write well. If you come across terms you don't remember, take the time to peruse a grammar book and relearn the rules. If you are up on your grammar, scan the checklist just to refresh your memory and to watch out for mistakes that even experienced pros make.

USAGE CHECKLIST

AGREEMENT

Subject-Verb Agreement

Numbers agreement, the agreement of subject and verb, is a problem I have seen so often that I'd like to tattoo the rules on every writer's wrist. I wouldn't care that the writer could cheat; at least the agreement would be right. As basic as it may seem, I remind you that the subject and verb must agree in number. If the subject is singular, the verb must be singular. If the subject is plural, the verb must be plural. The problem is that it's not always immediately clear to the writer whether the subject is singular or plural.

•*None is singular.* You wouldn't say, "No one are," yet that is what *none* means. None is never plural. I repeat: Not one none is plural.

•*Datum is one piece of information and is therefore singular.* Data are more than one piece. If you can't memorize the rule, try memorizing a rhyme: One datum has nothing to rhyme, two data do.

•*The number is five; a number is five; a number are sleeping.* A common mistake is to say, "A number is sleeping." If you're referring to a single entity (one of a kind or an integer), the subject is singular. If you're referring to more than one, the subject is plural. In the example above, "a number" may appear to be singular because of the article "a," but the implied subject is plural (many people are sleeping).

•*Each, neither, nobody, either, one, everyone, everybody, someone, or somebody* is always thinking that one of these words is plural. They are all singular, all the time.

Agreement problems most often occur when the subject is separated from the verb by a number of words, and it is especially likely when the subject follows the verb.

•Incorrect: The rope and shovels put on the wheelbarrow by the child was in jeopardy of falling off. (*Child* is closest to the verb, but it is not the subject. The subject is "the rope and shovels," which is plural.)
•Correct: The rope and shovels put on the wheelbarrow by the child *were* in jeopardy of falling off.

•Incorrect: Inherited from your *kids are* insanity. (*Kids* is not the subject, *insanity* is.)
•Correct: *Inherited* from your kids *is* insanity. (Of course, the clearer version is Erma Bombeck's: "Insanity is hereditary; you get it from your kids."

Contractions further muddle the picture.

- •Incorrect: Now there's eggs all over the floor.
- •Correct: Now there *are* eggs all over the floor.

- •Incorrect: Where's the bucket and mop?
- •Correct: Where *are* the bucket and mop?

Deciding singularity or plurality of collective nouns can be tough. If the bucket and mop in the above example are considered as a single unit, then you *would* use the singular (same with such go-together items such as "salt and pepper"). If you're dealing with a collective noun such as faculty, audience, or team, examine your intent when determining number. If you are considering the group a unit, the noun is singular. ("The faculty is meeting today.") If you are considering the individuals in the group, the noun is plural. ("The faculty are taking different courses to meet their State certification requirements.")

Next comes one of those deadly but critical rules. The verb agrees with the subject even when the subject is different from the predicate nominative (a noun or pronoun that follows a linking verb and refers to the same subject). This is most addling when you have a plural predicate nominative next to a single verb. Sometimes the best bet then is to rearrange the sentence until you get a version that is not only correct, but smoother.

- •Incorrect: The gift were puzzles.
- •Acceptable: The gift was puzzles.
- •Acceptable: The puzzles were the gift.
- •Better: The gift was a box of puzzles.

Pronoun-Antecedent Agreement

Also common are errors in the agreement of a pronoun and its antecedent (the noun to which the pronoun refers). This is particularly pervasive when the writer is using general pronouns, such as *everyone*, *someone*, or *anyone*; or using pronouns, such as *one* or *he/she*, to demonstrate a neutral gender. You can decide which solutions sound best.

- •Incorrect: If someone coughs, they should cover their mouth.
- •Correct: If someone coughs, *he* should cover *his* mouth.
- •Correct: If *they* cough, *they* should cover *their* mouths.
- •Correct: If *someone* coughs, that *person* should cover *his or her* mouth.
- •Correct: People who cough should cover *their* mouths.

- •Incorrect: One should eat their cereal.
- •Correct: *One* should eat *one's* cereal.
- •Correct: *One* should eat *his* cereal.

- •Incorrect: One should tie your shoes.
- •Correct: *One* should tie *one's* shoes.
- •Correct: *One* should tie *his* shoes.

- •Incorrect: He or she should eat their toast.
- •Correct: *He or she* should eat *his or her* toast.

Using *he or she* or *he/she* makes it difficult to be consistent and clear in voice or correct in agreement. It also makes for awkward style and extra baggage in the wording department. The writer of the next example (taken from an actual essay), couldn't decide how to settle these issues.

When a guy walks his girlfriend or boyfriend, he should be allowed to kiss her/him if he wants.

What he meant to say was this:

When a guy walks his girlfriend or a girl walks her boyfriend, he or she should be allowed to kiss her or him if he or she wants.

This last sentence is correct but still confusing and takes prizes for awkwardness. Many writers forget that *he* can mean both *he* and *she*, unless used in clear reference to a male. *She*, on the other hand, always means only a female. Therefore, you don't need to say "he/she" or "he or she"; by simply saying, "he," you avert both agreement and stylistic problems. On the other hand, however correct it is grammatically and smooth it is stylistically, this stance invites political problems. In *The Christopher Robin Birthday Book*, A. A. Milne offered an amusing solution to this dilemma: "If the English language had been properly organized...then there would be a word which meant both 'he' and 'she,' and I could write, 'If John or Mary comes, heesh will want to play tennis,' which would save a lot of trouble." Barring the invention of new words (surely on the way), you can take a neutral position by replacing pronouns with nouns and repeating the noun as needed. This is the tactic I have used as often as stylistically feasible in this book, repeating "writer," "reader," and the like instead of saying "he," which might offend some readers. There's that audience factor again.

Here is how our previous example could be rewritten, substituting nouns for the pronouns.

> When a teen walks a date, kissing should be allowed if both parties are willing.

Or, even better because it's clearer and more concise is the following.

> Teens should be allowed to kiss on dates.

Descriptive Nouns-Subject Agreement
Be sure that descriptive nouns agree with the subject.

> •Incorrect: I am a fresh<u>men</u>.
> •Correct: I am a fresh<u>man</u>. (There is only one of you. Also, apropos of the previous discussion, you are a freshman whether you are a male or female. Again, <u>man</u> can mean a male or all men and women, while <u>woman</u> can only mean a female, which makes it a wonderful and unique word.)

> •Incorrect: They are fresh<u>mans</u>.
> •Correct: They are fresh<u>men</u>.

> •Incorrect: They are in the fresh<u>men</u> class.
> •Correct: They are in the fresh<u>man</u> class. (There is only one class level.)
> •Correct: They are in classes for fresh<u>men</u>. (Many students attend each class.)

PRONOUNS

Pronouns must be in the correct case—nominative, objective, or possessive. Most writers grasp how to write a pronoun when it is the nominative case (when it's the subject), unless the subject is a compound one. For some reason, adding a second subject confounds readers. Whenever you doubt your choice of pronoun case, check the sentence by reading it with only one subject. I am giving many examples because this is a common error.

•Incorrect: My boyfriend and me are happy. (Would you say, "Me am happy"?)
•Correct: My boyfriend and I are happy. (You would say, "I am happy.")

•Incorrect: Kiele and him are friends. ("Him is a friend"? No way.)
•Correct: Kiele and he are friends. Or, He and Kiele are friends. (You would say, "He is a friend.")

•Incorrect: Cody and me have a lot in common. ("Me has"? Forget it.)
•Correct: Cody and I have a lot in common.

•Incorrect: The family and myself have great luck. (Saying "Myself has great luck" would bring bad marks, if not bad luck.)
•Correct: The family and I have great luck. ("I have great luck.")

•Incorrect: She and me have a lot going for us.
•Correct: She and I have nothing going if we speak that way.

The same problem occurs in the objective case; again, try the sentence with only the pronoun as the object.

•Incorrect: The owner paid him and I. ("The owner paid I"?)
•Correct: The owner paid him and me.

•Incorrect: The president paid the owner and he a compliment. ("Paid he"?)
•Correct: The president paid the owner and him a compliment. ("The president paid…him a compliment.")

When a pronoun is used in an appositive (as an explanation or identification set next to a noun), the pronoun must be in the same case as the noun to which it refers. Test the same way you did above.

•Incorrect: Many of the patients, especially Yolanda and him, accepted their illnesses with difficulty. (The objective case is incorrect, since "of the patients" is not the subject, "most" is. You wouldn't say, "Him accepted.")
•Correct: Many of the patients, especially Yolanda and he, accepted their illnesses with difficulty. (You would say, "He accepted….")

> •Incorrect: Certain scientists in our group, notably him and her, are challenging our notions of cell research. ("Him and her" are not appositives for "in our group," so they should not be in the objective case. They are appositives for "scientists," which is the subject of the sentence, so they must be in the nominative case.)
> •Correct: Certain scientists in our group, notably he and she, are challenging our notions of cell research. (You would say, "He and she are challenging....")

In the possessive case the most persistent error is using *it's* for *its*. *It's* is a contraction meaning *it is*: "It's a shame more people can't remember this rule." *Its* is the possessive of *it*: its teeth, meaning "the teeth of it." If you said, "It's teeth," you would be meaning, "It is teeth." The rule must be remembered the hard way, by memorizing it. Never use an apostrophe for the possessive of *it*. It's its way of confusing you.
Other possessive pronouns behave similarly.

> The girl's goat is hers; the boy's goat is his; your goats and my goats are ours; their goats are theirs, but once they're all together, I don't know whose goats belong to whom. It's all the same to the goats, I guess.

Use the possessive case of a pronoun before a gerund (a verb acting as a noun). Most people get this rule wrong in conversation, so it's easy to miss in your writing. If you imagine that the gerund belongs to the pronoun, it may be easier to remember to use the possessive.

> •Incorrect: I don't like them talking behind my back. (The talking belongs to them; it is *theirs*.)
> •Correct: I don't like *their* talking behind my back.

> •Incorrect: He going surprised me. Him going surprised me.
> •Correct: *His* going surprised me.

Reflexive Pronouns
When you combine a pronoun with the suffix *-self* or *-selves*, the new word becomes either *reflexive* or *intensive*, according to intent. If you mean to refer to the antecedent, the pronoun is used reflexively. The intent is to explain something about the antecedent.

> Reflexive: He cleaned the house himself. (In other words, he did it alone.)

If you mean to refer back to but also to emphasize the antecedent, then the pronoun is used intensively.

> Intensive: He himself cleaned the house. (This version implies that there is something special about the act, such as that a maid usually does it.)

Relative Pronouns and Relative Clauses

Who, whoever, whom, and whomever are relative pronouns used to introduce subordinate clauses. A subordinate clause (also known as a dependent clause) is a phrase that is used as a noun or modifier in the same way as a single word or phrase; it cannot stand alone. Deciding which case to use and remembering to include the relative pronoun, at least in formal writing, are the two main problems.

Use *who* or *whoever* (nominative cases) when the pronoun acts as the subject for the verb in your clause. When in doubt, look for another subject for the clause. If you can't find one, then you need to use the nominative case.

> •Incorrect: Check whomever leaves.
> •Correct: Check whoever leaves. (*Whoever* is not the object of *check*, as it may appear at first. Rather, "whoever leaves" is a subordinate clause, of which *whoever* is the subject. Therefore, you use the nominative case.)

> •Incorrect: Give a tardy slip to whomever arrives late.
> •Correct: Give a tardy slip to whoever arrives late. (*Whoever* is the subject of the verb *arrives*, not an object of the preposition *to*.)

> •Incorrect: I'm the kind of guy whom would buy a satellite if I could charge it.
> •Correct: I'm the kind of guy who would buy a satellite if I could charge it. (*Who* isn't the object of *I am*, it is the subject for the subordinate clause, "who would buy.")

Use *whom* or *whomever* when the pronoun acts as the direct object or indirect object for the verb in the clause.

•Incorrect: Jean does not care who she hurts.
•Correct: Jean does not care *whom* she hurts. (*She* is the subject of the clause; *whom* is the object: "she hurts whom" is the way to read this to double-check the case.)

An exception occurs with linking verbs such as *to be*, *to become*, and *to seem*. These are also called reflexive verbs; they tie the subject to the pronoun (or noun or adjective) that describes it. A clause using one of these verbs requires that both subject and object be in the nominative case.

•Incorrect: Does anyone know *whom* her fiancé is?
•Correct: Does anyone know *who* her fiancé is? (Here the subject is *fiancé*. Since the verb is naturally reflexive—turning back on itself—*who* is, in a sense, a second subject. The nominative case is correct.)

A relative clause explains an antecedent and uses a relative pronoun (including which, that, or whose) or an interrogative pronoun (who, whom, which, what, why, or whose) to introduce it. The problem is that writers tend to omit the pronouns, especially *that*, *which*, *what*, and *why*. In conversation this is passable because the listener can usually interrupt the speaker to clarify a point, but in written material the omission can confuse the reader. As mentioned earlier, using the relative pronoun also indicates a more formal tone.

•Conversational: I feel silly behavior is relaxing.
•Formal: I feel that silly behavior is relaxing.

•Conversational: He refused to go. The reason he refused is unclear.
•Formal: He refused to go. The reason why he refused is unclear.

•Conversational: She thinks the school should have week-long pep rallies.
•Formal: She thinks that the school should have week-long pep rallies.

In general, verbs of the mind—such as think, know, see, understand, feel, imagine, and perceive—call for the relative pronoun.

Pronoun Reference

When you proof sentence-by-sentence, can you find the antecedent for every pronoun reference? If you can't, your reader can't either. The reference is considered "unclear" or "weak."

> •Unclear reference: I spent hours at the community center's get-acquainted party, and I didn't meet a single one. (Meet a single what? Man? Woman? Anteater?)
> •Clear: I spent hours at the community center's get-acquainted party, hoping to meet an interesting girl, and I didn't meet a single one.
> •Clear: I spent hours at the community center's get-acquainted party, and I didn't meet one interesting girl.

> •Weak reference: We spent the day at the fair, but we didn't play them.
> •Clear: We spent the day looking at games at the fair, but we didn't play them.

Could your reference be one of several antecedents (ambiguous reference)? If so, rewrite the passage so that the reference is clear and unambiguous.

> •Ambiguous: Tonya nominated Shaquita for class president because she was so involved in school affairs. (Who was involved? Tonya or Shaquita?)
> •Clear: Tonya nominated Shaquita for class president because Shaquita was so involved in school affairs.
> •Clear: Because Shaquita was so involved in school affairs, Tonya nominated her for class president.

Are you using *which*, *this*, *that*, or *it* to refer to a vague or general idea rather than a specific object or idea (general reference)?

> •General: The ad listed a wedding dress, "worn once by mistake," which was a bargain for anyone but the bride. (The writer didn't explain what the bargain was—the ad, the dress, or the wedding.)
> •Clear: The ad listed a wedding dress, "worn once by mistake," only $25. That price was a bargain for anyone but the bride.

•General: She had legs the shape of frozen french fries, skin the color of dried mustard, and hair the color of congealed gravy, but this didn't bother her. (To what in the preceding sentence does "this" refer? It could be any or all of the three points.)
•Clear: She had legs the shape of frozen french fries, skin the color of dried mustard, and hair the color of congealed gravy, but her looks didn't bother her.

•General: Jefferson's mother was always asking him where he was going, and that irritated him.
•Clear: It irritated Jefferson that his mother was always asking him where he was going.

•General: A truck covered with flowers, an enormous floating balloon, and a noisy brass band came down the street. It was almost too much excitement for a three-year-old boy. (Does "it" refer to the street, the band, or everything?)
•Clear: A truck covered with flowers, an enormous floating balloon, and a noisy brass band came down the street. The parade was almost too much excitement for a three-year-old boy.

CONTRACTIONS, PLURALS, AND POSSESSIVES

Most beginning writers treat contractions, plurals, and possessives as though they were interchangeable brands of coffee, mixing one with the other without concern. Although the formation of the three is similar, they are as unalike as coffee, lint, and athlete's foot. When through haste, carelessness, or ignorance, you drop an apostrophe in one place and add it randomly in another, you give the reader the wrong clues for interpreting the material. As you edit, stop at each contraction, plural, and possessive. Ask yourself whether the formation of the word and your punctuation agree with your intent for the word.

Contractions
If you've formed a contraction, you should be using an apostrophe to indicate a missing letter or letters. If no letters are missing, you don't need an apostrophe. If a letter or letters are missing, you need an apostrophe where the letter(s) should be.

•Do not; don't: The apostrophe stands for the *o* in *not*, so it is placed where the *o* would normally be.

•He is; he's: The apostrophe is placed where the *i* would be. (Note: *He's* means *he is*, not *he has*. If you mean *he has*, you must write it out in full.)

•I would; I'd: The apostrophe stands for the missing *woul*, so it is placed in between *I* and *d*. (Contractions with *would* and *should* are too casual for all but personal writing.)

You cannot say *ca'nt*, although many people try; what letters are missing between the *a* and the *n*? None. You cannot say *Iam*, one word rhyming with Siam but not meaning I am. Nor can you say, *I'am*, because even if I am missing some brains, I am not missing any letters (so I don't need an apostrophe).

Plurals

Plurals do not take apostrophes unless they are possessive plurals. Double-check your plurals the way you would check to make sure you had turned off all the lights before you leave home.

•The *girls* eat and get gas. The *girls'* cars eat gas and get poor mileage.

•The *Greens* refuse to mow their lawn. Several children were reported missing in the *Greens'* lawn. Or was it the *Greens's* lawn?

•Men who wear *their* socks day after day don't keep their women long. The *men's* socks would have to be sandblasted to smell good again.

•The *sixties* was an era which many people struggled through. The *sixties'* era is one which many people struggled through but remember differently.

•*He's* betting on *sixty*, calling, "Come on, baby, it's *sixty's* turn to win!"

Possessives

If you are forming your possessives incorrectly, it may be due to poor spelling rather than poor grammar, but the net result is the same: miscues for your reader. Beware of words that sound alike but are spelled differently, particularly *there/they're/their* (only the latter is a possessive) and *you're/your*.

MODIFIERS

Adjectives that are modifying other adjectives or verbs become *adverbs* and their form reflects their use. Adding the suffix *-ly* is the usual way of changing an adjective into an adverb.

- You can't do "bad" on your math quiz, but you can do badly.
- You may think that you feel "real" bad, but you really feel really bad.

Feel, smell, taste, sight, and sound (verbs of sense) take an adjective, not an adverb.

- The cafeteria smells bad.
- They feel bad because they spell badly.
- The lobster looked delicious, and it was deliciously prepared.

The modifiers *less* and *fewer* also confound writers. The rule is simple: *Less* modifies a singular noun; *fewer* modifies a plural noun.

If there were fewer writers, there would be less writing. But would fewer words mean fewer mistakes, or simply less copy?

Good and *well* are two other words invented just to confuse you. *Good* is an adjective only, while *well* can be either an adjective or an adverb. *Well* means healthy, well dressed or groomed, or satisfactory. Check to see whether you are modifying a noun, a verb, or adverb; only *well* can modify the last two.

- He sang well; he has a good voice.
- She feels good about her new job. He feels good about her.
- He feels well today. He is taking the news well.

Hopeful is an adjective and can only modify a noun or pronoun. *Hopefully* modifies a verb; it is an adverb, as the suffix *-ly* indicates. Using *hopefully* to begin a sentence is incorrect 99% of the time, so if you find a sentence that begins this way, rewrite it.

- Incorrect: Hopefully, he will win. (What verb is *hopefully* modifying? He cannot win hopefully.)
- Correct: He talked hopefully of the Saturday night game. (*Hopefully* modifies the verb *talked*.)

•Correct: He is hopeful that he will win. (Now *hopeful* modifies the pronoun *he*.)
•Correct: Last week's win was a hopeful sign. (*Hopeful* modifies the noun, *sign*.)

The phrases *most important* and *most importantly* suffer the same misguided fate as *hopeful* and *hopefully*. When used as an opening transition, *most important* modifies the understood phrase, "What is."

•Incorrect: Most importantly, if the team loses, he will lose his chance for a scholarship. (What verb does *importantly* modify? There isn't one.)
•Correct: [What is] Most important, if the team loses, he will lose his chance for a scholarship. ("Most important" modifies the implied *what*.)
•Correct: He stuck his chest out importantly. (This is a horrible sentence, but it's grammatically correct. *Importantly* modifies the verbal phrase, "stuck out." If you are using *importantly* and can find the verb that it modifies, you can keep it. Odds are, however, that the sentence itself needs repair.)

VERBS

Pick the right tense for the job and re-check it in each sentence. Your tenses should be consistent unless the sequence or time period shifts. Then the tense should change accordingly.

Ask yourself whether you have selected the best tense for the events you're describing. The present tense, for instance, is difficult to maintain in a narrative, especially if the events have occurred before the moment at which you are writing. If you are using the present tense in a narrative, ask yourself why. What makes it the best choice? If your answers satisfy you, carry on.

Once you have established that your tense choices are okay, proof your past tense verbs to make sure that you haven't dropped the suffix *-ed*. Two words, *use* and *concern*, are frequent victims of the dreaded "no-ed" disease, as the following examples show.

•Incorrect: I use to drop the *d*.
•Correct: I used to drop the *d*.

•Incorrect: Later I got use to adding it.
•Correct: Later I got used to adding it.

•Incorrect: I am concern about education cuts.
•Correct: I am concerned about education cuts.

The vigilant writer guards against bad speech habits encroaching on writing habits. In addition to the mistakes above, which I suspect come from poor speaking skills, are the following travesties.

•Incorrect: I'm gonna have a good career one day. ("Gonna" is slang.)
•Correct: I'm going to have a good career one day. (Say "going to," and you'll have a chance at a career.")

•Incorrect: I wanta jog with you.
•Incorrect: I wanna jog with you.
•Correct: I want to jog with you.

An infinitive is not an atom. Splitting it won't produce power. Instead, it will weaken the verb. It's an old rule, and these days broken nearly as often as not, but don't split the infinitive.

•Incorrect: When they refused to quietly leave, the manager threatened to physically eject them.
•Correct: When they refused to leave quietly, the manager threatened to eject them physically. (Better: delete *physically*)

Shall vs. Will

When to use *shall* and when to use *will* is a question most people no longer ask. They just use *will*, perhaps believing it's the only choice or that it's too much work to learn the rules. But the rules are simple, and knowing them gives you one more weapon in your fight to make a point clear.

Use *shall* in the first person singular or plural, except when the statement is forceful or determined. Then use *will*. What may be difficult is figuring out when a statement demonstrates force and determination. Look at intent. Do you want a lot of "oomph" behind your words or are you making a mild point?

•Regular tone: I shall see to the matter myself.
•Forceful tone: I will correct this matter if it kills me.

•Regular tone: I should like to apply for the position of veterinary assistant.
•Forceful tone: I will be their next veterinary assistant. (This implies that the person will get the job despite the obstacles, no matter what.)

The rule for the second and third person is the opposite. Use *will* for a regular tone, *shall* for a forceful tone. (You would think that the people making up these rules could have been a little more consistent.)

•Regular tone: You will have to clean your room if you want to be able to find things in it.
•Forceful tone: You shall clean your room, now. (Or else.)

•Regular tone: They will probably make good grades this quarter.
•Forceful tone: They shall make good grades, or they shall never leave this house again.

Lie vs. Lay
   I hate *lie* (meaning to recline, not to tell an untruth) versus *lay* (to put somewhere). They confuse me. I forget the rules and have to recheck them nearly every time I use one of these dastardly words. One thing that helps me distinguish the two is to remember that *lay* always takes an object. You can lay something down, but you can't lie something down. Some people think of chickens to remember the difference between these words: Chickens don't lie down when they lay eggs. (They sit down.) Also tricky is remembering that the past tense of *lie* is the same word as the present tense of *lay*. Check tense formation as well as meaning when you use these words.

•He didn't want to lie down.
He is lying down.
He lay down yesterday too.
He has lain down every night of his life.

•She wanted to lay the package on the counter.
She is laying the package on the counter right now.
She laid the package on the counter an hour ago.
She should have lain it somewhere else.

ARTICLES

It is so easy to form and use articles that they often fall victim to carelessness. You can find and treat the victims if you take time to focus your eyes on every article you have written. Is each correct?

Use *a* before a word beginning with a consonant, *an* before a word beginning with a vowel or a silent *h* (an honor). The choice for the latter is not immutable. I have seen both "an historian" and "a historian" in published articles. Look in the dictionary for phonetic spellings or read your sentence aloud as one way to resolve any quandaries.

And, which of course means "in addition," often shows up as a substitute for the article *an*. Make sure you haven't misspelled this simple little word.

If a noun or gerund has a slew of adjectives or adverbs before it, it may still need an article. Use *a* or *an* when the word is general: a sin (any sin), an elephant (any elephant). Use *the* when the word is specific or refers to a specific group: the sin (a particular sin), the elephant (not just any elephant, a particular one), the Senate, the church. Use nothing when speaking categorically: Sin is defined by your religion. Elephants don't go to school.

COMPARISONS

Who hasn't thought about *like* versus *as* and gotten muddled? *Like* is used when modifying nouns or gerunds; it is used as an adjectival phrase to say that one thing is similar to another thing. *As* is used when modifying verbs or adding information to verbs, as in a verbal phrase. When speaking, people often use *like* as a filler, similar to "um" or "uh" and as empty of meaning. Try to eliminate *like*, the filler, from your speech, as bad habits will easily creep into your writing if you're not diligent. "Like you know what I mean like?"

•Adjectival: Homework was a chore like cleaning my room or washing the dishes—never a pleasure. (*Cleaning* and *washing* are gerunds—other chores—so you use *like*.)
•Verbal: I did my homework carefully as my parents wanted me to. (*Wanted* is a verb, so you need *as* instead of *like*.)

•Adjectival: The couple looked like their dogs
•Adjectival: The dogs looked like groomed humans.
•Verbal: The dogs looked well groomed, as show dogs should.

•Incorrect: I feel like I'll never catch up on my homework.
•Correct: I feel as if I'll never catch up on my homework.
•Correct: I feel like a frantic gerbil when I'm trying to catch up on my homework.

Have you used any metaphors? You recall, no doubt, that a metaphor is a comparison that doesn't use *like* or *as*; the comparison is implied rather than stated. I often have the problem, as do many other writers, of mixing my metaphors. To be logical, the action of a metaphor should match the context of the metaphor, and the metaphor should be consistent throughout the sentence. If you find yourself having a hard time making the metaphor "sound" right, it might be a sign that the metaphor is either mixed or weak. You need to start over or delete the sentence.

•Mixed metaphor: He was floundering in the woods. (This is mixed because the action, "floundering," is something that takes place in water, not on land. It is a fish metaphor, and fish, except perhaps for walking catfish, do not stroll through the woods.)
•Consistent metaphor: He was floundering in the pool.
•Consistent metaphor: He was lumbering through the woods.

The job of editing involves both quick scanning and careful rereading. You draw upon your memory of the rules as you proceed. Some of the rules will stay with you for life. The ones in this chapter tend to be those that, for many high school students, have already started to slip away. With red pen (or a pencil) in hand, you can poke them into place.

SUM UP
1. In one sentence write the thesis of this chapter.
2. List any rules you need to memorize.

REACT
1. What is editing? Why is it important? How can you improve your editing skills?
2. Why should you do your own editing (as opposed to leaving it to a teacher or someone else)? How can you develop an objective attitude toward your own words?
3. Why is it important to follow the rules of standard usage? Give examples to support your points.

4. What is your opinion on the issue of using "he" versus "he or she" or "he/she"? What problems arise when you replace pronouns with nouns to circumvent offending an audience (or yourself)? In what ways can you get around the problem? Name audiences that might have different opinions about this issue.

5. Learning to be a careful editor will teach you patience, industriousness, and attentiveness to details. What other traits will you need to develop to edit your own copy successfully? How can you apply these traits to other aspects of your life?

ACT

1. In "Notable Quotations," record two quotations that contend with ideas that you find difficult to write about yourself but that you think the author explains well. Credit your sources.

2. Edit all your journal copy (from the first day to today) for correct grammar. Date your revisions.

3. List the types of errors you've made more than once in your journal. Describe the problems in grammatical terms. Think about ways to fix the rules in your memory so that you don't repeat these errors. If you think of any useful tricks, write them down.

4. Exchange journals with a writing partner. Edit the partner's previously edited copy while the partner re-edits yours. (Use a pencil or pen of a different color.) List and label any problems you find that the writer didn't. Date and initial your revisions.

5. Look through the newspaper, a magazine, or a book, scanning for mixed metaphors. Bring at least two examples to class. (You can find mixed metaphors even in some classic works. Shakespeare has Hamlet use a mixed metaphor in his "To be or not to be" speech.)

6. Listen to yourself and others speaking in class. Can you identify poor speech habits that might become bad writing habits? Try to get through an entire class period speaking correctly. Make it a group effort to correct each other's speech (politely).

"Prose is like hair. It shines with combing."

Gustave Flaubert

thirteen

Editing: Checkpoints for Wording and Spelling

When your written thoughts are cohesive enough, you can review your wording and change any that is vapid, vague, or incorrect. I wish I could hand you a pill that would enable you to know the rules effortlessly. I can't. To edit, you have to know the rules and know the language, and the only way to do that is the dreary way. Learn them.

As an English speaker you have access to some 500,000 words, not including another half a million uncatalogued technical and scientific terms. The breadth of the language surpasses that of all other languages. German, for instance, has a vocabulary of about 185,000 words and French has even fewer. Imagine the thoughts, ideas, and feelings you would lose if you could express yourself only in Creole, which has a vocabulary of approximately 2,000 words. A language of precision, subtlety, and variety, English offers you every word you need to say exactly what you mean.

We get stuck anyway.

We get unstuck through editing. Even though I can't wave a wand over you to make your writing perfect, I can point out the most common wording problems. They aren't exciting to read or memorize, but knowing them and looking out for them will ease the pain of editing.

CHECKPOINT #1: IS YOUR WRITING SPECIFIC AND LIVELY?

Be on the alert. Insipid writing below. You won't find these exact lines in your writing, but you can read each of your own lines and ask, "Could this be more specific? Can the reader actually see this?"

•Vague: Romeo's parents had problems with revenge.
•Specific: Romeo's parents thought revenge against the Capulets was more important than his love for Juliet.

•Vague: Smoking kills people.
•Specific: Smokers are three times more likely to die of cancer than nonsmokers.

•Dull: Band was exciting.
•Vivid: Sitting in the midst of forty-five tubas, violins, drums, and other instruments being tuned up was ear-splitting, chaotic, and energizing.

•Dull: In Jack London's "To Build a Fire," the main character's adversary is the weather.
•Vivid: In Jack London's "To Build a Fire," the main character battles the murderous cold and loses.

CHECKPOINT #2: ARE YOU REPEATING YOURSELF?

Repetition is saying the same thing more than once. Redundancy is repeating yourself by saying something that sounds different but actually means the same thing. Cross out words or phrases that say the same thing you have already said (unless it is a deliberate and effective stylistic device). Read carefully to catch and eliminate redundancies, many of which are commonly used (such as, "around the world and back again"; if you get around, you are back again).

•Repetitive: Romeo and Juliet poisoned themselves. They killed themselves with poison. They then died.
•Concise: Romeo and Juliet poisoned themselves and died.

•Repetitive: This needless tragedy could have been prevented. Their parents could have stopped these sad, useless deaths by allowing the couple to marry. [Note: Any tragedy is needless, is it not?]
•Concise: This tragedy could have been prevented had the couple been allowed to marry. OR: Had their parents allowed them to marry, Romeo and Juliet would still be alive.

•Redundant: In my opinion, I think....
•Concise: I think....

Redundant: Our house was quarantined off limits.
Concise: Our house was quarantined. (Quarantined means "off limits," so you don't need to say both.)

CHECKPOINT #3: ARE YOU USING SLANG?

Take out any slang. It's acceptable in fiction or if your teacher says so, but otherwise it's taboo in formal writing. If you find any of the following, revise as suggested.

- •Slang: lots, lotsa, lots of
- •Acceptable: a lot of
- •Better: much; a great deal of

- •Slang: I got to
- •Acceptable: I have to

- •Slang: gotcha
- •Acceptable: I have you

- •Slang: kinda, sorta
- •Acceptable: kind of, sort of
- •Better: Cross them out and don't put anything else there. "Kind of" and "sort of" don't say anything important.

- •Slang: y'all, youse
- •Acceptable: you (meaning the reader; if you can, switch to the third person: he, she, it, they, or one)

CHECKPOINT #4: ARE YOU USING USELESS QUALIFIERS?

When you qualify your thoughts with apologies or useless adverbs, you bleed them of their power. If you have used *really*, *very*, *kind of*, or *sort of*, cross them out and don't replace them with anything. If your verb is weak, choose a better verb.

If you have said, "What I really mean is..." or "What I'm trying to say is..." then you need to cross out those phrases (or anything similar) and rewrite the sentences without them.

•Apologetic qualifier: What I really mean is that Jack London makes the cold seem sort of alive.
•Straightforward: Jack London makes the cold seem alive.

CHECKPOINT #5: ARE YOU USING THE RIGHT PREPOSITIONS?

Prepositions have particular meanings, and we forget this sometimes. They show relationships: how one idea relates to another, where an item is situated, how images are connected, and so forth. You can describe precise positional relationships with prepositions. Without a large variety of prepositions, you can only describe those relationships generally. In Spanish, for example, *sobre* means above, around, beside, and atop; the relationship between objects is loosely defined. In Hungarian you can't show exact place, where something is, because the language has only postpositions—whereabouts, therein, thereunto, hereabout, for example. English, on the other hand, has more than sixty prepositions. You can describe positional relationships with accuracy, but you may need a good dictionary if you have trouble picking the right one for the job or eliminating unnecessary ones.

Don't use *where* when you mean *in which, for which,* or *so that.* Don't use *at which* or *on which* when you mean *for which.*

•Incorrect: This is another situation where we goofed up.
•Correct: This is another situation in which we goofed up.
•Simplified: We goofed again.

•Incorrect: He has gotten where he never combs his hair any more.
•Correct: He has gotten so that he never combs his hair any more.
•Simplified: He never combs his hair any more.

Among and *between* are also bugaboos. Use *among* when the reference is to more than two people. Use *between* when the reference is to two persons only.

•Correct: We were still hungry since we had to divide one pizza among ten of us; Tom and Jane were full since they had a large pizza to split between them.

•Correct: A woman in the crowd turned to me and whispered conspiratorially, "Between you and me, there's a lunatic among us."

If you have used *beside* or *besides*, check your intended meaning with actual meaning. Use *beside* to mean, "at the side of"; use *besides* to mean, "in addition to."

> •Correct: "Although the telephone was conveniently located beside his desk, he had much to do besides answering the phone."

Have you used *on* when you meant *about*? They are used accurately here: "He stood on the stage while he spoke about his experiences." Could you eliminate an awkward phrasing altogether?

> •Incorrect: I should like to inform you on my opinion of the dress code, which is unfair.
> •Correct: I should like to inform you about my opinion that the dress code is unfair.
> •Better: My opinion is that the dress code is unfair.

Have you used *on* or *of* when no preposition is needed?

> •Incorrect: You should consider on having no dress code.
> •Correct: You should consider having no dress code.
>
> •Incorrect: Despite of a divorce, my family stayed close.
> •Correct: Despite a divorce, my family stayed close.
> •Correct: In spite of a divorce, my family stayed close.

Have you used *with* when you meant *in*?

> •Incorrect: I am a junior with good standing.
> •Correct: I am a junior in good standing.

Some words take particular prepositions. For example, *ignorant* takes *of*: "He was ignorant of the rule." *Refer* takes *to*: "They referred to a book which I had not read." *Except* takes *for*: "My mother is a saint—except for her temper, of course." When in doubt, look in the dictionary for a sample sentence.

Two or more prepositions together are a sign of imprecise wording. Try deleting one. Usually the meaning will be the same, but the wording will be crisper.

•Imprecise: The walk led up to the house.
•Better: The walk led to the house.

•Imprecise: Set the camera over on the windowsill.
•Better: Set the camera on the windowsill.

CHECKPOINT #6: ARE YOU USING THE RIGHT WORD?

The list below contains word pairs that are frequently confused. Sometimes the confusion stems from similar spelling, sometimes from subtle differences in meaning. If you find that you cannot remember the meaning and/or spelling of a word, invent tricks to help you. I have listed some of mine, but it is best to think of your own. Mine match my way of thinking; yours will match your way and so should be easier to remember. As you will notice, the definitions are casual, and I have given you the parts of speech only when it seemed helpful for distinguishing meanings. For precise definitions, use a dictionary.

Able	Capable of doing something.
Allowed	Permitted to do something.
Accept	To receive.
Except	To exclude. (My memory trick is that the prefix for both the word and the definition is the same: ex.)
Adapt	To adjust; to get used to.
Adept	Expert, proficient, very skilled. (I match the middle letters of each word to the first letter of the primary definition. Adapt matches adjust; adept matches expert.)
Affect	To alter, influence, or change.
Effect	(v.) To accomplish, to bring about a result. (I use the same trick here as above. Affect matches alter. Effect matches result.) (n.) The result of some action.
All right	Okay, fine.
Alright	Means *all right*, but is not standard English.
All ready	Completely prepared or ready.
Already	Previously, by this or that time. Now; so soon; so early.

All together	Everyone or everything together; in a group.
Altogether	Wholly, completely, entirely.
	A group of talking turnips all together would be altogether different.
Capital	The seat of government of a state or country; a letter in the upper case; money invested in a business.
Capitol	A building occupied by a state legislature; the building in Washington, D.C. used by Congress.
	Al invested his capital in aluminum. Ollie covered the state capitol with olive oil. (I know these are stupid, but the stupider the sentence, the easier it is to remember. Make up your own if you don't like mine.)
'Cause	Slang for because (note the apostrophe indicating the missing letters); unacceptable in formal writing.
Cause	(n.) Reason; (v.) to bring about.
Because	A conjunction that means for the reason that; an adverb that means by reason of. Don't begin a sentence with *because*. Why not? Because I said so. Besides, it's a fragment.
Cite	To quote or refer to; to summon to appear in court.
Site	A location.
	I copy and cite while I sit on a site.
Close	To shut; to bring to an end. Nearby.
Clothes	Garments; what you wear.
Cloths	Fabrics; what your clothes are made of, what you use to clean with.
Decease	(n.) Death; (v.) to die. (When you cease, you die.)
Disease	Illness. (Combine the prefix dis-, meaning *not*, with *ease*: When you have a disease, you are not at ease.)
Disinterested	Unbiased, not influenced by selfish motives.
Uninterested	Indifferent.
Disqualify	(v.) To declare ineligible or unqualified.
Unqualified	(adj.) Not qualified, not fit to meet specific requirements.
	She was disqualified because she was unqualified.

Emigrate	To move from (-e) an area or country. (e for exit from)
Immigrate	To move into (-im) an area or country. (i for into)
	Stanislav and Vladislav emigrated from Russia, worked several years in Europe, and eventually immigrated to America.
Eminent	Prominent, lofty, excelling in station or repute. (The e in excellent reminds me of the e in eminent.)
Imminent	Near at hand; projecting or leaning forward. (Although imminent need not be negative, I remember the im spelling by thinking of impending doom.)
Immanent	Inherent; remaining within.
Envelop	(v.) To wrap up in; to surround completely.
Envelope	(n.) A wrapper.
	You envelop a letter in an envelope.
Human	Pertaining to mankind.
Humane	Compassionate and sympathetic about humans and animals.
Imply	To indicate or suggest something without stating it forthrightly.
Infer	To deduce by reasoning.
	His absence implied defiance; they inferred his defiance from his absence.
Loose	Free, unfettered.
Lose	To misplace. (I seem to have misplaced an o.)
Moral	(adj.) Pertaining to right or proper conduct.
	(n.) Principles of right or wrong conduct.
Morale	(n.) State of mind.
	Her morale was high because she had held true to her morals.
Personal	Individual, private.
Personnel	The staff of an organization; the section of the staff which deals with hiring.
	The company policy stated: "Don't get personal with the personnel."

Precede	To go before. (<u>Pre-</u> means before, prior to; in front of.)
Proceed	To go on or go forward, especially after stopping. (<u>Pro-</u> means *forward*.)
Real	An adjective that describes the opposite of *fake*.
Really	An adverb (usually a needless one) used to emphasize an adjective or verb.
	Something is not "real cool," meaning, "not fake cool." If it is cool at all, it is "really cool."
Principal	A chief or a head; the head of a school; a capital sum. (Remember this ditty: "The princi<u>pal</u> is my <u>pal</u>." Or, if it is easier: "The princi<u>pal</u> is not my <u>pal</u>.")
Principle	A fundamental truth or doctrine; an accepted rule of conduct. ("<u>Ple</u>ase have princi<u>ple</u>s.")
Resume	To begin again.
Résumé	A summary; a brief account of qualifications and experience.
Salary	A fixed compensation paid periodically to an employee for regular work or services.
Wages	Money that is received or paid for services, as by the hour, day, or week.
Think	To form or conceive in the mind. Thinking is a cognitive process.
Feel	To perceive by touch or through the senses; to be emotionally affected by.
Believe	To accept on faith.
'Til	Slang for *until*; unacceptable in formal writing. Note the apostrophe, indicating that letters are missing.
'Till	No such word.
Till	Up to the time that or when, onward to (less formal than *until*); to plow; a money box.
Until	(conj.) Up to the time that or when.
	(prep.) Onward to.

Weather	The state of the atmosphere with respect to wind, temperature, rain, etc. (<u>Wea</u> as in, "Wear a raincoat.")
Whether	(conj.) Used to introduce the first of two alternatives, which may be implied. Saying, "Whether or not," is redundant, as "or not" is part of the definition.

CHECKPOINT #7: IS YOUR SPELLING CORRECT?

A funny thing happened when I went to rewrite this section. I had originally subtitled the sections in this chapter in the same style I had in others, but then I decided that "checkpoints" made more sense. When I deleted the heading, I realized that it had a typo. See if you can catch it (at least three editors didn't): SRAIGHTEN UP SLOPPY SPELLING.

To many writers, spelling errors seem insignificant, but misspelled words can change your content. A spelling error shakes the reader's confidence in the writer. You, the writer, lose credibility. Consider the loss of regard a friend of mine experienced for the teacher who wrote this note: "I caught your son John wandering around the halls without a past." John may have no past, but that teacher has no future. Even a single error can cost a college or job applicant the chance for an interview. Painstaking proofing is the only route to perfect spelling, but there are few things as frustrating as looking up a word to verify its spelling or meaning when you cannot spell the word well enough to find it. Take heart; there are dictionaries just for this problem, such as *The Bad Speller's Dictionary*, which provide multiple ways to find a word. Make the effort to become familiar with the rules of phonetics, too; "sounding out" a word is an old-fashioned method for figuring out spelling, but it is a method that works.

Remember the old "i-before-e" rule from grade school? Many people must not, because it's a rule often broken:

> I before e
> Except after C
> Or when sounded as A
> As in neighbor and weigh.

As with most rules, this one does not always hold true. Here are a few words which pay no heed to "i-before-e." When in doubt, check it out.

counterfeit
forfeit
neither
receive
height
leisure
seize
either
foreign
weird

The following list contains the words most frequently misspelled in the thousands of manuscripts which I have edited. In my experience, the errors that high school students make are the same ones that college students and business executives make. If your manuscript includes any of these words, double-check them for correctness. Make your own checklist of words you misspell frequently. Some errors may result if you type hastily or carelessly. For instance, I know perfectly well how to spell *the*, but it is a word which I often type as *teh*. When I read my copy, I always look for that error.

Some words are usually misspelled a certain way, and the incorrect forms are listed in parentheses and italics to help you find errors. In addition, words that are often mixed up with the spelling of other words are listed together.

I really don't expect most homeschoolers to have trouble with spelling, but I'd rather err on the side of prudence and ask you to review the list anyway, especially since many of these mistakes were made by honor roll students.

Homeschool, home school, and home-school are variant spellings that have been accepted by the press; no one has declared definitively how to spell this grass-roots word. With words such as these, or British/American spellings (such as analyze/analyse), pick one spelling and be consistent.

absence (*absense*)
absurd
achievement
accidentally
accommodate (*accomodate*)
across (*accrost, acrost*)

ad/add
advertisement (*advertisment*)
affected/effected
allowed/aloud
a lot (*alot*)
any more (*anymore*)
athlete (*athelete*)
athletics
at least (*atleast*)
attendance (*attendence*)
be able (*beable*)
beginning
believe (*beleave*)
brake/break
business (*busness, bisness*)
cafeteria
certain (*certin*)
committee (*comittee, commitee*)
condemn (*condem*)
conscious (*conscous*)
convenient (*convenent*)
convenience (*convenence*)
course/coarse
correspondence (*correspondance*)
counselor (*counsler, counslor*)
criticize (*critisise*)
definite (*definit*)
dependent (*dependant*)
descend (*discend*)
description (*discription*)
desperate (*desparate*)
develop (*develope*)
difference (*diference*)
disappoint (*disapoint, dissapoint*)
dispensable
embarrass (*embarass*)
environment (*enviroment*)
equipped (*equipt*)
escape (*excape*)
exaggerate
exceed (*excede*)
excellent (*exellent*)

existence
experience
familiar (*familar*)
fascinate (*fasinate*)
February (*Febrary, Febuary*)
feel (*fell*)
forty (*fourty*)
forward (*foward*)
further (*futher*)
government (*goverment*)
grammar (*grammer*)
guidance (*guidence*)
high school (*highschool*)
humorous
imaginary
immediately (*immediatly*)
independent (*independant*)
indispensable (*indespensible*)
interview (*intevew, intervew*)
its/it's
knowledge (*knowlege*)
license (*lisense*)
lightning/lightening
losing
lovely (*luvly, lovly*)
manager (*manger*)
misspelled (*mispelled*)
more (*mor*)
necessary
niece (*neice, neese, nease*)
nineties (*ninties*)
no/know
no one (*noone*)
occasion (*ocassion*)
occurred (*ocurred*)
occurrence
omitted (*ommitted*)
opinion
opportunity
parallel
parliament (*parlament*)
past/pass/passed

perform (*preform*)
performance (*preformence*)
permanent
persuasive
pleasant (*pleasent*)
possess
prefer (*perfer*)
prejudice (*predjudice*)
privilege (*privelage, privlage*)
professor (*perfessor, proffeser*)
qualifications
recommend (*reccomend*)
references (*refrences*)
remember (*rember*)
repetition
restaurant (*restrant, resterant*)
rhythm (*rythm*)
schedule
separate (*seperate*)
senior (*senor*)
significance (*significant*)
similar (*simlar*)
sincerely (*sincerly*)
something (*some thing, somethings*)
sophomore (*sophmore*)
spelling (*speling*)
success (*suksess, sussess*)
superintendent (*superintendant, supertendent*)
surprise (*suprise*)
than/then/that
thank you, thank-you (*thankyou*)
there/their/they're
there's/theirs
think (*thank*)
to/too/two
though (*tho*)
through/threw (*though, thru*)
tragedy (*tradgedy*)
truly (*truley, truely*)
villain
virtuous
wear/where

who's/whose
writing
your/you're

To recapitulate, these are the main questions to ask when editing for wording and spelling:

Checkpoint # 1. Is your writing specific and lively?
Checkpoint # 2. Are you repeating yourself?
Checkpoint # 3. Are you using slang?
Checkpoint # 4. Are you using useless qualifiers?
Checkpoint # 5. Are you using the right prepositions?
Checkpoint # 6. Are you using the right word?
Checkpoint # 7. Is your spelling correct?

Take care of these seemingly nitpicky but essential details, and you're two-thirds done with editing.

SUM UP
1. In one sentence write the thesis of the chapter.
2. Identify the problems which you find particularly vexing, and record them in your journal under the heading: "Watch out for these."
3. Review your journal for spelling errors. Correct any you find, and then make a list of your "most dangerous" words.

REACT
1. Discuss how your life would change if you had to think, speak, and write in a language of only 2,000 words. Give examples of some ideas that would be unavailable to you.
2. Why does precise wording have more impact than vague wording? Give examples.
3. Is it fair that a grammar, wording, or spelling error could affect a writer's credibility so much that a job opportunity would be lost? Is it fair that writing ability plays so large a role in college admissions? Support your views. What arguments could be made for the opposite viewpoint? Be sure to answer in full sentences.
4. Do you think that if you write and speak well you cut yourself off from your friends or from other people in your community? Is it affected or snobbish to speak correctly? Does it have to be?

ACT

1. Add quotations to "Notable Quotations" that demonstrate the power of precise wording. They should be short but dynamic.
2. Rewrite the following sentences so that they are not redundant or repetitive.

> 1) It is worth the effort to try one more time again to word with vigor, vitality, energy, verve, and life.
> 2) Rewrite your words and sentences when you revise copy while editing.
> 3) His victory in this race today would mean that he would win a race for the first time.
> 4) In my opinion, I think that, to me, a sense of failure is always qualified by a sense of growth that reduces the feeling of failure.
> 5) According to Tom Robbins, who said it, "Make it work is the only rule."

3. Rewrite the following sentences so that the prepositions are used accurately. Eliminate unnecessary prepositions and generally improve the sentences.

> 1) Cut twenty roses from out in the back gardens.
> 2) Except with commonly used expressions, there are times where the students' slang confuses the teachers and where the teachers confuse the students.
> 3) Put the cat that's out on the back porch out besides the fence.
> 4) She told him of her research showing where prepositions are required for mathematics to make quantitative comparisons among numbers.
> 5) As of this date, the sales department is twenty percent below under the monthly sales quota in which bonuses are given; last month over twelve bonuses were awarded.
> 6) The hole filled up with water.

4. Write a sentence demonstrating correct usage for each of the following:

Accept	Disinterested	Moral
Except	Uninterested	Morale
Affect	Imply	Think
Effect	Infer	Feel
Believe		

5. Discuss the implications of the difference in meaning of "think," "feel," and "believe."

6. Read the editorial page of your daily newspaper and look for errors in wording, grammar, and spelling, especially in the letters to the editor.

7. Begin collecting errors that appear in your local newspapers and present them in class. How many errors per issue can the members of the class find if they pool their examples? Pay particular attention to those which you did not spot but were caught by a classmate or the teacher. (Chances are you yourself are making those errors.)

Ode To Spell Checker

Eye halve a spelling checker
It came with my pea sea
It plainly marks four my revue
Miss steaks eye kin knot sea.

Eye strike a key and type a word
and weight four it two say
Weather eye am wrong oar write
It shows me strait a weigh.

As soon as a mist ache is maid
It nose bee fore two long
And eye can put the error rite
Its rare lea ever wrong

Eye have run this poem threw it
I am shore your pleased two no
Its letter perfect awl the weigh
My checker tolled me sew.

(Poem circulated on the Internet, author unknown)

fourteen

Editing for Punctuation, Capitalization, and Structure

Yes, more dreadful but necessary stuff awaits you in this chapter. You've lived through usage, wording, and spelling, and you thought that was bad. You've still got to review punctuation, capitalization, and sentence structure, because they've got to be perfect too. You can proof for one area of mechanics at a time or proof for all at once. Either way, start out by scanning for obvious errors, such as sentence fragments or omitted periods. Then scrutinize for problems in any category, revising as you read.

PUNCTUATION, ONE MARK AT A TIME

Colons
Often confused with a semi-colon, at least in practice, a colon can only join two independent clauses if the second is an explanation of the first (Example 1) or a lengthy quote (Example 2). In general, use it before a lengthy list—although never after a verb (Example 3). Or, use it to mean "that is" (Example 4).

Example 1: Their votes were taken by proxy: substitutes voted for them.

Example 2: She quoted from her research paper: "Early in 1849 Josiah Henson narrated his experiences to Samuel A. Eliot, who subsequently wrote *The Life of Josiah Henson, Formerly a Slave, Now an Inhabitant of Canada.*"

Example 3: The catalogue featured clown apparatus: bulbous noses, oversized shoes, horns, floppy hats, pancake makeup, flowers that sprayed water, and the like.

Example 4: She faced a moral dilemma: whether to prosecute her secretary for embezzlement or to let him go and cover for his actions.

Also use a colon (instead of a comma) in the salutation of a business letter.

- •Incorrect: Dear Sir or Madam,
- •Correct: Dear Sir or Madam:

Commas

Following are the comma rules broken most often.

Place commas on either end of a nonrestrictive (nonessential) clause, one which adds an idea but does not change or affect the meaning of the main idea. Use no commas with a restrictive (essential) clause, which has to be in the sentence as it influences the meaning somehow. The phrasing of a nonrestrictive clause may be the same as that of a restrictive clause; the difference lies in your intent.

- •Nonrestrictive clause: The barber, who came from Seville, claimed that he shaved one hundred men last Friday. (Where he came from is not essential.)
- •Restrictive clause: The barber who came from Seville claimed that he shaved one hundred men last Friday. (The barber making this claim is the one from Seville, not the one from somewhere else.)

Interrupters function the same way as nonrestrictive clauses. They are nonessential, and their role as such is defined by commas.

- •Interrupter: Mr. Dawson, I feel that life is unfair.
- •Interrupter: I feel, Mr. Dawson, that life is unfair.

The phrase "as well as" does not require a comma before it unless it is parenthetical (it interrupts).

- •Essential: Peanut butter, jelly or jam, and bread as well as a knife are needed to make a peanut butter and jelly sandwich.
- •Parenthetical: A wrench, a rope, and a candlestick, as well as a cast of would-be murderers, are featured in the game "Clue."

An appositive or appositive phrase should be set off from the rest of the sentence by commas. No commas are necessary if the appositive is so closely related that it seems essential to the word it modifies (restrictive appositive).

- Nonrestrictive appositive: The lavatories, even the ones upstairs, are unsanitary.
- Restrictive appositive: The lavatories upstairs are unsanitary.

An introductory prepositional phrase takes a comma only if there are two or more prepositions in the phrase.

- In the bathroom the sinks are grimy.
- During a long talk with the doctor last night, he learned that his father's condition was serious but not hopeless.

An introductory transition usually takes a comma, but it's not necessary. The choice is yours.

- He denied that he had any obsessive traits; nevertheless, he cleaned his fingernails constantly.
- In addition, he washed the car six times a day.
- In addition he washed the car six times a day. (Compare the rhythm of the two sentences.)

Use a comma after an introductory adverbial clause (a clause beginning with subordinating conjunctions such as *if*, *after*, *until*, or *when*).

- When in doubt, delete.
- After you delete, do not add more.

Do not use a comma if you are joining *dependent* clauses with a conjunction. Use a comma if you have *independent* clauses joined by a coordinating conjunction (*for, and, nor, but, or, yet, so*—easily remembered by Frode Jensen's acronym: FANBOYS). Place the comma before the conjunction. Do not forget the comma, and do not use a semi-colon if you have a conjunction. Test whether your clauses are independent by considering each clause on its own. If the clause forms a complete sentence, it is an independent clause. If the clause does not have a subject and a verb, it is a dependent clause.

•Dependent clauses: She put on her sneakers to mow the grass but otherwise wore only a bikini.
•Independent clauses: Her parents preferred that she wear a coat, but they were so happy she was doing some work that they did not intervene.

•Incorrect: She went to the video store but, she could not find a movie she liked.
•Correct: She went to the video store, but she could not find a movie she liked.

Use a comma after each dependent clause in a series of clauses.

•Incorrect: After her plastic surgery she was in much pain wore bandages for months and had to stay out of the sun.
•Correct: After her plastic surgery she was in much pain, wore bandages for months, and had to stay out of the sun.

You may groan at this reminder, but the following three rules are often broken.

1. Put a comma between the name of a city or town and the state. You also need a comma between the name of a city, state, or province and a country.

•Gary, Indiana
•Barrington, Rhode Island
•Sydney, Australia

2. Use a comma after the closing of a letter.

Very truly yours,
Pedro Garcia

3. Put a comma between the numerical date and the year if you are writing a date in the American style. The European style—which is being used increasingly in the sciences—does not take a comma and reverses the order.

•Incorrect: June, 29 1989 or June, 29, 1989
•Correct: June 29,1989 or 29 June 1989

Dashes
     Writers either neglect the dash or overuse it. I am guilty of the latter, and knowing this helps me guard against it. Dashes are used to indicate an abrupt break in thought or used before an explanation to mean *namely*, *that is*, or *in other words*. Dashes are less formal than colons.

> •Ruth had long dreamed of this possibility—a semester abroad—but had never expected to experience it.
> •There was nowhere left to go but down—to his sister's house.

Exclamation Point
     This mark should be reserved for truly forceful, dramatic, or expansive comments. Unfortunately, it is often used liberally. Do not use an exclamation point to bolster weak wording. Never use more than one exclamation point at the end of a sentence.

> •Stop! There's a car coming.
> •The Iron Curtain has fallen!
> •What a game Sammy played!

Hyphens
     Use a hyphen to form a compound adjective when it comes before a noun. Do not use hyphens when the compound adjective comes after a noun or with an adverb.

> •Correct: The freshman class held a fund-raising dance last week.
> •Correct: The freshman class held a dance for fund raising last week.

> •Incorrect: The newcomer was a barely-known competitor.
> •Correct: The newcomer was a barely known competitor.

     Use a hyphen when necessary to divide a word at the end of a line. There are two problems with hyphens and word division. Forgetting the hyphen is one, and dividing the word incorrectly is another. Check the words at the end of each line; if any are split between lines, be sure that you have used a hyphen. Do not split a word between two pages. Move the whole word to the subsequent page. As for proper division, sound out the word to locate the syllables and break after a syllable. When two consonants are together at a syllable break, the division is usually, but not always, between them. Sound out the word again, or check a dictionary for the correct division.

syl-la-ble   be-tween
con-so-nant   pro-nun-ci-a-tion

When you form a compound word (a single word made up of two or more words joined together) check the dictionary for the standard form. Sometimes the word will be hyphenated and sometimes not.

•Nonstandard: Doublecheck
•Standard: Double-check

Quotation Marks

When repeating someone else's words, use quotation marks. Place commas and periods inside the closing quotation marks as needed. Let me restate this, as few people remember the rule: If you have a comma or period next to an ending quotation mark, the comma or period will go inside the mark—ALWAYS. Use a comma before a quotation when introducing or continuing a full quotation.

•The linebacker said, "I think the game was rougher than usual."
• Ross said, "This year has been an odyssey for me," and added, "a trip I'll never forget."

Place quotation marks and exclamation points inside the closing quotation marks only if part of the quote.

•"Would Eastern Europe ever be the same?" they wondered.
•Is America's most important motto, "Let freedom ring"?

Always place the colons, semi-colons, and hyphens which are part of your sentence's punctuation outside the closing quotation marks.

•The paper labeled it, "The most radical economic reform ever attempted in modern history"; the business community would never be the same.
•The slogan of the program was "No experiments"—no doubt due to the administrators' fiscally conservative approach.

Only one end mark is used at the end of a quotation.

•Incorrect: The family moved to Timbuktu, but a friend said, "They were reluctant to go.".
•Correct: The family moved to Timbuktu, but a friend said, "They were reluctant to go."

Periods

Omissions are the primary problem, except when working on the computer. Then a common error is to type two accidentally. Check that you have a period at the end of each sentence, especially the very last one. For some reason, many writers omit the final period. Some writers put a period at the end of every line, particularly when writing letters. The only two places you need a period are at the end of a sentence and after an abbreviation. If an abbreviation is the last word of a sentence, just use one period.

Semi-colons

Two independent clauses can be joined by a semi-colon instead of a coordinating conjunction and a comma. If you find a sentence with two or more independent clauses, but do not see *and, or, nor, but, yet,* or *for* between them, you need a semi-colon.

•Incorrect: The topic at the meeting was the interstate speed limit the topic was hotly debated.
•Incorrect: The topic at the meeting was the interstate speed limit, the topic was hotly debated.
•Correct: The topic at the meeting was the interstate speed limit; the topic was hotly debated.
•Correct: The topic at the meeting was the interstate speed limit, and the topic was hotly debated.

Use a semi-colon between two independent clauses when they are joined by transitions such as *hence, on the other hand, nevertheless, in addition,* and so forth.

•Incorrect: My complaint is that dorm rules are enforced too strictly, to wit, first offenders are given the same punishment as repeat offenders.
•Correct: My complaint is that dorm rules are enforced too strictly; first offenders are given the same punishment as repeat offenders.

A semi-colon may be needed for clarity to make divisions within an independent clause if the clause contains many commas.

> The elderly students had significant potential arising from their innate capabilities, which in many cases was above average; their experience, spanning decades and continents; and their driving need to work, learn, and do as much as possible in the time they had left.

Underlining

A single line is needed, but often omitted, to indicate titles of books, periodicals, works of art, ships, and newspapers. (Printers take this underlining as a signal to place the words in italics; do not yourself put them in italics.) Do not run a continuous line under the entire title; underline each word separately. Double-check newspaper titles carefully to make sure you underline the city if it is part of the title. On the other hand, when you title a paper, do not underline your own title.

> •Incorrect: Please consider me for the position of grapefruit squeezer as advertised in Sunday's New York Times.
> •Correct: Please consider me for the position of grapefruit squeezer as advertised in Sunday's <u>New York Times</u>.

Also use underlining for words, letters, and numbers referred to as such, as well as for foreign words.

> When I was trying to read Italian, I pronounced <u>cinque</u> like the French word <u>cinq</u>. Both mean <u>5</u>.

Abbreviations

Unless you are positive about an abbreviation, check the dictionary for standard form. Many students, for example, mistakenly abbreviate *avenue* as *av.*, but *ave.* is the correct form. Except for Dr., Mr., Mrs., and Ms., abbreviations are usually reserved for informal writing and addresses. *Miss*, as in *Miss Ginger Sanford*, does not take a period since it is not an abbreviation.

Note that states have two possible abbreviations, a postal abbreviation or a traditional abbreviation. The postal abbreviation should always be used for mail, but it is also becoming standard usage for other forms of writing. See the Appendix for a full list of state postal abbreviations.

If you use an acronym, spell out the full name first (unless the name is something commonly known, such as the YMCA); give the acronym in parentheses if important or if you will be using the acronym later as a substitute for the word.

> The Stella Rondo Society (SRS) was formed in 1986. A monthly book club, SRS has a maximum membership of nine.

Capitals

With a few exceptions capitalization errors result from penmanship problems or carelessness. Check your copy for random capping—letters that you have capitalized mid-word for no reason, because of a typo, or because you hand-write certain letters the same way whether in capitals or lower case (typically, *R, D, A, T,* and *F*). All lower case letters must look like lower case letters. All capitalized letters must be clearly capitalized. Do not write in capitals only.

Capitalize the first word, the last word, and all the important words in titles of books, articles, essays, reports, periodicals, poems, stories, and so forth. Do not capitalize coordinating conjunctions, articles, or prepositions of fewer than four letters.

- <u>Little Toot and the Loch Ness Monster</u>
- <u>Fried Green Tomatoes at the Whistle Stop Cafe</u>
- <u>Because It Is Bitter, Because It Is My Heart</u>

Capitalize the first letter of each principal word in the name of a university, college, or school: University of Montana, The College of William and Mary, Jefferson High School. Do not capitalize the words *university, college, high school, junior high school, middle school,* or *elementary school* unless they are part of a formal name.

Do not capitalize a class level: freshman, sophomore, junior, senior. The whole class (e.g., the junior class) may be considered as a proper name; whether you capitalize is up to you and your teachers. Whatever you do, be consistent. Capitalize both words or neither word: Senior Class or senior class, but not senior Class or Senior class. When writing about courses you take in school, do not capitalize unless they are proper names or are followed by a number.

American history	French	Chemistry III
History 101	journalism	biology

Capitalize the first word in every sentence. Please remember this fundamental fact: A sentence starts with a capital letter and ends with a period. Within a sentence you usually do not capitalize the first word after a semi-colon unless it is a proper name, but some people will capitalize after a colon if an independent clause follows it. Do as your teacher recommends. If a formal statement follows the colon, capitalize the first word (second example).

> •Correct: The problem was simple: no leash laws had ever been established in the rural part of the county.
> •Correct: The problem was simple, the solution simpler: Henceforth, no dogs shall run unleashed in Wildesville County.

When writing letters be sure to capitalize the first letters of the month in the date, the street, city, and state in the address, and all names. Also capitalize the first letters of the opening salutation and the first letter of the first word in the closing.

INCORRECT:	CORRECT:
Very Truly Yours,	Very truly yours,
Sincerely Yours,	Sincerely yours,

Fragments and Run-ons

The most common structural errors are sentence fragments and run-on sentences. Fortunately, they are easy to spot. If you see a subject but no verb, or a phrase without a subject, you have found a fragment. (Such as this.) Fragments do not belong in formal writing. Run-ons are also easy to locate. Look at any lengthy sentences; if you find a comma but no conjunction between two or more independent clauses (called a comma splice), you have found a run-on.

> •Fragment: Easy to locate.
> •Standard: The knobs are easy to locate.

> •Run-on: Seniors have parking privileges, they can leave at lunch, they get out at noon.
> •Correct: Seniors have parking privileges; they can leave at lunch; they get out at noon.
> •Correct: Seniors have parking privileges, they can leave at lunch, and they get out at noon.

If you start a sentence with a subordinating conjunction, be sure to finish it with an independent clause. Often fragments begin with *if, though, when,* or *because.* Pay attention to your speech patterns, observing how often you voice a fragment as opposed to speaking a complete sentence. Practice using full sentences when chatting with your friends; doing so will help you to write in full sentences.

- •Incorrect: If I went shopping. I took a list to keep from buying too much.
- •Correct: If I went shopping, I took a list to keep from buying too much.

- •Incorrect: Though, I didn't buy anything.
- •Correct: Though I didn't buy anything, the chocolate candies tempted me.

- •Incorrect: When you were gone. I couldn't believe that you had ever been here.
- •Correct: When you were gone, I couldn't believe that you had ever been here.

- •Incorrect: Because I said so.
- •Correct: Because I said so, you shall not sleep on the roof.

Do not start a sentence with a relative pronoun. You will not only make a fragment, but you'll lose the antecedent.

- •Incorrect: That he had kicked.
- •Correct: The cow that he had kicked swatted him with her tail.

- •Incorrect: Whom he had told off.
- •Correct: His boss, whom he had told off in an undisciplined moment, fired him.

Proofing for punctuation will help prevent run-ons. In addition to searching for comma and semi-colon errors, look for periods omitted between sentences. Such an omission incidentally causes a run-on.

- •Incorrect: The roof leaked, and his mattress was the target of the downpour He awoke wet and grumpy.
- •Correct: The roof leaked, and his mattress was the target of the downpour. He awoke wet and grumpy.

Misplaced modifiers are more difficult to spot than run-ons. When you examine each sentence, check to be sure that each modifier is next to that which it is modifying. If the modifier is misplaced, the content will be skewed.

•Incorrect: They had pulled their swimsuits on barely before the door opened.
•Correct: They had barely pulled their swimsuits on before the door opened.

•Incorrect: At 5'11" and 195 pounds, you'd never guess George was a weakling. (As far as I know, you're not the weakling, George is.)
•Correct: You'd never guess that George, at 5'11" and 195 pounds, is a weakling.

Do not leave your modifiers dangling, that is, sitting at one end of the sentence when the related noun is at the other end or buried in a sentence.

•Incorrect: Teeth snapping hungrily, they were met by a dozen guard dogs.
•Correct: They were met by a dozen guard dogs, teeth snapping hungrily.
•Correct: Teeth snapping hungrily, a dozen guard dogs met them.

•Incorrect: Running madly, the car provided shelter for them.
•Correct: Running madly, they headed for the shelter of the car.

•Incorrect: Arguing with each other, the dogs interrupted them.
•Correct: Arguing with each other, they were interrupted by the dogs.
•Correct: The dogs interrupted their arguing.

Parallel Structure
Ideas of equal value, coordinate ideas, and compared or contrasted ideas can be expressed with parallel structure, but you must use the same grammatical form to express each idea. For example, a phrase should be paired with a phrase, a verb with a verb, and a gerund with a gerund. One option is to use a subordinating conjunction (such as *while*, *after*, or *because*) to form an adverbial clause with more than one idea in it; another is to use correlative conjunctions (*both...and, neither...nor, either...or, not*

only...but) to set up the structure. If you do not find any parallel structures in your writing, study the following models to learn how to write them, and then try a few.

> *Parallel structure expressing coordinate ideas:*
> •Faulty: The dog sang while *jumping* on his bones and *ate* them one by one. (gerund and a verb)
> •Parallel: The dog sang while jumping on his bones and eating them one by one. (two gerunds)

> *Compared or contrasted ideas:*
> •Faulty: *Studying* for a test is more useful than *to fret* about it for days. (gerund and an infinitive)
> •Parallel: To study for a test is more useful than to fret about it for days. (two infinitives)

> *Correlative conjunctions:*
> •Faulty: Too late he saw that his options were either pink *hair* or *shave* it all off. (noun and verb)
> •Parallel: Too late he saw that his options were either pink hair or a bald head. (two nouns)
> •Parallel: Too late he saw that his options were either to live with pink hair or shave it all off. (two verbs)

Whew. That's it for rules you've got to watch out for, although of course you still have to pay attention to all the rules I didn't mention because I've presumed that you've memorized them already. The more you can remember, the easier the clean-up job will be. Nevertheless, whenever you edit, you are likely to find something that could be improved. Go ahead and improve it. The effort will make you a better writer, one change at a time.

SUM UP
1. In one sentence write the thesis of the chapter.
2. Briefly summarize those rules of punctuation that you break most often. The list should serve as a reminder and a personal caution.

REACT
1. Although punctuation must adhere to strict rules to be correct, certain punctuation marks are somewhat interchangeable (such as dashes, colons, and parentheses). What criteria would you use for choosing one mark over

another when there are several options? What effect could one mark have as opposed to another? Give examples.

2. How does incorrect punctuation influence the work and the reader?

3. Do you read punctuation correctly? Practice reading aloud to yourself, using the punctuation as a guide for timing and pacing. Read one of your essays to a writing partner. Does your writing have a good sense of rhythm?

4. Think about acronyms and how often we use them. Draw up a list of those that you commonly use. Then consider how public and political uses vary. What is the strategy behind coining START (Strategic Arms Reduction Talk) or WIN (Whip Inflation Now)?

ACT

1. Add quotations to your "Notable Quotations" that demonstrate complex but fluid sentence structure.

2. Test your punctuation sense. Add or delete punctuation marks in the following sentences. When necessary for correctness or smoothness, replace one mark with another.

> 1) I couldnt help myself, I wanted to be a "one of a kind person"; a rebelling son
>
> 2) For movie extras, long days often spent standing around sometimes in hot costumes are, compensated, for when a star performs, nearby.
>
> 3) After sitting on the bench for a year; I looked forward to a better year; playing!!
>
> 4) In addition a college education could help Jack the big blowhard claimed to prepare his children for earning an income living life fully and moving out of the house as soon as possible.
>
> 5) (In her letter Ellen her mother) said the gift of music, is, in many ways, the gift of love and if I helped you to open up to classical music, then, I have given you a present that will last through life.

3. Test your sense of structure. Rewrite the following sentences so that they contain no structural errors.

1) Suddenly nervous, self-conscious, and shy, the phone shook in his hand.

2) Desperately, others watched as the swimmer crawled in the surf, searching for her lost contact lens.

3) His son glued tin foil on the walls spraying black paint on the floors without remorse.

4) After shopping at the grocery store, her choices were to go the bank or resting.

5) Neither the locals nor the ones who were touring the country responding well to the travel campaign.

6) Although he had inside plumbing. He often used the outhouse instead. Because he preferred the view from there.

7) While leaping for their lives the keys dropped on the floor the women were terrified.

4.   Recheck your journal looking for punctuation errors. Date your revisions and corrections.

5.   Begin a collection of dangling participles—the more outrageous the better. Check your newspaper. If you can't find good examples, create some in class.

"There's not much to be said about the period except that most writers don't reach it soon enough."

William Zinsser

"An author who assures you that he writes for himself alone and that he does not care whether he is heard or not is a boaster and is deceiving either himself or you."

François Mauriac

fifteen

Presentation: Appearances Matter

Imagine that you have a date tonight. It isn't a blind date that your cousin or best friend arranged, and it's not an, "Okay, I'll go out with you since I have nothing better to do" sort of date. You are meeting for the first time a date you consider hot. Really hot. How will you dress? You may spend five minutes or five hours getting ready, but the likelihood is that you will think about your appearance very, very carefully and dress to impress.

Each paper you present is like the first encounter with a hot date, albeit not as exciting. The reader takes appearance into account in a quick glance, and in that instant you either measure up or fail to measure up. If you do not measure up in person, you have the chance to explain why and to make excuses (although you still may not get a second date). Writing offers no second chance once the material is out of your hands. If the appearance of your paper is neat and orderly, the reader instantly credits you with a certain amount of respectability, credibility, patience, and savvy. If the presentation is sloppy, the reader instantly discredits you. The cost might be a job interview, a lower grade, a place in college, or a raise. Appearances do matter. And while presentation is not a matter related to content, as is the rest of this book, it's still part of the whole package. Like it or not, you have to deal with it every time you write for an audience.

Once you have finished the job of editing, the final task is to prepare the material for presentation. This means recopying it if you have handwritten it, retyping it, or keying the corrections into the computer and reprinting it. Then you must proofread your final copy for errors such as typos. On this final go-round, you must adhere to standards of proper appearance. Fortunately, the rules of presentation, like the rules of proper dress, are easy to learn and employ, or to review if you already know them.

CHECKPOINT #1: ARE CORRECTIONS DONE NEATLY?

Corrections

Messy corrections are the number-one problem in the appearance of high school and college papers. Corrections should be UNNOTICEABLE, even if you're just handing the paper across the kitchen table to your mother or father. Caked, flaky correction fluid is noticeable. Scratched-through letters are noticeable. Letters written or typed on top of other letters (strikeovers) are noticeable. It might seem to you that a lower case b can be turned into a capital B without notice, but you are wrong. The reader will see the strikeover and read, "Lazy."

Few people can get all the way through a paper without making some errors. If you shouldn't make corrections that are noticeable, what are you supposed to do? Here are a few options.

Use a single coat of *fresh* correction fluid. If the fluid flakes from the brush when you pull it from the bottle, you need to replace the fluid. Make sure that the correction fluid is a type that will work over pen, typewriter ribbon, or printer ink so that your error will not bleed through the correction. Wait until the fluid dries before writing or typing over it. Remember to complete the correction later.

Try using Pentel Multi-Purpose Correction Pen, or another brand of correction pen, instead of fluid. The brand mentioned here uses a point instead of a brush. It is easy to apply, fairly precise and quick, and it does not flake.

If the above options are not available and circumstances (and audience) allow, mark a single line through the error: ~~error~~. Then place your correction after the error if there is room. If not, mark the insertion with a printer's mark known as a caret, and place the correction above the space where it is meant to be read.

Blanche drove ~~form~~ from Tucson this morning.

•He made a ~~mistke~~ mistake ʌ but had no room for the correction.

You can make typewritten corrections as you go with correction tape or ribbon. Check to make sure that the error has been completely removed; if not, you will have to apply fluid or start over. If you have made many corrections (more than three or four in a two-page paper), it's best to start over. Those who work on a computer or an electronic typewriter with memory capabilities should make corrections on the machine and print a fresh copy.

If you are writing a letter of application, résumé, or curriculum vita, you will most likely type your final copy, and that copy must be perfect. Perfect means perfect. No errors.

CHECKPOINT #2: ARE YOUR MARGINS THE RIGHT SIZE?

Maintain at least a one-inch margin on all sides. If need be for hand-written work, lightly pencil in guidelines. Remember to erase these later. If your text is short, your lower margin may be larger than those at the sides or top; this is acceptable. If what you have written is lengthy, use additional sheets of paper. Don't write to the very edge or on the back. It is better to leave a larger lower margin and carry at least three lines to an additional page than to cram those lines at the bottom or to carry over only one or two lines.

If a word on the last line falls beyond the right margin, move the whole word to the next page rather than splitting the word between pages. It's okay if the final line has more space on the right than the other lines. You may split a sentence between two pages, but be sure to continue the sentence at the left margin on the subsequent page, several lines beneath the heading.

CHECKPOINT #2: ARE YOUR HEADINGS CLEAR AND APPROPRIATE?

When you have a title, center it on the top line of the first page if hand writing the material. If typing, leave a two-inch margin above the title. Skip a line or space, and write your first and last name, centering it beneath the title. Then skip one or two lines before beginning the first paragraph. The title should not be underlined unless it contains a formal title, and then only the formal title is underlined. You don't need end punctuation unless the title poses a question.

Silicone Implants: Lovely or Lethal?

by Susan Cohen

Mother-Daughter Relationships in <u>The Joy Luck Club</u>

by Robert Phan

If you are responding to an assignment question, write or type your name on the left or right side of the paper, being careful not to cross the margins. Beneath your name write or type any relevant class information, as required, and/or the date. Skip two lines or spaces and place the question flush with the left margin. If you are responding to more than one question, number the questions as they were numbered on the assignment or exam sheet. You may start your response on the first free line below the question, or skip one space.

> Wendell Shapiro
> Composition 102
> January 31, 2010

1. What are the elements of style? Name four and give an example of each.

The elements of style are coherence, conciseness, smoothness, and....

Subsequent pages must include your name (at least your last name and never just your first name) and the page number. Your material will survive most mishaps, such as an employer mixing one set of applications with another (your page one with Godzilla's page two) or a teacher dropping all the term papers on the floor, if you label each page. No page number is needed on the first page because the title format (or the address format of a letter) indicates that it is the first page. You have several choices, shown below, for placement and arrangement of your carry-over headings (also called "continuity headings"), but all headings must be at least one inch from the top of the page.

Holstein--4

Holstein--4

Holstein   Page 4

Holstein/Page 4

Holstein
Page 4

CHECKPOINT #3: WERE YOU CONSISTENT WITH YOUR SPACING?

Write on every line (single space) or every other line (double space) as expected or assigned. In general, double spacing is better because it is neater and leaves room for comments, corrections, and revisions. Whatever you do, be consistent. Don't skip a space between some lines but leave no space between others. Consistency in format is essential.

Except in certain letter formats, indent each new paragraph approximately half an inch from the left margin or five letter spaces on the typewriter or computer. (Use the tab key, set at the right point, so you don't have to count spaces every time.) Be sure to space each paragraph indentation the same way. All paragraph indentations must align.

Unless told otherwise, leave two letter spaces between sentences.

CHECKPOINT #4: ARE YOU USING THE CORRECT FORMAT FOR LETTERS?

Letter formats come in three styles: full block, semi-block, and block. The full block style is the one used most often in business. The semi-block is more traditional, and most people write personal letters using this format. The block is a mix of the first two and the one most easily confused. It is also the least used. All letters, regardless of format, have in common the following sections: the heading, the inside address, the salutation, the body, and the closing.

Business letters should be typed if possible, and the letter should be centered on the page (between the top and the bottom, not side to side). A long letter will fill in most of the page except for the margins, while a short letter would have the same left and right margins but larger upper and lower margins.

Heading

The heading includes your full address and the date. It does not include your name. Where the heading is placed varies according to letter style, but its left side will always line up. Check that you have included the full address, including street number and what type of street (Road, Lane, Avenue, etc.). The latter may be abbreviated, with the exception of *lane* which has no standard abbreviation. Consult the dictionary if you are unsure of an abbreviation. Also check: Did you include the full zip code? You may leave one or two spaces between the state and the zip code, as long as you are consistent, leaving the same number of spaces in the heading and on the envelope too.

Single space the heading, and skip two lines between the heading and the inside address.

> 320 Apple Tree Lane
> Hungertown, NJ 00000
> January 1, 2007

Inside Address

The inside address of a business letter includes the following: the addressee's name and the courtesy title (Mr., Mrs., Ms., Miss, or Dr.), the addressee's job title if you are not on familiar terms with the person, the name of the business, and the full business address. You have a choice whether to place the job title on the same line as the addressee's name or to place it on the next line. Your decision may be based on the length of both name and title. If you place the title on the same line, use a comma between the name and the title. Use no comma if you place the title on the next line. A personal letter follows the same format—name and courtesy title, if appropriate, on the top line; street address on the second; and city, state, and zip code on the third (or on the fourth if the address includes both a post office box and a street name). In either case, never end an address line with a "floating" punctuation mark.

The inside address is single spaced usually. Skip two lines between the inside address and the salutation.

INCORRECT

Dr. Gislaine deGraff,
Education Coordinator
P.O. Box 134.
Braintown, WA

CORRECT

Dr. Gislaine deGraff
Education Coordinator
Braindrain College
P.O. Box 134
Braintown, WA 00000

OR:

Dr. Gislaine deGraff, Education Coordinator
Braindrain College
P.O. Box 134
Braintown, WA 00000

Salutation
The salutation includes the word *Dear* plus the person's courtesy title and last name, followed by a colon in a business letter and a comma in a personal letter. If you do not know a woman's marital status, you may address her with the title *Ms*. If you do not know the person's name but do know the gender, you may write, "Dear Sir" or "Dear Madam" (without the quotation marks, of course). If you know the job title but not the person's name or gender, you may drop "Dear" and substitute the job title for the name (e.g., "Manager," or "Personnel Director," or "Editor"). Another choice, considered old-fashioned but to me clearheaded, is to write, "To Whom It May Concern." If you are writing to a company but not to a particular person or someone in a particular position, your options are below.

•Gentlemen: (if sure that the company is run by men)
•Dear Sirs: (if sure that the company is run by men)
•Ladies: (if sure that the company is run by women)
•Mesdames: (if sure that the company is run by women)
•Dear Sir or Madam: (unsure whether the company is run by a man or woman, but you know it's one person)
•Ladies and Gentlemen: (sure that it's run by both females and males)
•Dear Sirs or Mesdames: (same as above)

As you can see, the choices abound. To skip the "Dear," except as noted above, is unacceptable, as is to include the person's first name in the salutation. (You wouldn't say, "Dear Ms. Larena Muhammad," but you would say, "Dear Ms. Muhammad.") The body of the letter usually starts on the first line beneath the salutation, but skipping a line is also acceptable.

Body and Closing
The body of the letter is your content. The body is usually single spaced but may be double spaced as long as you do so consistently throughout the letter. Following the body, skip two lines before beginning your closing section. Never put the closing alone on a page; shift a few lines to go with it if need be.
The closing section includes the actual closing line (a sort of farewell), your signature, and your printed or typed name. Unless you are writing to a friend or to a close business acquaintance, the closing should be formal. Remember, too, that only the first letter of the first word of a closing is capitalized. The closing must be followed by a comma. Here are the wording options for a formal letter.

ACCEPTABLE	UNACCEPTABLE
Very truly yours,	Your friend,
Sincerely yours,	Thanks,
Respectfully yours,	Thank you,
Sincerely,	Truly yours,
	Yours respectfully,
	Yours sincerely,
	Yours very truly,
	Cordially,

Regardless of letter style, the signature is placed midway between the closing and the printed signature and should align with their left margin (*their* left margin, not necessarily the letter's left margin; that depends upon letter style). You'll need to skip three or four spaces between the closing and the printed signature to make room for the handwritten one.

Very truly yours,

Carlos Sanchero

Carlos Sanchero

Carry-Over Headings

How to write carry-over headings for letters is a subject of disagreement. Some people think it's acceptable to write your own last name and the page number on subsequent pages, using one of the formats suggested earlier. Other people believe that this is improper, that instead the addressee's name or the name of the company should be listed on each subsequent page, rather than the writer's name. Either way, the heading must also include the page number and should include the date (to help identify it). The layout of the heading is different from one letter style to another. Below is an example of a carry-over heading for a full-block letter.

Addressee's or company name
Page number
Date

Full-Block Style

Every letter section is aligned with the left margin in the full-block format. There are no indentations. Instead, skip two lines or spaces between each section (so that you begin on the third line or space) and one line or space between paragraphs. Skip two lines between the closing and the line on which you print or type your name. Place your carry-over headings one inch down and in from the left edge, as in the previous example.

An example of the full-block style is below.

FULL-BLOCK FORMAT

Your street or P.O. address
City, State Zip Code
Date

Addressee's full name, including courtesy title
Addressee's job title if relevant (here or on previous line)
Name of business if relevant
Addressee's street or P.O. address
City, State Zip Code

Dear _____ :

The body lines up with the left side also, and you leave a one-inch margin on both sides of the page.

Skip one space between paragraphs but don't indent them.

Closing,

[Your signed name]

Your printed or typed name
(If you printed your signature, don't print it again.)

Block Style

In the block style the spacing between sections is the same as for the full-block style. Skip two full spaces between sections and between the closing line and the line for printing your name. Skip a single space between paragraphs. The heading and closing sections align on their left sides, but rather than begin at the left margin, these begin near the center of the page and extend to the right margin. If you find that your heading information does not reach the right margin, do not spread out your letters so that it does so. Start over, and move the whole section to the right as needed, bearing in mind that the right side need not be straight. If, conversely, the heading extends into the right margin, move the section to the left as needed. To work out such problems, you may need to rough out your layout before you make your final copy.

Since the heading and closing sections align, you may want to imagine a dotted line extending from one section to the other so that your alignment will be true. On the typewriter or computer, take note of your spacing count or set your tab so that you can be consistent. The alignment must carry over even when the heading and closing are on separate pages.

The inside address, salutation, and body of the letter align with the left margin. Do not indent paragraphs.

Place carry-over headings on one or two lines within the top and side margins. Whether you include the addressee's name or yours is up to you or your teacher; including the first name as well as the last is also an individual choice, although you never use the first name by itself. Including the date is also an individual choice.

| Ms. Anjin Michaela | -2- | May 2, 2005 |

| Ms. Anjin Michaela--2 |

Because the block format uses elements of both the full-block and the semi-block styles, people tend to forget how to do it properly. If you are using this style, double-check that both your heading and closing sections are placed toward the right and align, even if they are on separate pages. Make sure that no paragraphs are indented. Below is an example of the block format.

BLOCK FORMAT

> Your street or P.O.
> City, State Zip Code
> Date
>
>
> Addressee's full name, including courtesy title
> Addressee's job title if relevant (here or on previous line)
> Name of business if relevant
> Addressee's street or P.O. address
> City, State Zip Code
>
>
> Dear _____ :
>
>
> The body lines up with the left side also, and you leave a one-inch margin on both sides of the page.
>
> Skip one space between paragraphs but don't indent them.
>
>
> > Closing,
> >
> > [Your signed name]
> >
> > Name printed or typed

Semi-Block Style

The heading and closing sections begin near the center of the page and extend to the right margin. As with the block style, if you find that your heading information does not reach the right margin, do not stretch it so that it does. Start over, and move the whole section to the right as needed. If the heading extends into the right margin, move the section to the left as needed. Both the heading and closing sections must align on the left side.

Remember, the left side is not the same as the left margin. Skewing the alignment is a common error.

Also similar to the block style, the inside address and the salutation line up with the left margin. But unlike the block style, paragraphs are indented, typically five letter spaces or half an inch. Subsequent lines begin at the left margin. Your teacher may want you to skip a space between paragraphs even though they are indented. Otherwise, the spacing is the same as with the other two styles: two lines or spaces between each new section and between the closing and printed name.

Any carry-over headings should run across the page, as shown in the section on block format, or should be placed to align with the right or left margin.

On the next page is the example of semi-block format.

SEMI-BLOCK FORMAT

Your street or P.O.
City, State Zip Code
Date

Addressee's full name, including courtesy title
Addressee's job title if relevant (here or on previous line)
Name of business if relevant
Addressee's street or P.O. address
City, State Zip Code

Dear _____ :

    Indent five letter spaces from the left margin, and leave a one-inch margin on both sides of the page.

    It is optional to skip one space between paragraphs, but you must indent them to conform with the semi-block format.

Closing,

[Your signed name]

Name printed or typed

Envelopes

    Business letters should be mailed in a #10 envelope. Fold the letter in thirds, folding the bottom third up first and then folding the top third over that. Place the letter in the envelope so that the copy faces the back of the envelope. The recipient should be able to pull the letter out, unfold it, and start reading it without having to turn the page or pages around.

    The address information and its placement are the same on all envelopes. The return address (your address, which in the letter is called the heading) goes in the upper left-hand corner of the envelope. Although you did not include your name in the letter heading, you must do so in the return address. Leave a one-fourth to one-half inch margin on the top and left sides. Place the address (the recipient's address, which is the inside address in the letter) so that it begins about one inch to the right of the return address (about four and one-fourth inches from the left side) and down two inches from the top of the envelope. These measurements are for a #10 envelope. Make adjustments for other size envelopes that will be proportionately the same.

Your full name
Your street or P.O. address
City, State Zip Code

        Addressee's full name, and courtesy title
        Addressee's job title if relevant
        Name of business if relevant
        Addressee's street or P.O. address
        City, State Zip Code

Traditional business format uses the upper and lower case, as well as punctuation, according to standard grammatical rules. The post office currently prefers that all information be placed in capitals and that commas and periods be eliminated.

ELDRIDGE MASON
77 HIP-HOP STREET APT 12
NEW YORK CITY NEW YORK 00000

        MR IRA J KOOL
        BUSINESS MANAGER
        SPLIT TUNE RECORDS
        2225 PLATTER ST
        CHICAGO IL 00000

CHECKLIST FOR LETTERS

1. Are the letter and envelope free of errors and obvious corrections?
2. Are abbreviations consistent?
3. Are margins and spacing uniform?
4. Are indentations consistent? Do they match the guidelines of the chosen letter style?
5. Do all aligned elements truly line up? Is the closing aligned with the heading, even if they are on different pages? Do all sections match the guidelines of the chosen letter style?
6. Did you use carry-over headings after the first page? Do the headings include both your last name and a page number or the addressee's name and a page number?
7. Does the last page have at least two to three lines of text plus the carry-over heading, the closing, your signature, and your typed or printed name? Remember that if you are writing the letter by hand, you only need to print your name in addition to your signature if your signature is illegible or marginally legible.
8. Are the closing, signature, and printed name aligned on their left side? Their left side is the same as the left margin if you are using a full-block or block format, but not if you are using the semi-block.
9. If you have included a courtesy title (Mr., Ms., etc.) in your signature, ask whether doing is necessary to clarify your gender. If it is, put it in parentheses: (Miss) Sam Chang. If it is not, delete it.
10. Is the phrasing of the salutation appropriately formal?
11. Is the phrasing of the closing appropriately formal?

One last bit of advice. Whether you are writing an essay, an exam, or a business letter, always look at it one last time before you turn it in. Always. The time and effort you expend on creating a spotless manuscript can buy you something a slovenly manuscript cannot: a reader willing to give you a chance.

SUM UP
1. Write a paragraph about the role that appearance plays in your life.
2. After class add any new ideas generated in the discussion.

REACT

1. In what ways does presentation convey attitude? What are the key elements in an effective presentation?

2. What is your attitude toward personal appearance? We have all heard the aphorism, "You can't judge a book by its cover," but how often do we judge or are we judged according to a first or superficial impression? Be candid.

3. To create a polished piece of work takes time. You cannot dash off an essay the night before it's due and hope to produce perfect copy. Think about how much time you need to do excellent work. Every person works at a different pace; be realistic in estimating the time you require. Then consider how you budget your time. Do you allow enough time to do what is needed? Can you organize your time better?

4. In our "information age" certain skills are especially useful: effective use of a typewriter, a computer, a library, and the Internet among them. How can you upgrade your skills? What other skills are important to your efficiency as a writer and a student?

ACT

1. Consult *The Concise Oxford Dictionary of Quotations* or *Bartlett's Familiar Quotations* for entries pertaining to appearance or beauty. Pick at least three and add them to your "Notable Quotations." Analyse them in class to determine which of them you really believe in practice. For example, we might all agree that "Beauty is only skin deep," but when we react or relate to people, do we place greater value on inner qualities or surface appearances?

2. Write a short descriptive, narrative, expository, or persuasive essay. You may build it from a paragraph you wrote for a previous exercise, use a "Notable Quotation" as a starting point, or start from scratch. Take the essay through the entire rewriting and editing process. Prepare a final copy that is correct in execution and perfect in presentation (typed if possible).

3. Redo the paper in letter format, addressed to your teacher. Include your filled-in envelope (also typed if possible) with the finished assignment.

"Learn to write by doing it. Read widely and wisely. Increase your word power. Find your own individual voice through practicing constantly. Go through the world with your eyes and ears open and learn to express that experience in words."

P. D. James

PART II: APPLICATION

SECTION 5: BRIDGE-BUILDING IN ACTION

CHAPTER 16, BRIDGES TO KNOWLEDGE

CHAPTER 17, BRIDGES TO OPPORTUNITY

CHAPTER 18, BRIDGES TO THE WORLD

"Continuous effort—not strength or intelligence—is the key to unlocking our potential."

Liane Cordes

sixteen

Bridges to Knowledge

You are now a bridge builder; you have all the tools you need to travel the gap between you and another person. But you can hone those tools with practice. Consider the following analogy.

Chefs whose meals are never eaten do not know whether the food is cooked to culinary perfection. Without feedback they cannot improve the combination of ingredients or seasonings. They would be food preparers, not chefs. Similarly, those who study and practice but never test the art of writing on a real audience never know whether their craft is sharp or dull; nor is it clear what needs to be improved. They are word crunchers, not writers.

At this point you are like a chef's assistant who has learned how to chop vegetables but not how to cook them. Since the point of writing is to communicate, you must now apply what you have learned. Practical writing covers three areas: education, opportunity, and daily needs. Each has its expectations and guidelines. This chapter discusses the typical assignments of school and college, which includes the book report and its counterparts, essays and essay questions, and the research paper. These are the typical bridges you must cross to make your way from school to the working world. All have aspects which are also common to business writing.

One purpose of assignment writing is to learn something, or to show what has been learned. A second purpose is to meet the requirements of a particular assignment in a way that satisfies the expectations of a teacher. If you fulfill the second purpose, you will also meet the first.

Most teachers provide specific guidelines and requirements for assigned projects. Pay attention to their expectations; ask questions and request examples if you are unsure of any points. The teacher is a tough audience, especially when it is a parent, but it is nevertheless a reader you must satisfy. And, while it is the teacher's responsibility to make sure that the assignment is clear, it is your responsibility to do your best.

BOOK REPORTS: LOOKING BEYOND THE COVER

Reports on books, for instance, are fairly formulaic, enough so that the same general guidelines apply to reporting on stories and plays. A report states the main thesis, briefly outlines the plot, describes the main character or characters, and discusses your reactions to the book or some element of the book. A typical assignment asking you to discuss one aspect of the book might require you to, "Discuss the use of mythical reality in Gabriel Marquez's *A Hundred Years of Solitude*." A summary—as opposed to a report—is a concise but comprehensive statement of the main points, relating plot and character to theme. A character analysis examines the role of a character in relation to the book's thesis or secondary themes. A typical assignment might read as follows: "Discuss the ways in which Willy Loman's family relationships, in Arthur Miller's *Death of a Salesman*, contribute to the theme of failure." A synopsis is a compressed summary of just the plot.

In all varieties of a report, be sure to include the title of the piece and the author's name when you introduce your topic. In addition, give the full name of each character you discuss, and support comments with brief, well-chosen quotations. A relevant quotation will not require a lengthy explanation to relate it to a point; the point should be obvious.

In the opening paragraph state the thesis of both the book and your paper—your thesis being your slant on the book's theme. While a book may have multiple secondary themes, it can, by definition, have but one *central* theme. You can usually approach that theme from several angles. Keep your writing focused on one angle only. You will probably have to try several times to transform your thesis from a vague stab at clarity to a cohesive, logical, and focused idea. If you're not sure whether you're being clear, ask someone to read your thesis statement and then explain it to you in different words. If the person fumbles a great deal, it may be that your message wasn't as obvious as you thought.

•Assignment: Write a book report on *The Road from Coorain*, placing particular stress on the role of the land in developing the protagonist's character.

•Vague thesis statement: *The Road From Coorain* is about a woman who struggles to find her identity and has trouble with her upbringing, especially her mother and the land on which she grew up. (This thesis statement covers too many points—the struggle for identity, trouble with her upbringing, trouble with her mother, and trouble with the land. It isn't focused on any one point.)

•Focused thesis statement: In Jill Ker Conway's memoir, *The Road from Coorain*, the land, both terrible and magnificent, inspires in her courage, then fear and powerlessness, and finally, indomitable courage. (Notice that this statement includes the author's name as well as the book's, and, although it mentions several emotions, the focus is on one point, the land in relation to those emotions. The thesis is now manageable.)

•Focused opening paragraph: The Australian grassland, as portrayed in Jill Ker Conway's *The Road from Coorain*, is a magnificent but relentless taskmaster, a place of riches and of ruin. The land and the inhabitants' attitudes are like its bitter winds, eroding the author's efforts for a better life until she almost gives up. Only when she recognizes that she can leave the land behind— by moving to America to continue her education—can she escape its hold on her. (This is a full introduction, with a slight twist on the theme compared to the previous thesis statement. The first sentence indicates the theme: The land gives and takes away. The second and third sentences indicate the major points which the writer will use as support.)

For assistance in determining the book's thesis or your own, or key elements of a character's nature (such as a fatal flaw), read the author's introduction if the book is nonfiction, the editor's comments, and/or the book jacket blurb. Book reviews, which you can find by using *The Reader's Guide to Periodical Literature*, can give you another writer's ideas on the subject. *The New York Times Book Review* is an excellent source. *Benet's Reader's Encyclopedia* also provides concise summaries of plot and major points. Remember, however, that these sources are meant only to prime the pump and to inspire you. You must present your own ideas in your own words. To this end, discussion with a writing partner or group can help you sort out your reactions.

In a general book report you should note a few aspects of the book, such as scenes, characters, plot, sense of place, emotion, or wording that especially appealed to you. You can also note the elements that did not appeal to you, or ones that could have been made more effective. If you have enough points on both sides of an issue, you may wish to use a comparison/contrast development scheme. (See Chapter 4.) Your report will be easier to write if you make notes as you read or after you finish reading a chapter. If the book is yours, and you don't feel squeamish about marking in your books, underline key sections as you read them and mark the corresponding page numbers in the back of the book. If the book is not yours, make your notes on a separate sheet. Either way will help you find vital points and supportive quotations when you write; as a bonus, the notes make studying for exams much easier.

Use the last paragraph or, in a lengthier report, the last few paragraphs to sum up your reactions to the book—your feelings about it and its impact on you. Tie these reactions to the book's thesis.

> Ms. Conway's determination to make her life her own made me re-examine my own lackadaisical attitude about life. I take it as it comes; she made what came bend to her rule. In a sense, she was as relentless as the land and every bit as magnificent.

In an analytical essay use your summary to re-emphasize your thesis and highlight its main points. A critical essay may be considered the same entity as an analytical essay, or it may be considered an examination of the book compared to other literature of the same genre or time period, or of the book's style.

> •Analytical: In sum, the harshness of the author's childhood and the survivalist nature which she developed to overcome the cruelties imposed by drought and poverty propelled her beyond the limitations placed on women in the late fifties.

> •Critical: The author's evocative style is reminiscent of other female memoirs, notably *West With the Night* by Beryl Markham.

For a character analysis, restate your thesis in relationship to both the character and the book. Conclude with a clincher that wraps up the piece dynamically.

> At the beginning of the book, the author describes her mother as someone with "boundless physical and intellectual energy," a woman who "reveled in blessed independence." Near the end of the book, Ms. Conway calls her mother "an angry and vindictive woman," someone who could not harvest and cherish "the experiences that nourish hope." Independence had become crushing dependence, and the drought in her mother's soul was far more devastating than any the climate had wrought upon the land. For the author to stay with her mother was to live in an emotional and intellectual desert. To leave was to affirm life.

A synopsis is a compressed summary of the plot, and you can't write it unless you understand what a plot is. A plot is not a static entity. Rather, it is a set of significant events that topple into each other like dominoes, moving the action from the beginning of the book to the end and leaving the characters in a different state than they began. The basic pattern for plot is conflict/resolution. The difficulties of the main characters escalate with each ensuing conflict. Sometimes conflicts occur without immediate resolution. These conflicts and resolutions make up the scenes of the book, story, or play. All the scenes are (or should be) important to the story, but some are more critical than others. The key scenes, or plot points as they are also called, are the ones you need to discuss.

Before you begin your first draft, make a list of the key scenes in sequence. Review the list. If you left out a scene, would a reader still understand how an event or an aspect of character development led to the next? If not, the item is likely essential. If so, the item can probably be omitted. Next ask yourself whether the reader needs more information than you have given; you may need to add a scene. Finally, ask yourself how important the scene is. Did it have a major impact on the main characters, or was its purpose to help set up a more important scene? For example, in Richard Wright's short story, "The Ethics of Living Jim Crow," the first scene portrays a fight near the main character's home. After this scene, the narrator discusses a move from Arkansas to Mississippi and his efforts to get a job. This move itself, while chronicling an event, is not actually a scene. It is background information necessary for the reader to understand the scene which follows, in which the main character encounters scathing prejudice. Your job is to discern the major scenes from the minor ones and to show, briefly, in what way the major scenes are critical to the book's plot. Use examples or quotations to support your belief that the scene is vital.

In your opening paragraph sum up the thesis in relation to plot. Mention three or four vital scenes that push the main character toward epiphany (a moment of determination or insight) or resolution of the conflict. The body of the paper will discuss those scenes in order. Below is a prototype for a synopsis, using *The Adventures of Huckleberry Finn*.

The Adventures of Huckleberry Finn by Mark Twain features Huck, a young boy, and Jim, a runaway slave. Through a series of adventures, many involving narrow escapes from danger, Huck learns about the value of human life and individual dignity. The book begins with his escape from his cruel father. When he runs away, he joins up with Jim, and they travel on a raft up the Mississippi River to help Jim to safety. They encounter desperate thieves and murderers on a sinking riverboat. After several frightening days on the river, they are found, and Jim is put back into bondage. The climax comes during a battle between two rivaling families, when Huck helps Jim escape. The story resolves with Jim a free man and Huck in a new home.

Paragraph 2 would describe briefly Huck's conflict with his father and the condition it sets up in relation to the thesis, that under Huck's father human dignity is nonexistent.

Paragraph 3 would explain how Huck and Jim hook up and why this pairing is necessary to plot development. Jim's presence ultimately forces Huck to question his own beliefs about slavery and human rights. Without Jim, Huck wouldn't have to think about these issues in personal terms.

Paragraph 4 would describe the encounter on the riverboat and how it serves to bring Huck and Jim closer together.

Paragraph 5 would describe Jim's recapture and compare it to Huck's becoming an adopted son and, in a sense, Jim's "owner." The scene is necessary to enable Huck to understand Jim's predicament and to deepen his own self-examination.

Paragraph 6, which could also be part of paragraph 5, would briefly recount the battle between families and the ensuing chaos. The point is to show how this event pushes Huck into noble action.

Paragraph 7 would be the conclusion. It would sum up the changes the plot has brought upon the main characters.

This example marries plot development with an examination of theme and character. In some cases, just noting the key scenes without discussing their relationship to the theme is all a teacher will want.

YOU CAN'T AVOID ESSAYS

Essays, including essay tests, are the mainstay of academic life. Every step outlined in the book thus far will help you write essays, whether your assignment is to meet a single purpose (to describe, to narrate, to explain, or to reason/persuade), to write about a particular topic, or to show what you have learned in class. Once you have licked the problems associated with developing sound content in a clear and logical manner, the main problem you may have with essays is developing a response that meets the various criteria of the assignment. A specific question or assignment has innate requirements and needs an "answer" that covers all of them.

Many students get started on an assignment or test question by repeating the question nearly verbatim in the introduction. This, I have found, is a stalling tactic used when the student is not yet sure what to write.

> •Assignment: List aspects of the society in Mark Twain's day which were of interest to him, and show how they influenced his writing.
> •Student's opening: Some aspects of the society in Mark Twain's day that influenced his writing are slavery, politics, and class structure.

What are the problems with the above opening? One problem is that it answers only the first part of the question—the list. Neglecting the second part of the question, examining influence, leads to another problem: The statement is. not a complete theme, for the information is not focused. Slavery, politics, and class structure are topics too large to develop fully within the space of an essay, and showing every influence or every aspect of all influences may also be too broad. Without focus the writer has no sense of developmental direction.

A useful tactic is to brainstorm first about the question and to form a thesis given the ideas that arise. Then you can write an opening which includes your thesis.

> •Revised opening: The morality of slavery, corrupt politics, and an elitist class structure stirred Mark Twain enough to write about them in all his works. He consistently took a view opposing that of the general populace and acted out his view through his characters.

The revision gives the writer a firmer direction. The paper will discuss Twain's positions on the issues listed and how his positions went contrary to much of society. For support the writer can mention stories and characters which show Twain's position. Since strong introductions usually lead to firm conclusions, the arrangement will also help the writer conclude more firmly:

> In every work from his first to his last, Mark Twain used his characters—their trials, their dreams, their flaws, and their courage—to prove that slavery was immoral, politics corrupt, and class elitism inhuman.

Apologetic wording is another problem in many essays. When you are unsure of your ideas, explore them more. Think about them and expand them logically. Avoid beat-around-the-bush phrasing such as, "What I really mean is…" or "What I am trying to say is…." Demonstrate faith in your ideas and word choices even when you do not feel confident. Dropping unnecessary qualifiers will automatically make you sound confident. Really.

Essay tests demand the same keen organization and solid content that every essay does, but usually you must put your response together in less time and space. If you are allowed, use scrap paper or the back of the exam to work out a rough outline (a simple list of key points will do) of your answer. Make sure that the major points of the question are covered in your outline and again in your essay. Avoid filler words such as adverbs, adjectives, and qualifiers; let your verbs, nouns, and examples do the talking. Be as concise as possible. If you are under a time constraint, it is better to include your main points and supportive examples than to spend time building a fancy introduction and conclusion. On the other hand, you always need a well-defined thesis statement: the answer to the question in one or two sentences, stated one way in the opening and rephrased in the conclusion to show the effect of the support and development on the thesis.

RESEARCH PAPERS: NOT A DISEASE

Most everyone I know views the research paper as a fatal disease. There are many reasons to try to evade writing one: They are long, complicated, a lot of work, and generally hateful—or so the rumors go.

It is true that they are long, complicated, and involve a great deal of work, not all of it interesting. But a great deal of the process should be interesting to most students. The problem often lies in the topic of the paper. Lackluster themes run rampant. If you choose a topic that rouses your curiosity, the work is—well, I can't say fun exactly, but it is at least less trying.

Finding something that interests you takes energetic exploration of the possibilities. If you relate well to your teacher, you may be able to discuss possible topics until you find some which stimulate your imagination. Or you can bounce ideas off a writing partner or group, a parent, or a friend. Try to come up with a long list of possible topics.

Once you have formed a list, visit the library. It is maddening to get mid-way through a research paper only to realize that you cannot find enough material for the required length. You need to make sure that enough material exists before you commit to a topic. Look for books, articles, and primary sources such as speeches. Look in the encyclopedia for suggested source material; look up the source material, too, as it may be listed but not available locally. Likewise, look through the *Reader's Guide to Periodical Literature* and *Magazine Index* (a computerized database) for articles, but be sure to check which magazines are carried by your library. (I once committed to a topic that had at least twenty relevant articles listed, only to find that not one of the magazines or newspapers was available locally.)

In your search, remember dictionaries, atlases, almanacs, the Internet, and the card catalog. Make sure at least three different kinds of sources are available. For now, make lists of the sources, but just scan the actual references to check the amount of information available on your possible topic. When you begin your focused research, you will return to them.

There are two questions to ask once you have finished this preliminary research. One, is there enough material available? Do not tackle a topic for which only one or two books and a few articles are available. Two, are at least three different kinds of sources available? When the answer is yes to both questions, you can whittle down your topic list and carve one that's right for you.

NOTE: Many people use the Internet for their sole or primary source of material. Much so-called "information" on the Internet is uncited, unsupported, or itself poorly researched. Don't use any information that can't be verified.

Find a Focus

The next step is to brainstorm for a well-defined focus. It may seem that you will need a miracle to find a thesis for a lengthy paper, but the process is the same as for any other paper. Examine your topic to determine whether you can find a slant on it, one of manageable but sufficient depth given the allotted time and page count. If you find that your topic is too small (not enough supportive information), yet you are still attracted to the subject, try working "backward." Think of larger and larger categories for your topic, until you can find a broader one to work with. Your initial topic will become a subtopic of the new topic.

•Topic too narrow to be developed:
Female printers in 1776 (too few female printers to write about)

•Broader topics:
Female printers during the American Revolution
Female printers from 1600 to 1800
Female printers up to the present

•Broader and developing an angle:
The role of women in printing, their specific contributions and changing statistics in terms of number of women involved and responsibilities

•Finally, the new topic:
Opportunities for American women in printing were far greater in the pre-Revolutionary and Revolutionary War days than in the nineteenth century.

Notice that the "new topic" has been written as a thesis statement. Your paper *must* have a single theme with a clear focus. That focus will direct your research, your organization, and your writing. A common problem with research papers is that the theme is not well defined. The length of the paper seems to short-circuit the normal thinking-through processes of thesis development. Follow the steps you would for any writing project. If necessary, re-read Chapters 3, 4, and 5 to rewire your memory. If you are still balking at pinning down your material into a single-sentence thesis (or even if you are not), try writing a list of questions about your subject. Examine the list and the answers for a slant on the topic. Had the writer working on the topic "Female printers in 1776" used this method, a different thesis might have emerged.

•Subject: Female printers in 1776
1. Who were they?
2. What was special about them?
3. What was the history of women in printing before then?
4. What was the status of women worldwide in terms of skilled employment as well as in printing specifically?
5. Did the printing industry offer them something different, or was the difference due to the times and circumstances?
6. How long did women "run the show"? Why did things change?
7. What other jobs did women take on during the war?

8. Were more opportunities always available for women during wartime?

•New topic:
Women at work: wartime opportunities, peacetime unemployment

•Thesis:
Until the past twenty years, women in America had their greatest employment opportunities during wartime, a phenomenon well demonstrated in the printing industry.

Once you have settled on a thesis, write it in one sentence and post it where you can see it whenever you are working. Next, begin your research; start by answering your list of subject questions. Track down information via the sources you located in your preliminary search. Look for information related to minor as well as major supportive points. As you take notes, remember that you are going to have to process, not merely report, the information, so don't simply copy your resource material. Select the key points as you read, and try, then and there, to write them in your own words on your index cards or notepad. You may find it useful to invent a shorthand script. (For instance, I leave out prepositions, articles, most modifiers, and most vowels when I take notes, unless I am recording a quotation.) The script will not only speed up your note-taking, but it will force you to think about what you have read and written when you flesh it out later.

Be sure as you conduct research to record sources on each card or section of notes; this will save you time later when you are doing your footnotes and bibliography. As you read a book or article, write the relevant source information at the side of your notes, or write it as a heading for a cluster of notes. Besides citing references in my notes, I often make a separate bibliography sheet when I begin research so that I can fill it in as I go instead of later on. This way, when I am in the final stages of preparing a paper, all I have to do is alphabetize the list instead of digging through notes for the references.

You need to record the following during your research:

> Author's full name, last name first
> Full title of the book (underlined) or article (in quotations)
> City of publication for a book, full title of publication (underlined) for an article
> Publisher and year published; if specific quotations used, write the page numbers
> For an article: Date of publication and page numbers (first and last, e.g., 23-31)

NOTE: If you are citing a source on the Internet, include the website in place of the city of publication. If the source is actually a quotation from a book, make sure you include all the standard information about the book, as well as the Internet information. If it is from an e-zine (an Internet magazine), note that it is such, and still include the publisher, year published, page numbers, etc. The rule of thumb is this: Include as much information as needed for someone else to find the same article. If this isn't possible, don't use it.

Also, label your notes as to the major or minor points which they address. Sometimes you will come across information you had not previously considered important but that you see now is relevant. Make a note to the side as to where it will fit and whether it is a major or minor point. Otherwise it's easy to forget how the pieces fit together. If you believe that it is a major point, explore your sources for sufficient support. A major point requires enough material to add at least two minor points, plus support.

The advantage of index cards over note paper is that they are more flexible as a working tool. When your space is limited, you are forced to write only essential information, and you naturally avoid copying large chunks of direct text. You can arrange cards alphabetically for your bibliography, or rearrange them to match the text when writing footnotes. Once ready to write your outline or first draft, you can easily shuffle them around to experiment with organization. Of course, you may not have a choice about your note-taking system, as your teacher may prefer index cards instead of notepaper or vice versa.

From Research to Draft, Step by Step

A research paper demands super-tight organization. You can't just drop your note cards and write about them in the order they fall. You must organize the material logically. Your paper could list every fact in the world (and many papers attempt this), but without organization the paper would be worthless. Organizing a research paper is no different from organizing any other multi-paragraph paper, but it seems daunting because it's so much longer than a standard essay.

Start by re-reading your thesis statement and your notes. Does the information truly support the statement? Or is another idea dominating? Don't be afraid to rewrite your thesis statement. It makes more sense to match your introduction and conclusion to the body of the material than to write an outline and draft that are not united in content. The writing process is one of discovery. Be sure to discuss your discoveries with your teacher to ensure that a new thesis won't be an unacceptable surprise.

Once you have ascertained that your thesis statement and research correlate, simply follow the steps laid out in Chapters 4 and 5 to write your first draft. Write major points and minor points in a sentence outline, and build from there. Once you have written a first draft, re-test your thesis against the development. Again, refine the thesis statement to match the content, and revise the content to match the thesis. Review Chapter 6 for the steps to rewriting effectively. A writing partner or group is especially helpful on a long project such as a research paper.

When you revise, you have the perfect opportunity to chase down and eliminate material that comes verbatim from other sources. Follow the steps laid out in Chapters 4 and 5. It may be tempting, and you may do so accidentally, but you must not plagiarise. If you use someone else's words, you must use quotation marks and credit the author either in the text or in a footnote. On the other hand, do not indulge in the tendency to use lengthy quotations. The teacher wants your thinking, in your words. Use only as many quotations as you need to back up your material.

If you use tables and statistics, use no more than absolutely necessary, and interpret them. Help us, your readers, to understand them. Don't stick them in there to fill up space. Superfluous material will detract from your paper's success (and, if you get one, your grade). Be sure to credit your sources for any graphics you use.

Wrap It up in a Pretty Package

After you have revised the paper to your satisfaction, type it according to your teacher's specifications or the general guidelines in Chapter 15. Put quotations of five or more lines into inset paragraphs, set two spaces down and ten spaces in. You do not need to indent the first line of a one-paragraph quote, but you should indent the first line five additional spaces for multi-paragraph quotations. You omit quotation marks in an inset paragraph, and single-space it.

Whether you use footnotes, endnotes, or parenthetical (internal) documentation is usually determined by your teacher. The last form of crediting sources, recently popular, puts the source reference into parentheses within the text. All three forms require a full list of references at the end of the paper.

Insert parenthetical documentation before the period at the end of the sentence using the material. This rule holds true regardless of whether the citation is a direct or indirect quote, unless the quotation is inset. In the latter case, the documentation goes two spaces after the period. Include the author's last name and the page number, without a comma between the two, when the author's name is not mentioned in the citation. Always skip a space before the first parenthesis. Below are three possible formats.

- Indirect quote: Nintendo was Franklin's passion, addiction, and downfall (Johnson 245).

- Direct quote: "His entire financial empire crumbled as he sat glued to his monitor, his thumb pinned to the control" (Johnson 245).

- Inset quote:
    Nintendo games were Franklin's passion, addiction, and downfall. His entire financial empire crumbled as he sat glued to his monitor, his thumb pinned to the control. A massive network of telephones rang without response. (Johnson 245)

When the author's name is mentioned in the text, put only the page number in parentheses.

Johnson believed that Nintendo games were Franklin's passion, addiction, and downfall (245).

Footnotes and endnotes are typed in the same manner but placed elsewhere. Footnotes go at the bottom of the page (single-spaced); endnotes at the end of the paper (double-spaced) on a separate sheet. Both are numbered consecutively as they occur in the text, with the number typed after the period and a step above the line of text.

> Throughout the war, roving gangs of armed brigands on both sides, Patriot and Loyalist—such as the "Skinners" and "Cowboys" of upstate New York—used the war as an excuse for random villainy.[1]

The citation for the footnote or endnote must give the following information, in order. Use a semi-colon between items if the note includes more than one source.

- The author and, if relevant, the translator (if the author is anonymous, start with the title)
- The title of the article or book and any subtitles, underlined
- The name of the magazine or newspaper if an article, underlined
- The city and year in parentheses if a book
- The volume if a magazine
- The date in parentheses if a magazine or newspaper
- The page number, followed by a period

A book footnote or endnote, such as for the previous quotation, would look like the following. Notice that the two authors are listed in the order their names appeared on the book.

[1]Forrest McDonald and Ellen Shapiro McDonald, <u>Requiem: Variations on Eighteenth-Century Themes</u> (Lawrence, 1988), 50.

When you cite a work more than once, but not consecutively, you do not need to repeat the full reference. The second time, and all subsequent times, use a short citation: the author's last name, a shortened title, and the page number.

[2]McDonald and McDonald, <u>Requiem</u>, 121.

A magazine footnote or endnote would look like this:

[3]Marcy McDonald, "Can Our Children Write, and Who Cares," <u>The World & I</u>, Vol. 3, No. 4, April 1988, 670.

Use the Latin abbreviation ibid., for *ibidem* ("in the same place"), when two or more consecutive footnotes or endnotes refer to the exact same source. (A different book or article by the same author is considered a different source). If the page number is different, include the new number.

    [4]Ibid., 671.

Sometimes your citation will include a quote by someone besides the author of the main text. You need to cite both sources, as follows.

    [5]Georgia Holtz, "Literature that Laughs," <u>Literary</u> <u>Weekly</u> <u>News</u>, 2 (Summer 1978) quoted in Caldwell, <u>Rise</u> <u>and</u> <u>Fall</u> <u>of</u> <u>Humor</u>, 34.

Occasionally writers make a footnote to enter a personal comment about something not directly related to the material. Such digressions may be useful, but they should not be made often and should never go in the text of a formal term paper.

Use a separate page or pages at the end of the paper for a list of works cited (specific references) or the bibliography (all the sources that you actually consulted). You include the same information as in a footnote but without footnote numbers or page references.

List the citations in alphabetical order (according to the author's last name, which is placed first on each line). If the author is anonymous, place alphabetically according to the first word of the title (do not count articles). If the author has more than one entry, use a long dash in place of the name after the first item. For articles, list the first page and the last page numbers (for example: 23-27) for the whole article rather than just the page numbers specifically used. Single-space within an entry; double-space between entries. Entries which occupy more than one line should be indented on the second and ensuing lines.

Follow the same format for your bibliography, but list all sources, not just the ones from which you quoted. Don't list a source you reviewed if the source turned out to be irrelevant. Center a heading on the top of the page which identifies the material (Works Cited or Bibliography). The example below uses a different style than used previously for footnotes. This is done to give you an example of another model. It's okay to use a different *style* but not different *styles*. Be consistent with whatever model you choose or are required to use so that footnotes, endnotes, bibliography, and works cited will be in the same format throughout the paper.

Bibliography

Kiell, Norman, The Adolescent Through Fiction (New York: International Universities Press, 1959).

Carpenter, Frederic, "The Adolescent in American Fiction," English Journal, XLVI, 1978, 314-318.

Giannetti, Louis D., "The Member of the Wedding," Literature Quarterly, IV, 1976, 27-30.

McCullers, Carson, The Heart Is a Lonely Hunter (New York: Bantam Books, 1978).

-----, The Member of the Wedding (New York: Bantam Books, 1979).

White, Barbara Ann, "Growing Up Female: Adolescent Girlhood in American Literature," Dissertation Abstracts International (University of Wisconsin), 1974, 616-657.

Check your final package against your teacher's guidelines for the paper to make sure you have done everything according to specifications. Before you turn in your final draft, be sure to edit the entire manuscript using the checklists in Chapters 12-15.

SUM UP
In one sentence write the thesis of this chapter.

REACT
1. Why do writers need readers?
2. Discuss the long-term value of writing assignments.
3. What kinds of information are usable as support in a research paper? Why would one type of support carry more weight than another? Why might one source have more credibility than another?
4. What are primary and secondary research materials? You'll have to do research to find the answer.

ACT

1. Add to your "Notable Quotations" some quotations dealing with issues that fascinate you. Select from both fiction and nonfiction.

2. Write a summary or synopsis of a movie you have seen recently. Discuss the success or failure of the plot as a development for the movie's thesis.

3. Write a critical or analytical essay on a book (or story or play) you have read. Choose any theme for your discussion; be sure to tie your paper's theme to the central thesis of the book.

4. Practice primary research. Interview an eyewitness or eyewitnesses to an event or time period. Take notes throughout the interview; if possible, use a tape recorder. Write a summary of the interview and include a few choice quotations. (You might ask questions about home entertainment in the early 1900s, for example, or what it was like to survive the Holocaust, to fight in the Gulf War, etc.)

5. Write a list of possible research topics that interest you. Go to your library and list potential source material for several topics. Select a topic based on availability of reference material.

6. Use the two methods in the chapter (in the "Find a Focus" section) to find two different focuses for your topic. Choose one and write your thesis in a single sentence.

7. Write a schedule for a research paper. Plan specific dates to finish each stage, from research to final copy. Write a paper according to the chapter's guidelines and your teacher's criteria. You may be able to write a research paper that meets the requirements of another class, such as history or science.

8. All finished assignments should meet the criteria for presentation given in Chapter 15.

"The trick is leaving out everything but the essential."

David Mamet

seventeen

Bridges to Opportunity

I would be a liar if I said that I've had to write something to get every job I've ever had. Once I walked onto a job site, asked the foreman if he needed help, and was hired on the spot to help clean up an oil spill. The man never even asked my name until the end of the day when he paid me. Another time I talked to the art director on a movie set during his coffee break. "Can you paint?" he asked. "Sure," I replied, and I was soon doing so. Both of these jobs were exciting, and neither required writing as a prerequisite.

Then again, neither lasted more than a month or paid well. To make something out of the experiences, to make more of them than what they were, I would have to prove that I gained from them something of value. The proof would come in the form of a personal narrative, letter of application, cover letter, or résumé, and the aim would be to gain employment, a position in college, or entrance into a special program, such as an internship. I could use the experiences to demonstrate the characteristic of assertiveness, for instance, or adaptability. Learning to make the most of who you are and what you have done relative to a specific goal is the crux of writing for opportunity.

Writing for opportunity differs from writing for assignments in that you write for your own benefit, out of your own motivation, and for an audience that will give you a "real world" grade: a position or no position, a promotion or no promotion, a raise or no raise.

THE NARRATIVE: KEEP IT PERSONAL BUT GIVE IT A POINT

The personal narrative is essentially a persuasive essay. Its peculiarity is that it asks you to be, on the one hand, creative and personal and, on the other hand, well-organized and analytical. The point of both sides is to persuade the recipient (a college board, an employer, or some other review panel) that you are the right person for the position. You must show that you are interesting, self-motivated, and able. Your content, organization, and logic must be solid and clear. And your style must demonstrate your personal values and qualities.

Are you sweating yet? Relax. It's a cinch. Just follow the writing steps outlined in earlier chapters, particularly in Chapters 8, 9, and 10. Then consider the challenges and practice the solutions discussed in this section. You'll blow 'em away.

College or job narratives require that you address a specific question in full. Most narratives require some analysis—explaining the *why* of something—and this part of the essay is where most students fall short. View the question as though it were a test, with points taken off if you do not respond to all parts. Look for key words, such as *define*, *evaluate*, and *describe*, which signal the direction your response must take. If, for example, the question were, "Describe a person who has influenced you and say why," you would not just give a description of the person. You would intertwine description and analysis, describing only those elements that you would need to show how the person was influential.

The tone of a narrative is "familiar," in that the subject matter is personal. Yet the audience is formal; slang or informal sentence structures such as fragments are unacceptable unless of obvious benefit to style. Instead, use examples that have universal appeal. You may use contractions (sparingly) in a personal narrative for a college application or graduate school, but avoid them in a business, educational, or professionally directed narrative.

Take a look at some sample narrative questions. Notice the key words in each, such as *discuss* and *explain* in the first question. Some of these are for college and some for jobs; all are culled from genuine application forms.

1. Discuss the pressures to conform that you face and explain how you handle them.
2. Write a detailed statement indicating your reasons for wishing to enter this program, your reasons for choosing our program, and how you believe that the program will influence you professionally. Describe your background and analyse the strengths and weaknesses of your preparation for the program.
3. Which of your values would you most want to pass on to your children or be remembered for by your friends? Why?
4. Discuss your biggest mistake and evaluate its impact.
5. Describe a personal experience that has caused you to change. Explain why and how you have changed.

6. Discuss your definition of a good employee and explain the contributions you will make as a good employee.

7. Discuss your career goals. Explain what steps you will take toward those goals in this position. Explain what contributions you will make to the company as you strive to meet your own goals.

8. Evaluate a significant experience or achievement that has special meaning for you.

9. Identify some personal item that you have saved for years; explain why you keep it. Under what circumstances would you throw it away?

10. Describe the most difficult obstacle you have overcome and what you learned in the process.

11. Discuss one or two activities or hobbies that have been important to you. Explain why, and explain how they add to your qualifications for this position.

12. What single adjective best describes you. Why?

13. What is the most meaningful book you have read. Why?

14. What three objects would you place in a time capsule to represent the decade of the 1980s? Why?

If you are given a choice of topic, explore the possibilities before deciding which attracts you most. You want to pick a question you can answer well but will also challenge you. Dig deep into the "why" of your subject and choose a meaty topic. Warning: If you are going to write about the memorability of your teddy bear, bunny, or rocking horse, you are going to have to dig really deep. Essays on such topics are like fast-food french fries. It is nearly impossible for the reader to tell one from another or for the writer to make the essay meaningful. Both the question and the response should allow you to demonstrate your writing and analytical skills as well as to show off some of your character strengths; all these are "selling points."

When you brainstorm, look for enough information to write about, a slant on that information, and the answers to these two questions: What are my strengths? What distinguishes me from other applicants? Write down everything positive you can think about yourself. Include, too, anything negative that you have worked on improving. You may find a thesis in the answers to these questions, but what you are looking for primarily are a few points that will reveal something vital about your character. Look for an angle that will allow you to blend in these points.

Your essay will not survive without a thesis, one that is more than a restatement of the question. Make sure that your opening addresses your thesis and provides a strong hook. The example below addresses the question, "What single adjective best describes you. Why?"

> •Ineffective opening, because it gives neither the writer nor the reader a sense of direction:
> The adjective that best describes me is <u>inquisitive</u>.

> •Effective:
> I am inquisitive. The cat, poking its paw under a door; the puppy, falling into a tub; the toddler, squeezing behind a couch: This is me. I look for more; I search for answers, and I search for the joy of searching.

See how the second opening provided a clear direction for the essay's development? The style of the essay is successful, too, because its gentle and slightly humorous tone is rich in imagery.

Use Fresh Ideas and a Crisp Style
Being creative without being cute is a challenge for narrative writers. You must be in tune with your emotions, thoughts, and ideas so that you can relate them freshly. Timed writing exercises (see Chapter 5) can help you find new images. Concise material will be crisper. You do not have to be avant-garde. Speak honestly and precisely. A few telling details will add more richness and creativity to your essay than a non-stop barrage of big words or a series of outlandish examples.

> •Overblown style:
> When my emotions react with a song that I most enjoy, my passion is exuberantly affected by my affections and desires, and every note vibrates with meaning.

> •Concise and fresh:
> Sometimes a song pierces me, and I find myself singing as though every note counted as much as a heartbeat.

Your style should be enticing. Replace vague wording such as *a lot*, *great*, *many*, and *things* with specific phrasing and concrete examples. Play with your introductions and conclusions. Variation, richness, boldness, or subtlety can have great impact in a personal essay. The first section draws the reader in; the other leaves an imprint on the reader's mind.

•Vague and undeveloped:
My mother has influenced me a lot and in many ways.

•Specific, visual, and clear:
I wanted to go to the senior prom desperately. My mother, a single parent, had no extra money for frivolities such as a dress to be worn for one night only. At the same time, she wanted me to have the same chances that others had. Without any obvious regret, she ripped down her new curtains that she had saved months for, and she sewed them into a stunning dress for me. Her resourcefulness, unselfishness, and ability to think swiftly and act energetically are her gifts to me.

The example transforms the empty phrasing of "a lot and in many ways" into a clear, vivid picture. By opening with an anecdote, the narrative lures the reader into involvement even before the thesis is directly stated. The last sentence states the thesis in a way that will direct development. Laid out like that, the thesis statement becomes a guidepost enabling you to check your bearings as you write. It's your North star.

Keep in mind at all times as you write that the personal narrative gives the reader something which statistics about grades and awards cannot—a snapshot of the inner you. Choose what you share carefully, and before you turn in a narrative, ask this question of it: Does this present a portrait of a strong candidate for the position? If not, rewrite it. Believe in yourself. Write confidently.

Whether your readers are in academia or business, they will be picky. Before they even read your essay or letter, they will instinctively examine the paper's appearance. A sloppy presentation will signal a lazy, uncaring attitude. You will not be there to offer excuses or explain why you could not recopy or reprint it. No matter what you have written, it will count just a little less than a paper equally or less brilliant but perfect in appearance and the conventions of standard English. So, edit your essay and have a friend edit your editing. Your friend shouldn't rewrite your essay, as that would be unethical, but merely point out any rough spots.

Redo the paper until it is impeccable. The reward may be an opportunity that will change your life.

COVER LETTERS UNCOVER YOUR POTENTIAL

Chutzpah helps when you write a letter of application or a cover letter (a letter accompanying a résumé). Used alone, with a narrative, or with a résumé, the letter of application is a fantastic tool for persuading someone to give you a chance to prove your abilities. The prospect at stake may be a grant, an internship, or a job, but the overriding thesis of each is the same: "I am the most qualified, and this is why." To develop this thesis, you must explore the requirements for the position, the expectations of the employer or review board, and your relevant qualifications. Then you must sift through the information to pull out that which fits the pattern of a letter of application. (For the sake of simplicity, I will use the example of employment. The process is applicable to a variety of situations.)

Qualifications are characteristics or accomplishments that fit you to a function or situation. They can be viewed as the job duties or requirements. Qualities are traits, attributes, or features, in this case positive. Most positions have specific *qualifications*, but often you can find indirectly related *qualities* within yourself that will enable you to meet those requirements.

In one way or another, you must address all aspects of the position, including some which will not be listed. An ad for a tennis instructor, for instance, might ask only for an experienced player. But a tennis teacher must be more than someone who plays tennis well; it must be someone who has the qualities—patience, articulateness, and energy, for example—to teach tennis. Qualities are only qualifications if they are needed for the job.

In the ads below, the qualifications and requirements are underlined, and the qualities are double underlined.

> Child care: Mature, dependable woman to care for infant in home. Must be experienced. Must do light housework, including cooking. Monday, Thursday, and Friday morning.

> Courier: Full time. Will load and unload packages and supplies. Must be able to perform basic preventive maintenance on vehicles and keep performance records. Needs valid license, perfect driving record preferable, strength to lift 55 lbs. required. Reliability, neat appearance, and good manners important.

Read the ad or guidelines carefully before preparing your letter. Try assembling your material into a chart to sort it out. One way to do this is to make two columns on a piece of paper. In the first column, list every actual requirement of the position. Below that note any optional qualifications, and below that list the unstated qualities you think are needed to perform the job well. In the second column, beside every point you can, note where or how you gained the experience or attribute (for example: through a class, job, or outside activities).

> Ad: Computer sales associate. Part or full time. Must have two years' Apple Macintosh experience. Must have at least one year working with Microsoft Word, any version. Pagemaker experience optional but desirable. Should be familiar with competitors; peripheral software knowledge helpful. Must have sales experience. Should be personable, punctual, and assertive.

The following "chart" responds to the ad above and would be for your eyes only:

QUALIFICATIONS:	MY EXPERIENCE
2 yr. Apple	2 years' school computer classes (Apple)
1 yr. Microsoft Word	Have own Mac & use Microsoft (3 years)
Sales exp.	2 summers: 1990 at Hard Hat Hardware 1991 at Video & TV Marketplace, and part time senior year
Hours: full or part time	Could work full in summer, part time during school year
QUALITIES:	
Personable	"Employee of summer" award, 1991
Punctual	Never late, work or school
Assertive	Most sales two months in a row, 1991
OPTIONAL:	
Pagemaker	No
Familiarity w/other software	Yes, subscribe to 3 monthly computer mags so have read about them; tried MacDraw at school
Familiarity w/competition	A little, from magazines
UNSTATED QUALITIES:	
Ambitious	Putting self through college
Self-motivated	Part time senior yr. at Video Place; kept up 3.0 average
Reliable	Perfect attendance, jobs and school

Your own notes may be more or less formal than the chart above; the idea is to match your skills and your potential to the job. When finished, compare it to the ad. Can you meet the essential requirements? If, for instance, the job calls for typing 60 words per minute, and you can only muster 20 with half the words wrong, you are not qualified. If the job requires you to work from 4 to 8 p.m., and you volunteer as a tutor at 7, do not apply for the job. On the other hand, if you are close to meeting a specific requirement (you could be there until 7 and could come at 3 to compensate, or you have 22 months of computer experience when the job calls for 24), then you might give it a shot.

Drafting the Letter

Once you have established your qualifications and proof of them, you can write your first draft. It should follow the outline below, and it must be in business letter format (see Chapter 11). Many phrases within the letter are conventions; these are standard ways of saying something. Don't monkey with them.

PARAGRAPH 1: You *must* state what you are applying for. You *can* mention your source of information about the job (which newspaper, a friend if an important friend, a campus listing, etc.).

> I should like to apply for the position of computer sales representative, as advertised in Sunday's <u>Yekaterinburg</u> <u>Express</u>.

PARAGRAPH 2: You *must* identify yourself in relation to the position. Do not identify yourself by saying, "Hi" or "Hello, my name is…"; state only those points about age and education that are relevant. State when you are available to work and begin the job if your time is restricted, or what shift you prefer if a choice is offered.

> I am a college freshman available for part-time work now, weekdays after four and any time on the weekends. Beginning May 5, I can work full time.

Then begin building your argument for employability, naming your qualifications and your relevant qualities. You're trying to prove that you can fulfill the requirements in the best possible way. Mention the most direct and relevant points first. If you have more than one major point to develop, you may need to write several paragraphs to develop them adequately. You might, for instance, develop qualifications in one paragraph and qualities in another. Be sure to support whatever you say.

PARAGRAPH 3 (or whatever number you are on): If you have had several employers, and you are not including a résumé, mention employment in one or more paragraphs. Use transitions to tie your paragraphs together. Mention volunteer activities or aspects of jobs or activities that help qualify you. Be sure to make a connection between the information and the requirements for the job. If you are including a résumé, you will use this section to develop any important information not made clear in that format.

SECOND-TO-LAST PARAGRAPH: If you are not including a résumé, but the job requires references, provide them here after making the conventional remarks regarding them:

> The following people have given me permission to use their names as references.

References are especially important if you have little or no job experience or no directly relevant experience. In a sense they provide experience by substantiating your characteristics and potential. Include two or preferably three references, choosing people who will be able to vouch for you in a persuasive way. Don't use close relatives for references, except when circumstances dictate (your uncle is your only supervisor, for example). Skip a space before the list of references and one space between each reference. You may block them horizontally (two or three in a row from left to right) or vertically (two or three in a row, one beneath the other), whatever looks better.

List the information like this:

> Full name with courtesy title
> Job title or relationship (e.g., "Neighbor" or "Former supervisor")
> Business name if relevant
> Street or P.O. address
> City, State Zip Code
> Telephone (Home)
> Telephone (Office)

Give the area code only if the reference is out of state. Designate home, office, or cell phone in parentheses (if relevant). If you just have one phone number, you don't need to identify where the phone is.

LAST PARAGRAPH: You can state that you look forward to an interview, but if this is irrelevant or physically impossible, don't mention it. If you are available for an interview, note when. Include your home or work telephone number and the hours you can be reached. Don't say that you are available at the employer's convenience unless you truly are. To close the letter, mention any materials you are including (such as a résumé or separate list of references) and thank the employer for considering your application.

> I look forward to an interview. My telephone number is 000-0000, and I am available every day after noon. Thank you for considering my application.

The formula for the letter is easy to follow. The challenge is to fit your material into it so that it makes sense for you and the job. One problem that many people face is the challenge of building something marketable out of seemingly nothing. The chart method described earlier will help, but if you are unsure about your own positive qualities and how they are valuable in the workplace, the next exercise may work better.

On one side of a sheet of paper, list every activity which you have participated in or organized or even observed closely over the last three years. Leave several spaces between activities. Now consider each activity objectively. What skills, qualities, or attributes did each require or teach? List them on the right. If you cannot think of much for the right-hand column, ask a writing partner, friend, teacher, or guidance counselor to help. Once filled out, the chart provides proof of your abilities. Refer to it when building your argument for employability. Keep the chart and update it regularly.

Below is a model of a sample chart.

Community Band, 2 years	Teamwork
	Take directions well
	Self-discipline (to practice, keep it up)
	Reliability (punctual, didn't miss practices or performances)
	Well organized (kept up studies despite demanding schedule)
Rap group	Self-motivated (started group myself)
	Organizing skills (set up rehearsals)
	Ambitious (arranged performances)
	Creative (wrote lyrics)
	Responsible (civic awareness: played anti-drug, anti-crime songs; promoted literacy)
	Reliable (made all rehearsals and performances; never missed school even after late-night performances)

Positive wording is a must. Edit out pejorative language and negative experiences. If you have no job experience, do not say, "I have no experience," or "I have never worked or had a job." (This is redundant, anyway.) Sidestep the issue if possible, or word the point so that you look good anyway. Compare the language in and impact of the two paragraphs below.

•Negative and lacking confidence:
I am only seventeen and still go to high school (Badger Home School for Boys), but I think I might be able to do your job if you give me a chance to try it out so I could see how I'd do. I'm not too bad at math since I have to teach my younger brothers (grades 6 - 9). I'm pretty sure I can do your job because I've been taking accounting at the local community college and do okay. I was treasurer too, for our synagogue's youth group.

•Positive and confident:
I am a seventeen-year-old student at the Badger Home School for Boys. I have gained the attributes needed for the accounting position from several sources. One, I have had to teach my three younger brothers math for the last two years, so I am well organized, articulate, and efficient, as well as generally fast with numbers. Second, I have maintained an <u>A</u> average throughout two years of accounting courses at the local community college, where my classmates were an average of three years older. Finally, as treasurer for the youth group at my synagogue (160 members), I have used the same accounting skills which your job requires.

Similarly, do not mention points that are not in your favor, such as low grades or no transportation. Of course, don't waste time applying for jobs for which you have neither the skills nor the aptitude, and never lie.

If you have left a job recently, state your reasons in a positive manner. The future employer will want assurance that there is no underlying problem.

•Negative:
I quit working as a cashier at Gunga Din Burgers because the bosses were jerks, and the hours stunk. Dino's was better, and besides, I wanted more money.

•Positive:
Last summer I gained cashier experience working first at Gunga Din Burgers and later at Dino's Pizzeria. I shifted from the first to the second to gain more hours of employment, necessary since I am putting myself through college.

Be precise. If you have experience in an area, say what the experience is and how you gained it.

•Vague and redundant:
I was employed as a cashier. I have experience in this area.

•Precise:
I was employed at Hunky-Dory Toys as a cashier from 2000-02.

•Precise:
My volunteer experience last summer included running the cash register in the hospital cafeteria.

Letter of Application Checklist

1. Have I named the specific position (or fellowship, apprenticeship, etc.) for which I am applying?
2. Have I addressed all requirements (both qualifications and qualities)? Have I supported my statements?
3. Have I named my relevant employers?
4. Is my reference information complete?
5. Have I followed conventional phrasing?
6. Have I spelled "want ad" correctly? (Not "wanted ad" or "want add.")
7. Have I written "Very truly your<u>s</u>" or "Sincerely your<u>s</u>," (not <u>your</u>)?

You may be asked to include a résumé with your application. In this case, put your data in the résumé and write a shorter letter of application, called a cover letter. This follows the basic formula for the application letter, but it will not include your job history per se or references. It can and should refer to aspects of your jobs, volunteer work, or activities that can prove your claim that you are an outstanding applicant—in other words, relevant material that's not adequately covered in the résumé. For instance, your résumé might list that you were captain of the bowling team, but your cover letter would mention that you organized a winning team and did the team's accounting.

Below is a sample cover letter, accompanying an application for work in child care.

3451 Hope St.
Newport, RI 02806
October 14, 2012

Mrs. Brandi Forrest, Director
Preschool Palace
34 Appian Way
Newport, RI 02806

Dear Mrs. Forrest:

I should like to apply for the position of child care worker, as advertised in The Newport Daily, October 13.

I have a number of experiences which have prepared me for work within a center. Last summer I participated in a two-part, ten-week series on "Discipline and Development of the Preschool Child." The series was sponsored by the YMCA under the direction of Gelsey Lamoureaux. In the spring I participated in a four-week parenting and family workshop, also at the YMCA. I have been actively involved in a "mothers' morning-out program" at my church, where I volunteered as a child-care worker.

These activities have provided me valuable lessons in guiding children toward healthy interaction and independence. For example, while young children may not understand the principle of sharing, they can be taught the behavior. I have used the following technique successfully: When a toy becomes a battleground, one child is given a turn for a specific time, say two minutes. Providing a manageable time limit allows the child a turn as well the opportunity to give up the toy independently.

I have worked since 2010 in part-time child care in the home, watching children for two families. The position required that I work closely with two mothers, who were not always in accord on child-rearing issues, and that I understand the individual needs of their children. I made myself available before and after work to discuss issues, read materials they gave me, and research specific questions.

Besides my direct child-care skills, I play guitar and sing. I have a background in performing arts and can conduct a variety of fun and creative activities, such as sing-alongs, dancing, and storytelling. These activities help the young child develop a capacity for self-expression and independence and would benefit as well as entertain the children at your center.

I look forward to hearing from you. Thank you for considering my application.

Very truly yours,

Johannah Reimer

Johannah Reimer

Use the same checklist as for letters of application. Be sure to compare your letter to your résumé to make certain that you aren't needlessly repetitive.

RÉSUMÉS: SHORT AND NEAT

There are a zillion ways to lay out a résumé—and as many books to tell you how. Study the sample lay-outs in this chapter, and either pattern yours after one of them, or hit the library for other ideas. The only important rules are to keep the lay-out well spaced, the presentation IMMACULATE, and the information short and to the point. A one-page résumé is ideal.

As for content, certain elements must be included, while others are optional. Put your name at the top of the page; below that, put your full address and telephone number. Next comes either education or employment, dealer's choice. If you have had few jobs and are still in school, put education first. If you have worked a great deal, put employment first. Begin with the current or most recent information, and place it below a heading marked *Education* or *Employment*, as appropriate.

Give the full name of each school you have been in, beginning with high school. If you are homeschooled, say so; give the name of your school if it has one, making sure it is clear that it is a homeschool. If you take (or have taken) classes at a college or community college, list them. If you have graduated from a certificate or degree program, note the year you did so and the certificate or degree you received. You may also mention activities, outside training, special educational opportunities, experience, or awards that are relevant to the job or that show generally positive attributes.

List your employers chronologically from most recent to the earliest. You may wish to list only relevant employers, but do not do this if it creates gaps that might make an employer wonder why you were out of work so long.

Provide the name of the company, your job title, the time span of your employment, and any special (i.e., not obvious) duties, achievements, or awards. If you have many experiences but not much paid employment, you can cluster both categories together under the heading "Experience."

A section for activities, such as school or volunteer activities, is optional, unless you included this information under education. If the list is short but the information important, mention the activities in your cover letter and show a clear connection between them and the job's requirements. Give the *full* name of any organizations; mention the time span of your involvement and say what you did (or do) if it is not otherwise clear. Other optional inclusions are a statement of career goals or position desired, age, hobbies, workshops, or scholarships. You are not required to state your race or gender.

Lastly, provide your references. Unless you have listed considerable experience, it is prudent to include three, fully detailed references. It is acceptable, however, to say, "References available upon request" at the end of the résumé. If an ad says, "Include references," then you must. In many instances, not doing so may automatically cost you the job. Provide at least two references but no more than three. If you run out of room, as I did, you can mention that more references are available, or use a second sheet for all your references. If you do so, be sure to include your name on the second sheet as well, and title it: REFERENCES.

Following are two sample résumé lay-outs. Usually you will double-space between sections and single space within a section. Capitalizing all letters of a section title is optional; another option is to underline the title. Do one or the other but not both. Leave at least a one-inch margin on all sides.

RÉSUMÉ

First and last names
Street or P.O. address
City, State Zip
Telephone number, including area code

EDUCATION:

Current   Plateau Junior College. Freshman standing.
                                  Major: Early childhood education.

1991   Homeschooled. Academic degree.
                                  Special classes: Preschool teaching, two years.

EXPERIENCE:

Summer 1991   Workshops in "Children and Discipline" and
                                  "Play Skills for Preschoolers," at YMCA
1990 to present   Nanny for Mrs. Holly Austell.
                                  Responsibilities include caring for triplets, age two;
                                  house-cleaning; preparing lunch.

Summer 1990   Volunteer at Children's Hospital.
                                  Responsibilities included directing daily
                                  creative play for twenty children.

SPECIAL INTERESTS: Dance, playing guitar, singing, and juggling.

REFERENCES: Mrs. Holly Austell
                    Current employer
                    P.O. Box 234
                    Anytown, MI 00000
                    Tel.: 000-0000 (Home)/000-0000 (Work)

                    Mr. Ross Hunter
                    Workshop leader, YMCA
                    345 Drummers Court
                    Anytown, MI 00000
                    Tel.: 000-0000 (Home)/000-0000 (Work)

Additional references are available upon request.

RÉSUMÉ

First and last names
Street or P.O. address
City, State Zip
Telephone number, including area code

<u>Education</u>

Current
Plateau Junior College. Freshman standing. Major: Early childhood education.

1991
Homeschooled. Academic degree. Special classes: Preschool teaching, two years.

<u>Experience</u>

June, 1991
Workshops in "Children and Discipline" and "Play Skills for Preschool Children," Reeves Baptist Church.

1990 to present
Nanny for Mrs. Holly Austell. Responsibilities include caring for triplets, age 2; house-cleaning; preparing lunch. Help one child with physical therapy activities.

Summer 1990
Volunteer at Children's Hospital. Responsibilities included directing daily creative play for twenty children.

<u>Special Interests</u>
Dance, playing guitar and singing, juggling.

<u>References</u>

Mrs. Holly Austell	Mr. Ross Hunter
Current employer	Workshop leader, Reeves Baptist Church
P.O. Box 234	345 Drummers Court
Anytown, MI 00000	Anytown, MI 00000
Tel.: 000-0000 (Home)	Tel.: 000-0000 (Home)
000-0000 (Work)	000-0000 (Work)

Additional references are available upon request.

You don't have to typeset your résumé, but you should make copies on a good quality paper, preferably 25% white cotton. Send a copy rather than the original. Before you mail your résumé, proof it one last time. Even one mistake, however small, will make you look bad.

The résumé and cover letter really have one purpose, and it's not exactly to get the job. It's to get an interview. You sell yourself at the interview, but getting the chance to do so hinges on your writing ability.

LETTERS THAT ASK FOR MORE

When you write a letter seeking promotion, continuation of project funding, a raise, or the like, you will loosely follow the cover letter format. Instead of proving that you have the capacity to do something, you are proving that you have already been doing something, and doing it well. Use standard business letter format.

PARAGRAPH 1: State your current position, duration of employment, what you are seeking, and why. Make your thesis clear, firm, and concise.

> I have been working for seven months as a cashier. My wage has been $6.00 an hour since I began. Because of my strong employment record, I am seeking a raise.

PARAGRAPH 2 (and more, if needed): In a few paragraphs defend and support your request. If seeking a raise, cover past duties and performance of them. Mention any employment awards. If you are seeking a promotion, mention job performance and show that you have the skills and attributes needed for the new position.

> I have met all the requirements of the job. I am punctual, and I frequently come in half an hour early to do extra work such as prepare my station and clean my area. My immediate supervisor, Yolanda Jones, can verify this. In addition, my bank balance has always been accurate at the end of the day. I have a good attitude and am courteous to the customers. My courtesy has twice won me the employee of the week award, and last month I was elected the co-worker of the month by my fellow cashiers. I am enthusiastic about my job and the company, and my enthusiasm shows in my work.

LAST PARAGRAPH: Tie your points to the thesis, ending with a request for action and closing courtesies. Do not threaten the employer with quitting if you do not get the action you desire.

> Because I have worked long past the three-month trial period, and I have received both awards and compliments for my work, I believe that I am qualified for your standard first raise of an additional fifty cents an hour. I should be happy to meet with you at your convenience to discuss this matter. Thank you for considering my request.

Check your letter against the editing guidelines in Chapter 14 before mailing.

Trying to gain a place in college, an internship or fellowship, or a job can be daunting, but as you learn to make the most of what you have done, you will gain confidence. Your letters, narratives, and résumés will improve. Keep a file of all the material you write when seeking placement or position; doing so will save you time when writing future applications, and one day will provide an interesting record of your life's work.

SUM UP
1. In one sentence write the thesis of this chapter.
2. Describe the opportunities available to you in the past year and the ones you hope to have available in the future.

REACT
1. Personal narratives, letters of application, and even résumés are persuasive in purpose; their common goal is to sell your experience and qualities to someone else. How do you feel about having to "sell yourself"? In what ways might the sales pitch change according to audience? What aspects of the "pitch" would be constant?
2. What are values? How do your expectations of yourself affect your perception of your own values? Are your expectations high or low? What impact do you imagine your expectations will have on your life? What impact have they had thus far?
3. Successful writing for opportunity depends upon meeting high standards. Is this fair? Should people be given chances to prove themselves even if they cannot communicate their own worth, prove their qualifications, or present their information professionally? In what ways do high standards make you expand your capabilities? In what ways do low standards diminish your capabilities?

4. What is the difference between qualities and qualifications? What are some desirable qualities in a college student? In an employee? Should someone with poor grades, low test scores, but a high IQ be accepted to college? Who is the better choice for a job, someone with the qualities which make for a great employee but without the requisite skills, or someone with a lousy attitude but the necessary skills? What is *your* attitude toward work of any kind (homework, work at home, jobs, and so forth)?
5. What distinguishes you from your peers?
6. Why must personal narratives, letters of application, and cover letters have a thesis?
7. After class discussion add any new ideas to your notes.

ACT
1. Look up the words *opportunity*, *possibilities*, and *quality* in *Bartlett's Familiar Quotations*. Add three quotations to your "Notable Quotations" relevant to this chapter and your class discussions.
2. List your personal strengths. Include everything positive you can think about yourself and anything negative you have worked on improving.
3. Write a personal narrative, choosing your topic from the sample list.
4. Find an ad for a job that you could apply for and possibly get. Try to choose a challenging position. Make a two-column chart like the one in the chapter, matching qualifications, obvious qualities, and unstated qualities with your experience.
5. Make an activity/attribute chart such as the one in the chapter.
6. Write a letter of application for the job or a cover letter and résumé.

"Be daring, take on anything....Technique holds a reader from sentence to sentence, but only content will stay in his mind."

Joyce Carol Oates

eighteen

Bridges to the World

One Christmas I gave my niece a magazine subscription. The following April she told me that she had never received the magazine. I typed a letter to the customer service department and explained the situation. I included a copy of my cancelled check and made a duplicate of the letter for my records before mailing it. A week later the company responded with an apology, and within another week service was started. My letter of adjustment did its job.

Protecting your consumer rights is but one of the many circumstances in life that require writing. Whether you stay at home for years, marry early or late, or stay single for life, you alone are responsible for your affairs. No teacher, parent, or friend can consistently intercede for you, communicating your interests to the world. It's up to you.

Letters will be the primary vehicle for your personal concerns. You need to know how to write letters of inquiry, complaint or adjustment, and opinion, along with letters expressing thanks, condolences, and friendship. The first three follow standard business style as to format, lay-out, and tone, and all are written pretty much according to a set pattern.

LETTERS OF INQUIRY: INFORMATION VIA MAIL

The purpose of a letter of inquiry or request is to obtain information which cannot or should not be requested in person or by telephone. Travel brochures, college catalogues, government pamphlets, and research materials are examples. While some of these you could contact via e-mail, you would still need to follow letter format and print a hard copy for your records. Either way, e-mail or postal mail, your letter should be short and to the point. Typically, the introduction, body, and conclusion occur within a single paragraph. State the subject of your inquiry and what you are requesting. Give the reason for the request if that will matter to the recipient of the letter. End with standard closing courtesies.

The following example is in the full block style. If your letter is short, begin it about one third of the way down the page to center it. Use a formal salutation and closing.

Box 2A
Pierre, NJ 00000
July 18,1992

Centers for Disease Control
1600 Clifton Rd., NE
Atlanta, GA 30333

Dear Sir or Madam:

I work full time as a house painter. Given recent stories about lead poisoning, I am concerned that I may be at risk when I strip and burn paint. The local health department has limited information about the matter. Can you tell me whether I am endangering myself, what the risks are, and how I can protect myself? Also, I would like general information about the effects of lead poisoning in adults. Thank you for your help.

Very truly yours,

Jhodessa T. Hespian

Jhodessa T. Hespian

In this letter, the reason for writing is relevant because it helps explain what is needed.

Note on a calendar the date you mail the letter so you can track the response and write again if necessary.

LETTERS OF COMPLAINT: PROTECT YOUR RIGHTS

Letters of complaint and adjustment point out problems, often with consumer issues. A letter of complaint may make a suggestion for improvement or a request for change, but its main purpose is to demonstrate that a problem exists and to get your statement about it on record. A letter of adjustment requests that a problem be corrected. Again, e-mail might be your chosen method of communication, but you would still use the same format, and you would still need to make a hard copy for your records.

Both types of letters require a firm but courteous tone and accurate details about the problem, in addition to accompanying supportive documents (which may be easier to submit with regular mail). Both should be brief. Depending on the issue at hand, the letter may require one or several paragraphs. Address the letter to the complaint department of the company or to a specific person in charge of the area of concern. Use standard business letter format, and remember to date the letter.

Here is the formula for letters of complaint/adjustment. The introduction should briefly describe the problem. If the problem is with a consumer product, describe the product, including product name, serial and model number, the size, color, or style (whatever is appropriate for the product). Also note where and when the item was purchased. If the problem is with a service (such as delivery or customer service, or a bill that has been paid but not acknowledged as paid), describe the transaction, and give the full names of any persons involved. Include all relevant details (catalog number, time involved in delivery, date of payment, and so forth).

In the next paragraph (or the same paragraph if the previous details were covered in a few sentences), describe action taken to date, if any, such as telephone calls or previous letters. If the dissatisfaction is related to a product, mention warranty terms or return policies as applicable. Mention and include *copies* of documents such as warranties, contracts, cancelled checks, sales receipts, bills, etc. (You don't want to send the original materials because then you have no record for yourself.) If you are sending any documents, you will type the word *Enclosures* on the line beneath your printed name. If attempting to send your copies via e-mail, you would need to scan and download your copies. (The recipient, if not on the same Internet server, may have problems downloading your attachments.)

Conclude by stating what you want done about the problem. In a letter of complaint, your statement may be merely that you want acknowledgment of the problem. In a letter of adjustment, you may ask for a specific action such as a notice stating that your account is clear, or you may request a refund, replacement, or exchange. Urge a swift response, but be reasonable. Action is likely to take a couple of weeks for local businesses and thirty days for national. Include your telephone number if a more immediate response is desired.

If you are returning a product, ask the merchant for shipping instructions and address. When you mail or ship the item, enclose a copy of your receipt if you are requesting reimbursement.

Below is a sample letter (salutation and body).

Dear Manager:

On October 19, 1992 I purchased a portable tape player, XYZ Brand, Model #12345 from your store in the Redwood Mall. The tape player worked well for twenty-nine days. On the thirtieth day, one speaker stopped working.

The day the tape player broke was Sunday, and your stores were closed. Therefore, I took the tape player back to the store the next day. The manager stated that the tape player had a thirty-day warranty, and that it "was not his problem that it stopped working on a weekend." He added that if I had been smarter, I would have bought your company's extended warranty policy for $49.95. Since I had not bought the plan, he said that I could take it to the store's repair shop, which would charge a $50.00 basic fee just to look at it. Actually fixing it would cost more. Given that the tape player cost only $79.99, either option seems extreme.

I have, then, several complaints. One, your store advertises "quality merchandise only." A machine that breaks the day its warranty expires is not "quality merchandise." Two, your store policy states that "satisfaction is guaranteed." Your manager's attitude was insulting and his solution far from satisfactory. Further, the charge for examining the tape player is excessive, and the cost of your extended warranty policy makes it unfeasible.

I would like you to replace or repair my tape player without charge. The problem of the warranty's being expired one day is hardly comparable to the problem of a dissatisfied customer. If you do not satisfy my request, I shall write to the Oregon Attorney General to complain about your unfair business practices and false advertising. Copies of my receipt, warranty, and your store policy are enclosed. I expect a response within two weeks. If you prefer, you may call me during the day at 222-2222. I look forward to becoming a satisfied customer. Thank you.

Keep a copy of your letter in a file, and on a calendar mark the date you mailed it. Mark, too, the date you could reasonably expect a reply—usually three weeks. If you have heard nothing within a few days of that date or are dissatisfied with the response, take additional action. Depending on the nature of the problem, you might write a second letter to someone with more authority in the company, or to a local or state consumer office, the Better Business Bureau, the state Attorney General, or your state senator or legislator. If you take a secondary step, include copies of all previous correspondence and documents.

LETTERS THAT SHAPE THE WORLD

Do you have an opinion on any of the following statements?

- You should/should not be twenty-one or older to be allowed to drink alcoholic beverages.
- Females under eighteen should/should not by law be required to have parental permission to have an abortion or to obtain birth control.
- Minority groups should/should not have different testing standards than Caucasians.
- Sex education should/should not be taught in middle or junior high schools.
- First consideration for a job or college should/should not be given to women and minorities, regardless of qualifications.
- Profiling should/should not be used to identify possible terrorists.

The above issues play a part of your life in some way, regardless of your stand on them. Like it or not, the world around you has an impact on your life. Your choice is whether to have an impact on the world. Letters of opinion provide an opportunity to do so.

A letter expressing your opinion is essentially a persuasive essay in business letter format. It can be written to the public (as an editorial), to a business or institution, or to someone with whom you are personally involved. The letter must have a single thesis, adequately supported and developed. Its tone should be forceful but not bellicose or insulting, and it should be targeted toward the expected readership. Before you begin, make sure that your reason for writing is clear; after you write your first draft, check to see whether you have stayed true to that purpose. Review the section on writing to reason/persuade in Chapter 9 and follow the guidelines below.

First, write to the appropriate party—someone who oversees policies, handles problems, or prints editorials, for instance. In the introduction identify the problem or issue, your stand on the issue, and, if relevant, your identity in relationship to the issue. The following two introductions take into account different reasons for concern about an issue.

- I am a member of the school board that voted last month to give money for teachers' raises instead of seat belts for school buses. Our position is that without teachers, there would be no need for school buses. Therefore, teachers' needs come first.

•My children must ride to school in buses without seat belts. Why, when it is a state law that all drivers and passengers must wear seat belts, are buses exempt from this rule? All buses should have an adequate number of seat belts, and children should be required to wear them.

In the ensuing paragraphs develop your argument. Your aim is to persuade the reader of the validity of your position, so consider your support and tone carefully. To be persuasive, show the "why's" behind your thinking and the "why not's" behind theirs. Contrast opposing views, as relevant, or use anecdotes, quotations, statistics, or description. Develop the argument fully but concisely. A lengthy editorial usually will not be published or will be condensed by an editor.

In the next example, the writer uses an anecdote and a quotation to support a point.

Last week the school bus I was riding had a flat tire. The bus skidded off the highway, and many students were flung from their seats. Fifteen students had to be treated for injuries such as broken bones, cuts, and bruises. Dr. Ian Kursel, the emergency room doctor, said, "Had seat belts been available, no one would have been injured."

Conclude by providing a possible solution (or solutions) to the problem, or by stating what you wish to be accomplished, changed, or noticed. This statement should match your intent in writing. What action(s) do you want the reader to take? Then close courteously, in either the concluding paragraph or a separate one, as demonstrated below.

The time has come to forego excuses and take action. The budget comes under review next month. I urge the city council to think first of our children, and I urge other citizens to write the council immediately with a plea for seat belts in all school buses.
Thank you for considering my letter for publication.

Here is the body of a sample letter of opinion.

Dear Editor:

I am a senior high school student in the Taylor County school system, where the teachers have been on strike for more than three weeks. The teachers are protesting what they deem unfairly low wages, and I agree that they are grossly underpaid. I am writing, however, with a protest of my own: Their strike interferes with my education. I believe that this is even less fair than their wages.

The teachers have three chief complaints. One, they have not received raises for three years, although the cost of living has risen 15% in that time. Two, due to a hiring freeze and natural attrition rate, all teachers have had to take on at least one extra class a week. Three, teachers who have been in the system for over ten years are making the same amount as teachers who were hired last year. All three complaints are legitimate. Teachers shape the future of America. A job with such responsibility should pay well.

As for me, it is my senior year. I am supposed to be preparing a personal narrative for college applications that are due beginning next month. I am supposed to be studying for my final round of SATs. I am concerned that my needs are not being met. Am I supposed to skip college next year just because the teachers need more money?

If our county does not have enough money for our teachers, then the county must raise the money through a tax referendum, car washes, bake sales, or whatever it takes. Our voting citizens should promise a resolution of the teachers' complaints, and our teachers should return to school immediately on good faith. A lot of futures are at stake.

Thank you for considering my view.

As always, use the checklists for editing and revising before mailing, and keep a copy for your records.

SOME THOUGHTS YOU CANNOT BUY

While you cannot buy a greeting card for an inquiry, complaint, or opinion, you can buy one for nearly every other attitude, event, or emotion. Although costly, greeting cards are handy. Even more convenient is a phone call. So why not use prewritten cards or simply "reach out and touch someone" through a telephone line?

Quick contact methods leave much to be desired, that's why. You cannot hold a phone call in your hands to read a second or third time. You cannot read personal meaning into a signature, which is usually the only handwritten part of a card. Any mail is great, it's true; but mail without anything personal—no news, no thoughts, no worries, no piece of the sender for you to smile about or ponder—is hardly mail.

Don't get me wrong. I buy greeting cards. I especially like the funny ones, since I'm not always that funny myself. But I mostly use cards to let people know I'm thinking of them, and I usually write something personal on them anyway. What's more, if I need to say, "Thank you," to offer condolences, or to let a friend or relative know how much I care, I always write a real letter. It might be short, and it might be written on a stock card, but it will say in my own words what I am feeling. Fortunately, there are patterns for such letters, although you must, of course, do your own thinking about what to fit into the pattern.

That pattern applies to e-mail too, but even more than for business letters, personal letters need the imprint of the writer. I find that e-mail is great for a quick query to a colleague or for keeping up to date with family members spread across the continent and sometimes hard to reach. But truly, it's not any faster than writing a letter, and while it's cool to read a missive from my brother while he's traveling through Ukraine, when I'm done, the experience is essentially over. I can print it out, sure, but that's never as warm and satisfying as holding paper he has written on, imagining his pen scrawling across the page, and being able to revisit as often as I wish the experiences he is conveying. You may feel different.

Saying Thank You Is a Gift to the Giver

A thank-you letter need not be long, but it must be specific. Always name the gift or deed. Mention in a sentence or more how you are using or enjoying the gift, or say how the deed influenced you or made you feel. If the gift was money, say what you did with it or plan to do with it. If you are not sure yet how you will spend it, it is okay to say so, but you might mention a few possibilities.

Here is an example. Note that the punctuation after the salutation is a comma, as this is not a formal letter. The closing, too, is informal. You should still include a heading and a date. Such a letter is usually handwritten, so you don't need to sign it twice. (But please, if your writing is illegible, type the letter so you spare the recipient the misery of trying to read it and failing. In this case, of course sign your name.)

31 Grateful Way
Kindness, ND 00000
October 29, 2003

Dear Grandma,
   Thank you for the birthday gift. Fifty dollars is a lot of money, and it has taken me a while to decide whether to save it or spend it. I have decided at last to do both. Half I put in savings toward a new bike. I plan to bicycle across the country next summer, and I'll need a better bike than Dad's old one. The other half I used to buy America's Guide to Best Bicycling Routes—a great book and an essential one for my trip. There was a little money left over, so I treated myself and my boyfriend to lunch. I guess that was a bit frivolous, but it was fun. So, thank you again for everything.

Love,

Paris

You may hate to write a thank-you letter, but a letter says that you care about the giver as much as the giver cared for you. It matches effort with effort, care with care. Besides, if you want to keep getting presents, you say thank you nicely.

Sympathy Letters Uplift the Reader

A letter of condolence is also short and follows a basic formula. It is much harder to write, however, because of the emotions involved. Even if you are writing to someone you do not know well, the circumstance can make you uncomfortable. On the other hand, if you are writing to someone about a special person in your life, the process can be wrenching. Yet write you must, because the recipient of the letter needs your support.

Usually the letter is not read carefully at first. The bereaved is grief stricken but busy with funeral arrangements. Nevertheless, the moment will come when the confusion has subsided, and the emptiness that the bereaved feels then can be overwhelming. That is when the person will re-read the letters of condolence: when the need is strong to connect with friends and family, and to reflect upon your relationship with the deceased. The bereaved is not drawn back to a card, to the rhymed verse of someone who had never met, touched, or been touched by the life of the deceased. The person will come back to the bond your words give: a link to moments that stay alive because you wrote them down.

Start by saying, "I am very sorry to learn of your loss," or something similar. (Note that contractions are inappropriate for the formal tone of the letter.) Then say one or two personal things that you remember about the person. This could be a habit: "It always tickled me the way Grandpa's lip and mustache twitched when he was about to laugh." You might mention a custom: "I remember the way Uncle Charlie always put me on his lap as soon as I arrived, and he always said the same thing, that I was the most beautiful girl he had ever seen. I was only five or so, but it made me feel so special." Or, you might relate an anecdote, such as something that the two of you did together. "You never knew this, but Aunt Nora and I were the ones who put the ice cream in your shoes. We were sorry about it, but we laughed about it for years." You might say something that you admired about the person. "I always admired Kwame's independence. Sometimes this made your life rocky, I know, but at school his independence was coupled with his energy. He was the main person responsible for getting our after-school lecturers' program started, and you know that has been a big success." As you can see, there is room for flexibility here. As long as the content is brief and true to its purpose—to remind the bereaved of the deceased's living moments—then your letter will be comforting.

After the section about the person, say something to the effect of, "That is how I think of Antonio, sharing a warm moment together," or whatever is appropriate and matches how you really do think of the deceased. Close by saying, "I am thinking of you warmly," or "fondly," or whatever is appropriate for your relationship with the person to whom you are writing. It will be obvious that you are thinking of the person, because you took the trouble and time to write a real letter. Believe me, the bereaved will always be grateful.

Although there is no specific category for a letter to someone gravely ill, there should be. People who are sick and possibly dying need support. In a "Dear Abby" column one day a person complained that the messages on greeting cards often ignore the nature of the situation. Someone who is terminally ill, for instance, is not cheered by foolishly optimistic messages such as, "I hear you're coming home soon," or "Get well fast." In the case of someone critically or terminally ill, a letter can bring a badly needed connection to life outside a hospital.

Again, such a letter should be warm in tone but formal in language. Begin by saying that you are sorry about the illness or injury. Then relate in a few sentences (or paragraphs, if needed) why that person is special to you. If the person may recover, close by saying that you hope or pray for a recovery. If the person will not recover, close by saying something about your relationship and your reason for writing, such as, "I just wanted you to know how much your friendship means, and will always mean, to me." Or, "You are my favorite aunt, and I wanted to thank you for the love and guidance you have given me through the years." A letter along these lines can make bearable someone's last moments.

Keep Friendships Alive Through Letters

A letter of friendship is something you write to build or maintain a special relationship. It is a chance to share your private thoughts and feelings, your interpretation of the events in your life, and your fears as well as your hopes. A letter from a friend is something to savor. For each moment you spend reading it, your friend is sitting beside you. Perhaps now most of your friends are on your block, in your dorm, or only a subway or bike ride away, but this will not always be the case. As you age, your world will grow, as will the physical distances between you and your friends. One friend I have had for 35 years lives in Iowa, more than 800 miles from me; another lives in Scotland—more than 4000 miles away. And my baby brother—one of dearest friends—for a while lived in Poland; a phone call to him could run fifty bucks, and when it was over, it was gone. I have to write to these people if I am going to hold onto them through time.

There is no formula for writing to a friend. Say what you are doing, thinking, or feeling. Give the person a glimpse at who you are, right then. Let your friend know what your day is like; describe where you live. It is marvelous for me to envision my friend Emma cooking muffins in her sunlit kitchen, or my friend Rick standing on a misty knoll above his stone cottage. What they have given me in their letters I can give back in mine—a piece of my life.

These days most people write their letters via e-mail. That's fine for casual conversing; you might consider printing some of your better letters and keeping a file for various friends with whom you communicate often. But an e-mail will never match the excitement of opening a real, not virtual, mailbox and finding a letter, nor can it compare with the sensation of touching the actual letter as you read and reread it. Try it.

A Voice of Your Own

Once you can communicate through the written word (and I firmly believe that you—yes, you—can do this), you have the ability to learn more about yourself and your world than you would otherwise. You can discover what it is you have to say that is important and uniquely yours. You can be confident, because you have a voice of your own that you can activate at will.

That voice enables you to take stock of yourself and to record and analyse your actions and thoughts throughout your life. You can keep notes on your travels, whether they be downtown, into the woods, across a meadow, or over the ocean. Send yourself postcards when you travel, and the words awaiting you at home will be a reusable ticket, available at any time for a trip into your memory. You can keep a journal or make observations on a calendar about memorable days or thoughts, and one day re-reading even a single line may bring the past into the present.

Whether you are an *A* student, a *C* student, an ungraded student, or a student at all, if you know how to write, you can make a difference in this world. Use your writing as a vehicle of change and for change. Write your way off a farm or onto a farm, out of the city or into the city, or somewhere in between. If you practice the guidelines in this book, you should be able to say on paper what you are thinking in your mind. And what you are thinking will continue to gain in quality.

The process of writing is ongoing. The more you write, the better you write and the clearer you think. The more clearly you think, the better you write, and so on in an infinite spiral of improvement. Improvement is a series of small successes. Greatness is not the call of genius; it is the call of work.

The first bridge of writing is into your own mind. From there, you can build bridges anywhere, anytime.

SUM UP

1. In one sentence write the thesis of this chapter.
2. Write, in one sentence, the thesis of this book.
3. Write a paragraph noting how the book's conclusion ties into its introduction. After class discussion revise your summary as needed.

REACT

1. Why write? Why write well? Think seriously about the need for writing in your life.
2. How would you define exemplary writing?
3. Review your journal, bearing in mind the statement, "The more you write, the better you write and the clearer you think." Pull out examples from your writing that support this maxim.

4. Can you apply the statement to other disciplines besides writing? In what ways has this course influenced your work in other classes? Can you apply the principle to other areas of your life? Give examples.

5. Have you changed since you started this class? In even so short a time have you grown, matured, developed? Has your writing also matured?

ACT

1. Add some quotations to your "Notable Quotations" that demonstrate exemplary writing. Then review your journal, other writing which you have done, or conversations you have had. Can you add to "Notable Quotations" some of your own best lines?

2. Write a letter of persuasion about an issue that inflames you. Address the letter to an appropriate—and real—audience. Prepare the letter for presentation and review it in class. Then mail a copy to the right person, whether a newspaper editor, your congressional representative, or a state official.

3. What present would you most like to receive on your next birthday, and who would send it? Pretend that your wish comes true, and write a thank-you letter for it. Alternatively, write a thank-you letter for a gift you have actually received recently.

4. Write a personal letter—to yourself. In it describe the changes that you have undergone in the past semester or year. End by voicing your aspirations. Seal the letter and put it in a safe place. Let it be a private time capsule to be opened ten years from now.

5. Remember in the first chapter, when I said I had never written to thank the woman who helped me so much when I was in high school? After telling you that, I felt so guilty that I found her address and wrote a long letter explaining how much she had helped me. I thanked her sincerely, and then I told her some about how I have felt her influence over the years. I heard back from her soon thereafter; she couldn't thank me enough, in return, for the impact that the letter had had on her, especially now that her children had grown up and she had been widowed. It was a rewarding response.

So now it's your turn. Write a thank-you letter to some person who has genuinely contributed to your life. (Why wait? When someone is dead, it's too late to say thank you.) You can be brief, but you should include enough detail to show your sincerity. Go ahead and mail the letter.

6. Discuss what you have learned about writing from reading this book. Evaluate yourself. In what ways have you most improved your writing? Do you need to attend to any specific areas? If so, in what ways can you continue on your own to improve your writing?

7. Write a letter to me, the author, via the publisher. The address is in the front of the book. Let me know what you liked or didn't like about the book, and what (if anything) you'd like to see added. If I've made any errors, point them out (tell me the page number too, please). Send me an example of your writing at the beginning of the course and at the end; let me see how you have improved.

"What is the secret to writing?"
"There isn't any secret. You sit down and you start and that's it."

Elmore Leonard

EDITING SYMBOLS

MARK   EXPLANATION

ℒ   Delete character or characters indicated.
stet   Let a previously deleted character or characters stay.
Insert space.
⌣   Close up space.
tr ⁓   Transpose; switch places. Place switches.
caps or ≡   Use capital letters. washington
lc or /   Use lower case letters. the Ǥiraffe

∧   Insert something that has been omitted.
gr   Error in grammar.
ref   Error in pronoun reference.
t or tense   Error in verb tense.
p or punc   Error in punctuation.
ital or ___   Use italic type or underline.
⊙   Put in period.
ss   Error in sentence structure.
frag   Sentence fragment.
rs   Run-on sentence.
w or wording   Problem in wording.
nc or ?   Not clear; question to author.
sp   Spelling error.
spell out   Spell out an abbreviation or acronym.
¶   Start paragraph.
no ¶   No paragraph break; run together.
ms or format   Problem in manuscript form or neatness.
‖   Even out lines.
⊢ or ⊏   Move the line left.
⊣ or ⊐   Move the line right.

Standard State Abbreviations (Postal)

Alabama	AL
Alaska	AK
Arizona	AZ
Arkansas	AR
California	CA
Colorado	CO
Connecticut	CT
Delaware	DE
Florida	FL
Georgia	GA
Hawaii	HI
Idaho	ID
Illinois	IL
Indiana	IN
Iowa	IA
Kansas	KS
Kentucky	KY
Louisiana	LA
Maine	ME
Maryland	MD
Massachusetts	MA
Michigan	MI
Minnesota	MN
Mississippi	MS
Missouri	MO
Montana	MT
Nebraska	NE
Nevada	NV
New Hampshire	NH
New Jersey	NJ
New Mexico	NM
New York	NY
North Carolina	NC
North Dakota	ND
Ohio	OH

Oklahoma	OK
Oregon	OR
Pennsylvania	PA
Rhode Island	RI
South Carolina	SC
South Dakota	SD
Tennessee	TN
Texas	TX
Utah	UT
Vermont	VT
Virginia	VA
Washington	WA
West Virginia	WV
Wisconsin	WI
Wyoming	WY

EVALUATION/CRITIQUE GUIDE

Students and teachers might find it helpful to use this guide as they acclimate themselves to the task of critiquing one another. You may copy it freely to use alongside a draft, or just use it to direct your comments while you write on the draft itself (in pencil, please). It may help to number the paragraphs so that you can refer to them without confusion (for example, ¶ 3, insufficient support).

If you find yourself refining this guide, please send me your improvements to incorporate in future editions. Thank you.

Introduction:
Clear?
States thesis?
Sets up development?
Starts with a strong "hook"?
COMMENTS:

Body:
Each idea presented clearly?
One idea per paragraph?
Uses logical development?
Develops all points stated
    in introduction?
Supports each major idea with
    at least two points?
Includes supportive examples?
Uses supportive quotations?
Uses supportive anecdotes?
Needs additional support?
COMMENTS:

Conclusion:
Restates thesis in new way?
Sums up key points?
Ends with a "clincher"?
COMMENTS:

Style (add after Ch. 7):
  Flows smoothly?
  Varies sentences?
  Appeals to senses?
COMMENTS:

Purpose and Audience
  (add after Ch. 10):
  Purpose clear and focused?
  Tone and attitude appropriate
      for audience?
COMMENTS:

Wording (add after Ch. 12):
  Uses concrete language?
  Any points ambiguous?
  Any points unclear?
  Any points redundant?
  Any points repetitive?
  Could wording be more
      concise?
  Could wording be more
      precise?
COMMENTS:

Grammar, mechanics, and appearance (add after Section 4):
COMMENTS:

Selected Bibliography

Bauer Jessie, and Bauer, Susan Wise. *The Well-Trained Mind: A Guide to Classical Education at Home*. New York: W. W. Norton & Company, 1999.

Bolton, Robert. *People Skills*. New York: Simon & Schuster, 1979.

Bradbury, Ray. *Zen in the Art of Writing*. New York: Bantam Books, 1992.

Calkins, Lucy McCormick. *The Art of Teaching Writing*. Portsmouth: Heinemann Educational Books, 1986.

Cheney, Theodore A. Rees. *Getting the Words Right: How to Rewrite, Edit, & Revise*. Cincinnati: Writer's Digest Books, 1983.

Conway, Jill Ker. *The Road from Coorain*. New York: Vintage Books, 1989.

Fowler, H. W. *A Dictionary of Modern English Usage*. Revised and edited by Sir William Gowers. Oxford: 1983.

French, Christopher W. (ed.). *The Associated Press Stylebook and Libel Manual*. New York: 1987.

Gibson, Walker. *Persona: A Style Study for Readers and Writers*. New York: Random House, 1969.

Goldberg, Natalie. *Writing Down the Bones*. Boston: Shambhala Publications, 1986.

Gordon, Karen Elizabeth. *The Transitive Vampire: A Handbook of Grammar for the Innocent, the Eager, and the Doomed*. New York: Times Books, 1984.

Keyes, Ralph. *The Courage to Write*. New York: Henry Holt and Co., 1995.

Lamott, Anne. *bird by bird*. New York: Doubleday, 1995.

McCullers, Carson. *Member of the Wedding*. New York: Bantam Books, 1979.

McDonald, Forrest. *The Phaeton Ride: The Crisis of American Success*. New York: Doubleday & Company, Inc., 1974.

Minto, Barbara. *The Pyramid Principle: Logic in Writing and Thinking*. London: Minto International, 1982.

Rico, Gabriele Luffer. *Writing the Natural Way*. Los Angeles: J. P. Tarcher, 1983.

Shertzer, Margaret. *The Elements of Grammar*. New York: Macmillan Publishing Co., 1986.

Strunk Jr., William, and White, E. B. *The Elements of Style*. New York: Macmillan Publishing Co., 1979.

Warriner, John E. *English Grammar and Composition (Complete Course)*. New York: Harcourt Brace Jovanovich, Publishers, 1982.

Winokur, Jon (ed.). *Advice to Writers: A Compendium of Quotes, Anecdotes, and Writerly Wisdom from a Dazzling Array of Literary Lights*. New York: Vintage Books, 1999.

Zinsser, William. *Writing to Learn*. New York: Perennial Library Edition, 1989.

INDEX

"Read, read, read. Read everything—trash, classics, good and bad, and see how they do it. Just like a carpenter who works as an apprentice and studies the master. Read! You'll absorb it. Then write. If it is good, you'll find out. If it's not, throw it out the window."

William Faulkner

ORDER FORM

Fax orders: 434-955-2479. Send this form.
Telephone orders: Call 866-268-1361 (toll-free). Have your credit card ready.
Website orders: www.popularweaselpress.com
Postal orders: Popular Weasel Press, P.O. Box 247, South Hill, VA 23970, USA. Telephone: 434-955-2478.

Please send the following:

_____ copies of Writing: The Bridge Between Us, @ $22.95 each
_____ copies of Teacher's Manual, @ $14.95 each

_____ Total copies   _____ **Total Cost of copies**

Shipping: U.S.: Add $4.00 for the first book and $2.00 for each additional product. Virginia residents multiply by .045 for sales tax.
Tax: $ _____
Total enclosed: $ _____

Ship to:
Name: _____

Address: _____

City, State, & Zip: _____

Telephone: _____

email address: _____

Payment: Check _____   Visa _____   MasterCard _____

Card number: _____

Name on card: _____ Exp. date: ___/___

Please send information about upcoming publications:
Yes _____   No _____

"Write even when you don't want to, don't much like what you are writing, and aren't writing particularly well."

Agatha Christie